The History of
Women's Football

The History of
Women's Football

Jean Williams

PEN & SWORD
HISTORY

First published in Great Britain in 2021 and reprinted in 2022 by
Pen & Sword History
An imprint of
Pen & Sword Books Ltd
Yorkshire – Philadelphia

ISBN 978 1 52678 531 2

A CIP catalogue record for this book is
available from the British Library.

Typeset by Mac Style
Printed in the UK by CPI Group (UK) Ltd, Croydon, CR0 4YY.

Pen & Sword Books Limited incorporates the imprints of Atlas,
Archaeology, Aviation, Discovery, Family History, Fiction, History,
Maritime, Military, Military Classics, Politics, Select, Transport,
True Crime, Air World, Frontline Publishing, Leo Cooper, Remember
When, Seaforth Publishing, The Praetorian Press, Wharncliffe Local
History, Wharncliffe Transport, Wharncliffe True Crime, White Owl
and After the Battle.

For a complete list of Pen & Sword titles please contact

PEN & SWORD BOOKS LIMITED
47 Church Street, Barnsley, South Yorkshire, S70 2AS, England
E-mail: enquiries@pen-and-sword.co.uk
Website: www.pen-and-sword.co.uk

Or

PEN AND SWORD BOOKS
1950 Lawrence Rd, Havertown, PA 19083, USA
E-mail: Uspen-and-sword@casematepublishers.com
Website: www.penandswordbooks.com

Contents

Acknowledgements

I would like to thank Simon, and our little cat, Bubby, for their longstanding support and, in Simon's case, patience. The cat found my tip-tapping away on the laptop while he snoozed rather irritating and would often sit on the keyboard to maintain a serene silence. This gave me cause for quiet reflection. And some additional characters which may have made their way into the manuscript. He was my first, and most severe critic.

I would like to thank the women who have shared their stories with me, and the staff of the National Football Museum, past and present who have helped to collect the oral histories. This is precious stuff, often neglected and so all the more valuable. Thank you, and I hope to have done your story justice.

Introduction

You may well find preconceptions that women's football is 'new' or recently developing challenged in this book. The first chapter concerns the beginning of the modern history of women's football, focusing on Nettie Honeyball who played in the early matches, the first of which took place in 1895 at Crouch End in front of 10,000 paying spectators. The initiative proved successful and would expand. Later, Mrs Helen Matthews became an important leader of a breakaway team, as did Nellie Hudson. Altogether, between 1894–95 and 1902–03 these teams played over 166 fixtures, as well as practice matches, covering the whole of England, Scotland, Northern Ireland and Wales. Most were played on significant grounds in front of a paying public to raise as much money as possible: an emerging professional formula for women's football.

But before we cover the success of the Honeyball business model for women's football in more detail, we must pause. Many people consider women's football to be a more recent innovation and would be surprised that it was played in the late nineteenth century. But Nettie, Nellie and Helen would not be the first women to play football. For that, we have to go back much further in time.

Women's Folk Football, *Cuju* and Barley Breaks before 1863

Women have been known to play ball games for as long as ball games have existed. There were many unregulated forms of women's football before the establishment of the Football Association (who wrote the modern Laws of the Game in 1863).

One such example was the centuries-old games in China known as *Cuju* (pronounced 'shoo-ju') in which the main skills and rules changed. In *Cuju*'s varied history there were women's teams, and female expert players such as Peng Xiyun, who juggled the ball with her feet, head knees and chest, much in the same way that Freestyle champions do today.

Folk football games took many forms in the Americas, Europe and Africa, often staged as part of fertility rites, especially linked with harvest and the agricultural calendar. Egyptian hieroglyphs and Greek artifacts show women taking part in ball games. In Europe, and particularly Britain, Whitsun was a traditional time to play matches, to celebrate abundance or potency, and here the ball was symbolic of the seed being successfully sown into the earth and harvested. Fixtures that rejoiced in a good harvest were often called barley breaks, popular with both men and women agricultural labourers, and often linked with feasting, dancing and celebration. There were also married women versus single women matches. Folk football was played with many different kinds of 'balls', from skins inflated with pig's bladders to more solid objects. Because folk football was often violent and linked to drinking, people could get hurt, so it was often banned by monarchs in favour of more useful activities such as archery, which could be used in times of war.

The Football Association's simple rules, the Laws of the Game, differentiated kicking codes from those that authorised handling the ball. Modern football had written rules and was gradually regulated under the Laws of the Game from 1863 onwards. Many football codes, such as Rugby Union Football, Rugby League Football, American Football, Australian Rules, Gaelic Football and so on, shared aspects of the same rules early on and increasingly differentiated their rules so that each game form became quite different.

In the transition from folk football to modern football, sometimes teams would play one half of a game under one set of rules and the other half under a another set of rules. This can make it difficult to say, definitively, that a particular match in the mid-nineteenth century was a game of Association Football because newspaper reports were not clear which code was being played, or even if it was a mixture. But we know that women have played various forms of football for centuries. As with games played on village greens and street football, there are often few newspaper sources, and no photographs, so evidence can be sketchy.

What we can also be sure of is that women helped to promote football during the period when it was becoming standardised and modernised, roughly between the 1840s and the mid-1860s. For instance, the Foot Ball Club Spa in Liege, Belgium, was an experiment undertaken in 1863 by Scottish aristocrats Sir Edward and Lady Helen Hunter-Blair as club patron and patroness with their friends the Fairlies. Although it does not seem to have been long lived, more of a holiday project, the Hunter-Blair's sons and daughters were listed as ordinary members. There may well be other similar examples.

Like many of these games, Association Football is essentially an invasion game, where a team takes the territory of the other by moving the ball. The scoring system involves placing the ball in the opponents' net, and so winning the most important territory that each team defends, the goal. Football is a relatively low scoring game. The rules are 'designedly inefficient'. Without the rules, it would be much easier to be able to stick the ball up your shirt, run the length of the pitch and place it in the goal. But the laws prevent this from happening. So they make the players combine as a team to try and invade the opponents' territory, through a combination of speed and skill. Sometimes the teams can be drawn, and, with two teams of eleven, there are a high number of player interactions over 90 minutes of play, making it hard to predict.

The Football Association, or FA, was an upper-class club for university graduates initially. It was dominated by the Oxford and Cambridge graduates who played mainly for their own enjoyment. When professionalism came, it came from Northern businessmen who understood that football could boost their local town, mill or business. The FA Cup enabled comparisons across the nation. Grudgingly, in

Wall painting of women playing *Cuju*. (*National Football Museum Zibo, China*)

1885, the FA accepted professionalism, and the formation of the Football League followed in 1888.

Women's football began outside the control of the FA, and this image (see plate x), dating from *Harper's Weekly* in 1869 is intriguing because it shows a fashionably dressed group of women players having a kick-around, presumably on a holiday or weekend. Of course, this is not photographic evidence of women's street football, but it intrigued the artist sufficiently that they took the time to record it. We also know of married women versus singles matches, such as one played 23 June 1877 in Scotland.

The increasing urbanisation of Britain in the 1880s and 1890 led to the rapid growth of organised sport. Skilled working-class jobs provided for the Saturday half-day at work, leaving time for matches, and middle-class entrepreneurs began to exploit opportunities to draw large crowds with new stadiums developed in urban centres, and increased links with transport infrastructure. So we see more women in football crowds, often enticed by cheaper entry fees or enhanced spectator experiences like sitting in covered stands. We also see more women as 'ordinary' shareholders of clubs like Arsenal, or running food- and drink-related businesses in or near grounds. Women were very much part of this new entertainment industry.

Glass bottles depicting women and men playing *Cuju*. (*National Football Museum Zibo, China*)

Chapter Two concerns why so many people consider that women's football is a new phenomenon. This was caused by an FA ruling on 5 December 1921 which requested that the clubs affiliated to it withdrew their pitches from use by women's teams, on the understanding that it considered football 'unsuitable' for delicate female frames. The FA also ruled that too much money had been absorbed in expenses by players and clubs and there was a danger of professionalism. The precise FA Council wording was: 'Complaints having been made as to football being played by women, the council feel impelled to express their strong opinion that the game of football is quite unsuitable for females and ought not to be encouraged.'

Without access to FA pitches, women's football moved to public parks, losing the opportunity to charge spectators for entry. This new tradition, contrary to the fact that crowds of 20,000 that had been regular during wartime, held that women's football was unspectacular and lacking in entertainment.

Chapter Three focuses on an important club, globe-trotting Manchester Corinthians Ladies Football Club, who were able to sustain a range of overseas tours and domestic matches in spite of the FA ban. Using a range of methods, including oral history, family history interviews, a reunion of the surviving players and player memorabilia, the chapter provides a history of Corinthians and their second team, Nomads, from 1949 onwards. Corinthians travelled twice to Germany in 1957, and other overseas trips included to Portugal and Madeira, and in 1959 two weeks to The Netherlands. The most ambitious tour, supported by the Red Cross, was twelve weeks in South America and the Caribbean in 1960, followed by one month in Italy in 1961, playing on the grounds of Juventus, Milan and other major clubs. During their existence, both Corinthians and Nomads, toured extensively, including to Ireland in 1962, Morocco in 1966, and France in 1970, in all winning more than fifty trophies. Who were the players, and what were their experiences?

Chapter Four concerns Harry Batt's Touring Teams 1968–72, as he sought to establish a more ambitious international future for women's football. This was a brave experiment, and it almost succeeded. Held outside the auspices of FIFA, there was a speculative series of games in Italy, where there had been professional leagues established by businessmen in 1968. Harry Batt could speak several languages, and was probably the most overqualified coach driver in history. He was also a visionary for women's football. Harry led an England team to the European Women's Championship in Italy in 1970, which proved the business case for women's football as a crowd pleaser. In 1971, only one year after Mexico hosted the men's World Cup, Harry took a team, which he was forced to call British Independents, to an even more ambitious tournament in Mexico, at a time when most ordinary people had not yet been on a plane to Spain. The opening games in Mexico were played in front of crowds of 80,000, demonstrating a large commercial market for women-only tournaments. But who were the players, and why were they and Harry banned on their return?

Chapter Five follows the establishment of The Women's Football Association in 1969, just as the European governing body, UEFA, and the world governing body, FIFA, gradually supported women's football. The glacial rate of change, and the lack of financial support meant that any progress was slow, and often challenged. Key personalities are described, such as Pat Dunn, Arthur Hobbs, Flo Bilton and Pat Gregory. Even church mice would consider the WFA poor. The first paid secretary, Linda Whitehead, was appointed in 1980 and moved office from London to Manchester to be more frugal. In 1993, having made such a dedicated contribution to women's football, Linda was made redundant by the FA as they took full control of women's football, because they thought they had people in place who knew better. In the short term at least, this proved not to be the case.

Chapter Six concerns the generation of Lost Lionesses between 1972, when the first 'official' England women's team was formed, and 1998, when Hope Powell was appointed manager. This generation is explored through the lives and careers of the first four England captains: Sheila Parker, Carol Thomas (the first woman to reach 50 caps), Gill Coultard MBE (the first woman to reach 100 caps), and Debbie Bampton MBE. We see how the growth of international tournaments helped players to play football and see the world. What were their competing club and country commitments, and how, as amateurs, did they train and play?

Girls of the Period Playing Ball featured in *Harper's Bazaar*, August 1869.

Chapter Seven concludes the book with a look at different forms of professionalism, and the migration patterns of those women who pioneered professional careers. This has more of a British perspective, and shows a growing globalisation of the women's game, as new opportunities became established. Finally, the chapter considers the creation of the Women's Super League, and the approaching Women's Euros 2022, as new opportunities for players. Perplexingly, an activity that began as a professional entertainment in 1881 is now seeking new audiences in 2021 in a more digital age. I hope you enjoy the story of these diverse history makers.

Chapter 1

The Honeyballers and Lady Florence Dixie

Nettie Honeyball and 'The Sporting Sensation of the Hour' in 1895

Nettie Honeyball was an astute entrepreneur, as well as a formidable midfielder. As club secretary, and later captain, Honeyball began to promote her newly founded team, The British Ladies' Football Club, or BLFC, well before their first game in 1895 in front of a paying crowd. While she joined the players as they trained before the match in 1894, Honeyball also began to talk to the press about the upcoming fixture, and in so doing used the media to obtain free advertising for her venture, building anticipation amongst spectators and achieving a larger crowd. In many ways late Victorian newspapers and magazines were like the social media of today: for every edition bought, it is estimated that it would be read aloud to those who were not literate, and for those who could read, passed on through several hands to a much wider audience.

A noted journalist, going only by the initials SDB, met with Honeyball at her home and found her to be impressive, writing in *The Sketch* on 6 February 1895:

> 'Miss Honeyball, putting aside an ominous batch of correspondence to give me some detail said; there is nothing of farcical about The British Ladies Football Club. I founded the association late last year, with the fixed resolve of proving to the world that women are not the ornamental and useless creatures men have pictured. I must confess my convictions on all matters, where the sexes are so widely divided, are all on the side of emancipation, and I look forward to a time when ladies may sit in Parliament and have a voice in the direction of affairs, especially those which concern them most.'

The interview continued, with SDB asking: 'I suppose you had a good deal of trouble in obtaining members?' to which Honeyball replied:

'Not at all. I have players from all parts of London, and a few even have to travel from the farther suburbs [sic]. They number close upon thirty, and three or four are married, the ages varying from fifteen to twenty-six. Of course, when we first began, complaints were made of stiffness and soreness, but that soon wore off, and you would be surprised to see the energy thrown into the game. Our original idea was to play our first match on Jan 12, but a good many difficulties stood in the way, so we decided to postpone it until the end of this month, on the Crouch End Ground, and we will call it North v. South. Then, if we attain any sort of success, we hope to visit a few of the provinces and endeavor to foster the game among the ladies there.'

Photograph of Nettie Honeyball, Captain of the British Ladies Football Club, in her football costume.

SDB: 'You may expect an amount of adverse criticism.'

Honeyball: 'I know it. Already the comic papers have burlesqued the notion right and left. All the members are of the middle class, else how could they spare the time and expense to indulge in practice?'

SDB: 'How did you go about getting the team together?'

Honeyball: 'Well in the first instance I advertised, and, as you can guess, I received a few bogus applications from young men. However, I called all the ladies to a meeting, and we soon proceeded to business. None of them, of course, had previously played, but, like myself, had gained all their experience and love of football from frequent onlooking. Then came the question of ground. The committee of the Oval refused to allow us the use of that ground, and eventually we made arrangements with Mr C.W. de Lyons Pike to practice and play on the Nightingale Lane enclosure. We have been out so far very regularly, no matter what the weather, and each time the improvement in style is more marked. Mr J.W. Julian, the well-known half-back, is acting as coach and rendering valuable assistance.'

SDB: 'Then I may take it that there will be no withdrawal – that the club is come to stay and astonish creation?'

Honeyball: 'You need have no fear of the collapse of the association. I told the girls plainly at the outset – they were all strangers to me except my sister – that if they ever wished to give up to tell me at once, and I would get others to take their place; but so far from that, the attendees

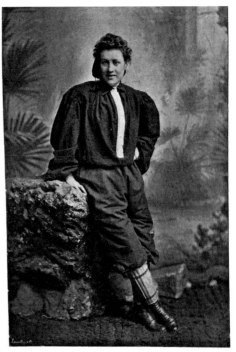

MISS NETTIE HONEYBALL, CAPTAIN OF THE BRITISH LADIES' FOOTBALL CLUB, IN HER FOOTBALL COSTUME.
FROM A PHOTOGRAPH BY MESSRS. RUSSELL AND SONS, BAKER STREET, W.

Photograph of Nettie Honeyball with football, taken at the Delman Art Studios in 1894.

at practice is astonishingly good. We had a little test game day one, and one side won by eight goals to six; but of course, all interest is being centred on the day we admit the public, for, as you may guess, our practice is strictly private. Lady Florence Dixie, who has evinced great interest, will doubtless be present, and has offered to present the winning eleven with copies of her *Gloriana*, a work which will appeal to us all. In addition, a weekly paper has offered timepieces to the successful ones also, so a hotly contested sixty minutes can be promised.'

SDB: 'Since interviewing Miss Honeyball I have had the pleasure of witnessing the members of the BLFC at practice and must confess to feeling of surprise at the amount of ability already attained. Although the occasion of my visit was not favourable, meteorologically, the ladies went about their various duties pluckily and energetically, skill and shooting power making up for any lack of speed and force.'

So SDB appeared to be initially dazzled by Honeyball's determination, and found himself in agreement with her aims, writing:

> We live in an age of progress, and the New Woman is the latest evidence of the advancement. Anybody who had predicted the appearance of ladies "between the lines" would have been looked at more in sorrow than in anger. Yet are we already in possession of a group of fair performers styled The British Ladies' Football Club with Lady Florence Dixie as the President.

If aristocratic support were not enough to entertain his readers, SDB then resorted to a combination of patronizing titillation, and flattery:

> Miss Nettie J. Honeyball is the secretary and captain of what may be fairly described as the sporting sensation of the hour, and, if energy and enthusiasm can command success, then the association is already assured of victory. As I saw her in her pretty little study in Crouch End, a thoughtful-looking young lady, with a strong personality, I at once dispelled the suspicion of burlesque that came into my mind.

The media coverage of women's sport, therefore, has a long and not particularly distinguished history of trivializing and sexualizing female athleticism, in spite of SDB's efforts to supportive gallantry in this piece.

Lady Florence Dixie President of the British Ladies Football Club

When the British Ladies Football Club was formed in London in 1894, there were several non-playing members as the club was part of the wider social changes calling for increased women's rights at the end of the nineteenth century. Lady Florence Caroline Dixie (née Douglas) had been born in 1855, and married Sir Alexander Beaumont Churchill Dixie in 1875. ABCD, as her husband was affectionately known, had homes in Mayfair and Bosworth, but the enormous fortune he inherited did not give him a great sense of how to manage money. The couple had two sons, George and Albert, born in 1876 and 1878 respectively. Dixie was an adventurer, an advocate of women's rights and a writer. An 1877 portrait by Andrew Maclure showed her wearing 'rational dress', and she later supported this for her football players.

Lady Florence Dixie has accepted the presidency of the British Ladies' Football Club. The members of the club do not play in fashion's dress, but in knickers and blouses. They actually (says Lady Florence) allow the calves of their legs to be seen, and wear caps and football boots!
NEWBY-STREET CHAPEL.—Under the auspices of

Newspaper Cutting, 'Lady Florence Dixie Has Accepted the Presidency of the British Ladies Football Club'.

Florence had done her duty by her rather dissolute, but nevertheless charming, husband by producing 'an heir and a spare' child to take over what was left of the family fortune. The children were left in what were hopefully good hands when, in 1879, Dixie went to Patagonia with Beau, her two brothers and a friend, publishing *Across Patagonia* in 1880. Rejecting a life of domesticity, Florence bought home a jaguar cub, which she called Affums, before he killed several deer in Windsor Great Park and was sent to London Zoo. On her return from South America, Dixie was the first woman ever appointed as a field correspondent for the *Morning Post* (later the *Daily Telegraph)*. She reported on the first Boer War, and later moved with her family to Cape Town in order to investigate the aftermath of the Anglo-Zulu war. She had clearly lived a lot and was something of a celebrity in 1895 when she supported the British Ladies Football Club.

Women's Football begins as a Professional Entertainment in 1881

In April 1881 newspapers in Scotland began to report that an 'Enterprising Advertising Agent' was going to organize a women's football match with two teams called England and Scotland, although there they were only nominally national representative sides. International matches between the two countries had become increasingly popular with the first unofficial game played eleven years before in March 1870, so the idea was to exploit the existing rivalry in staging a women's match. Women's professional cricket matches had already used some of the same techniques, with players appearing under pseudonyms, often organised by male professional cricketers as 'penny entrepreneurs.' The tour was scheduled to start in Glasgow in May and end in England in June, and would be widely publicised to make the most of the countries' rivalry.

On 7 May 1881 a crowd of about 2,000 gathered at Hibernian FC's Easter Road ground in Edinburgh to watch Scotland win 3–0. Though widely reported, we have to be cautious in using the newspapers as source materials since not all of the information was accurate. But we do get some useful insights.

The *Edinburgh Evening News* reported favourably on the fixture on 9 May 1881:

> The teams are composed of young women of excellent physique in most cases, and the somewhat fantastic costumes in which they were attired made the scene very charming and effective. The Scotch team, which was made up in Glasgow and neighbourhood, were dressed in blue jerseys, with crimson sash round the waist knickerbockers, and blue and white hose, and high laced boots. A badge with two Union Jack flags was sewed on the breasts of the jerseys. The English team had crimson jerseys with a blue sash, white knickerbockers, crimson and white hose, and high laced boots. They wore badges, with the English standard of the lion rampant. Both teams wore crimson and white woollen "couls". Several of the English team come from London. The number of spectators was good for an ordinary match, but a larger number might have been expected to turn out for to witness such an unusual spectacle. As the teams have only been in training about a fortnight, the play could not be expected to be brilliant, and there was the appearance of bashfulness and hesitancy about the ladies at the start. The game was, on the whole, a very mild kind of football; but the players warmed to their work, the running and dribbling received the commendation of the spectators. A general feeling was apparent, however, to make fun of the match, and when the Scotch team, which kicked off, played the first goal, the spectators cheered ironically. The match ended in a win for Scotland by three goals against nothing.

The *Edinburgh Evening News* reported the Scotland team as: Ethel Hay in goal; Bella Oswald and Georgina Wright in defence (or backs as the term was then); Rose Raynham and Isa Stevenson as midfield (or half backs); and forwards Emma Wright, Louise Cole, Lily St Clair, Maude

Riverford, Carrie Balliol, and Minnie Brymner. This was evidently an attacking line-up and not so unusual at the time, with the idea that a dribbling attacking player would be reinforced by supporting forwards. For this reason, although Louise Cole is reported as scoring the second Scotland goal, the newspapers recorded that Maude Riverford/Isa Stevenson 'combined' to score the third. Whether one gave an assisted pass for the other to score, or in some other way supported remains unclear. For England, the line-up was: May Goodwin in goal; Mabel Bradbury and Maude Hopewell in defence; Maud Starling and Ada Everstone in midfield; and forwards Geraldine Ventner, Mabel Vance, Eva Davenport, Minnie Hopewell, Kate Mellor, and Nellie Sherwood. But were these the players' real names?

An intriguing aspect of these fixtures is that many of the women players had similar, or identical, names to young actresses on the stage at the time, players such as the scorer of the first Scotland goal, Lily St Clair, though the names of some of the other players – Louise Cole, Kate Mellor and Emma Wright – were not that unusual. Whether these names were borrowed as pseudonyms, merely coincidence, or evidence that these actresses had a go at professional football remains to be definitively proven with careful genealogical research. We may never know. Certainly, girls were used to performing in front of a paying public as actresses from a young age, so this, along with theatre contacts, suggests that it was certainly possible. With infant mortality rates high, names were often recycled in families who used names like Mabel, Maud, Kate and Minnie fairly commonly. Some historians have gone further and argued that the women in 1881 were putting on a performance of a football match as actresses, but this is unlikely as anyone who has experienced the spontaneity of sport, compared with a rehearsed theatrical performance, can appreciate.

There is also the suggestion that some players, like Mabel and Minnie Hopewell, shared surnames, which was not unknown in theatrical families, whether or not the actors concerned were actually related by blood. Either way the series of matches was short-lived, as in the case of professional women's cricket, which was also often organised by male professionals who then absconded with the takings leaving the female players high and dry.

Nine days after the Edinburgh game, on 16 May 1881, 5,000 spectators turned up at the Shawfield ground in Glasgow to watch the second match. This did not go so well. Football hooliganism arrived early in women's football and the match was abandoned after 55 minutes. The *Athletic News* reported:

> A few roughs broke into the enclosure, and as these were followed by hundreds soon after, the players were roughly handled and had to take refuge in the omnibus. The crowd then tore up the stakes and threw them at the departing vehicle, and but for the presence of the police some bodily injury to the female might have occurred.

Undeterred, on 21 May England recorded their first victory – 1–0 – at Hole-i'-the-Wall, Blackburn, home of Blackburn Olympic (who would go on to win the FA Cup – the first northern working-class side to do so – in 1883, defeating Old Etonians at Kennington Oval in front of a crowd of 8,000).

Scotland were again victorious 2–1 on 30 May at the Queen's Hotel Ground, Sheffield, followed by a 1–1 draw on 3 June at the Cattle Market Inn Ground, Liverpool, and at Windhill, Bradford, recorded a 2–0 victory. However, Cheetham in Manchester was less hospitable, and two games on Tetlow Fold on 20 and 21 June were abandoned: the first after 30 minutes and the second after 55 minutes. This encouraged the tour to return to the Cattle Market Inn Ground, where the final two matches, on 25 and 26 June, were decided in favour of Scotland by 2–1 and 2–0 respectively.

It is not recorded what the takings were, how much players were paid, or who benefitted financially from the whole enterprise. What is clear is that there was enormous topical interest in women's football and that British players were global pioneers. Australian and New Zealand press coverage reported matches at the time, but we cannot always be sure if these were the Scotland versus England matches discussed here, or home fixtures, or if the reports were about Association Football as opposed to other codes. The tour, however, was hugely important symbolically, proving the existence of a paying public for the women's game.

Was a young Nettie Honeyball inspired by reading about these matches? We do not have a reference from her to them. But being physically active and assertive on a public stage was important to 'New Woman', as Nettie and others were often called, and like the players in 1881, her modernity been so much of the funds absorbed, but it was unavoidable.—The accounts were passed.

FOOTBALL FOR WOMEN.

BY LADY FLORENCE DIXIE IN THE "PALL MALL GAZETTE."

There is no reason why football should not be played by women, and played well, too, provided they dress rationally and relegate to limbo the straight-jacket attire in which fashion delights to clothe them. For, for women to attempt any kind of free movement in fashion's dress means the making of themselves ridiculous, even as men would so make themselves did they play cricket or football arrayed in skirts and their attendant flummeries. I cannot conceive a game more calculated to improve the physique of women than that of football. I refer, of course, to the Association game, which to my mind is the only legitimate representation of this most excellent sport, for I have never been able to see any justification for the word football as applied to the Rugby method of play, which would be better represented by the application "harum-scarum scrummage." In Association football a player must be light and swift of foot, agile, wiry, and in good condition; and are not these physical requisites just the very characteristics of good health most to be desired for women. To lack them is a misfortune, to attain them an ambition, which all lacking them should have; and certainly football is the surest way of securing them. In that school of the future, which, looking ahead, I see arising on the golden hilltops of progress above the mists of prejudice, football will be considered as natural a game for girls as for boys, as will also cricket, athletics, and all national games in pursuit of which the hideous fashions which crush women with their barbarous and unnatural rule will receive their severest checks and final dethronement. It was, therefore, with pleasure, that I accepted the presidency of the British Ladies' Football Club, when I was approached and asked to do so. I stipulated, of course, that if my name was to be associated therewith, the principles of the club must coincide with my publicly-expressed ideas and well-known advocacy of rational dress for women. The members of the club do not play in fashion's dress, but in knickers and blouses. They actually allow the calves of their legs to be seen, and wear caps and football boots. Terrible! is it not? "Quite too shocking!" as an old society dame remarked to me with a shudder, adding squeakily, "And I certainly should never allow dear Mynie to so demean herself!" I looked at her and "dear Mynie," whom she was chaperoning to the ball, and said nothing, though I said a good deal. And amidst my thoughts I wondered which looked most decent, my lithe, agile football teams, in their dark-blue knickers and cardinal and pale-blue blouses, and this old slave of fashion and her unnaturally-attired charge, with her naked grotesque and arms, pinched in waist, high-heeled shoes, and grotesque balloon-like shoulders, hunched and thrown out for all the world like huge tumours? I could only come to one conclusion, and that one may be readily guessed. If the British public will only give encouragement to the idea, which is now being put into practice, of football for women it would soon take a firm hold and become an approved custom. I am in hopes that the British Ladies' Football Club will be able to furnish teams to travel about the country and endeavour to popularise the sport by playing some matches in different localities, which a little encouragement of a practical character will enable them to do. Let women, therefore go in for this excellent game, and earn for themselves that improved physique which will not only improve their appearance, but their health as well, and act as an incentive to the rising generation to go and do likewise. "Hunting," said Mr. Jorrocks, "is the sport of kings, the image of war." "Football," says the president of the British Ladies' Football Club, is the sport for women, the pastime of all others which will ensure health, and assist in destroying that hydra-headed monster, the present dress of women." May it live and prosper is my fervent hope and wish.

Newspaper Cutting, 'Football For Women' by Lady Florence Dixie from the *Pall Mall Gazette*.

extended to wearing a recognizable football kit.

The football industry for men was still in its infancy. The men's professional Football League would be formed in 1888, after the FA accepted professionalism in 1885. So, although male professionals were around at this time, the media furore over women players who drew large crowds of paying spectators to watch their matches meant that the story went global, inspiring other women to play around the world. Though marred by crowd violence and a lack of financial transparency, the matches were staged on major grounds or sites of public entertainment.

Although this was a short-lived experiment, there were many similar matches organised in the 1880s, with Madam Kenney's Famous Edinburgh Team winning 1–0 over Grimsby Town Ladies on 23 April 1887 at the Thornes football field in Wakefield. On 2 February 1899 a six-a-side game saw Greener's Violets win by eight goals to two over Greener's Cutters, both teams coming from a glassworks in Sunderland. Carl's Original French Footballers and the Midland Ladies Association also staged matches. There was talk of a Canadian women's team coming to the UK, but financially this seems to have been optimistic. There are probably many more planned and actual matches yet to be uncovered. This was clearly an entrepreneurial and professional beginning for women's football.

Nettie Honeyball and the British Ladies Football Club Business Model

Although Nettie Honeyball had originally launched the British Ladies Football Club as an amateur team, she was able to consistently draw large crowds on a regular basis and so money became more important. This, in turn, led to new rival teams being established by Helen Matthews and Nellie Hudson. Intriguingly, Brighton High School also recorded a girls' team in 1894 but this doesn't seem to have been as long-lived as the BLFC.

There were around fifty members of the club, of which about thirty were players. Wearing blouses instead of the regulation shirts, and blue serge knickerbockers, shin-pads, ankle protectors and boots, the team trained before their first match, with ex-professional coach J. W. 'Bill' Julian, who had played for both Royal Arsenal and Tottenham Hotspur before finishing his career at Dartford and then opening a sports shop in Plumstead. Florence Dixie would say of the British Ladies Football Club players: 'There is no reason why football should not be played by women, and played well too, provided they dress rationally and relegate to limbo the straitjacket attire in which fashion delights to attire them.' Hence the idea of rational dress. The women covered their heads with fisherman's caps, as it would have been the convention of the time to appear in public with some form of headgear.

THE LADY FOOTBALL PLAYERS.

On Wednesday evening the lady football players visited Doncaster, and played a match on the Intake ground. It was calculated that there would be from 2,500 to 3,000 persons on the ground. The ladies divided themselves into reds and blues. During the first part of the game play was fairly equal, though generally in favour of the reds. Just before half-time, however, the blues, by a capital dribble, carried the ball three-parts of the length of the field and scored, the lady goal-keeper being too far away to prevent the ball going through. The second half was much the same as the first. There was a good deal of chaff and banter, and the play was very moderate. No further score was made, so the game ended in favour of the blues by one goal to none.

Newspaper cutting of a BLFC Match Report at Doncaster, drawing a crowd of 3,000 spectators.

Unlike women's hockey, which had been established by the rather middle-class All England Women's Hockey Association (AEWHA) in 1894/5 season as an all-woman committee, rational dress meant that football players wore breeches, not skirts. Although the American Amelia Bloomer did not create the style of split skirts, later known as Bloomers, she did popularise them from 1851 onwards as a campaigner for women's rights. The style, also known as rational or reform dress, Turkish or American dress, or culottes, was important throughout the nineteenth century for the growth of women's sports and transport, particularly cycling and equestrianism. Certainly Florence Dixie rode astride her horse rather than using a side saddle, and it may have been her affection for equestrian pursuits, especially hunting and blood sports, that cemented her commitment to dress in this way.

In 1894, asked to respond to SBD's question about how her players would handle the public gaze of women in this challenging costume, Nettie Honeyball responded:

> Why not? There is nothing at all questionable in our costume. When Lady Florence Dixie consented to become president, she specially stipulated that, if the club were to attain its end, the girls should enter into the spirit of the game with heart and soul, "I will have nothing to do with balloon sleeves and trained skirts, and anything like that. Don't court ridicule by ridiculing yourselves." Accordingly we all have our costumes of divided skirts – a sort of blue serge knickerbocker – and the teams will be distinguished by wearing, respectively, cardinal and pale blue blouses. You will detect no nervousness in the girls when they make their first public appearance. We practice twice a week.

Women football players who played in matches from the earliest days wore more or less the same football strip as men, with boots, shinpads, blouses or shirts. Although you will often see photographs of women wearing different kinds of divided skirts and caps, this was because most people appeared in public with covered heads at the time. Many of the early men's teams, especially in public schools, often covered their heads as a sign of modesty in public. And, of course, football was mainly played in the Autumn, Winter and Spring months when clothing would have been needed because of cold public outdoor spaces.

Cartoon drawings: 'The Lady Footballers: An Anticipation', from *The Sketch*, 24 October 1894.

Largely due to Honeyball's shrewd PR campaign, the first BLFC match was between North and South, held on 23 March 1895 at Crouch End Athletic ground in Hornsey, drawing over 10,000 spectators. There was a full programme of entertainment, with the women's game preceded by a match between Crouch End and the Third Grenadier Guards, and so the BLFC did not kick off till nearly quarter to five.

It was considered a financial and sporting success, and *The Shields Daily News* of 25 March told its readers that 'the players mainly belong to London and the suburbs but a few hail from the country.' Many were of independent means, the paper went on, but a few were married women. We now think the social mix was greater than this, and the youngest player was about fourteen years of age, with the eldest being around twenty-eight.

North v South meant North London versus South London, and the teams, as reported by *Lloyds Weekly Newspaper* on 31 March 1895, were not always given full first and surname: 'North: Mrs Graham, in goal, Misses Nettie J. Honeyball, Lily Lynn, P. Smith, E. Edwards, Daisy Allen, Ruth Coupland, Williams, Rosa Thiere, B. Fenn, Nellie Gilbert. South: Misses L. Clarence, Annie Hicks, Ellis, Obree, Emma Clarke, Eva Roberts, Lewis, Alice Hicks, A. F. Lewis, E. Potter, Ellis.'

It wasn't clear if the reporter at the match for *The Sketch* on 27 March 1895 was SDB, but it is evident that he wasn't impressed:

> It would be idle to attempt any description of the play. The first few minutes were sufficient to show that football by women, if the British Ladies be taken as a criterion, is totally out of the question. A footballer requires speed, judgement, skill, and pluck. Not one of these four qualities was apparent on Saturday. For the most part, the ladies wandered aimlessly over the field at an ungraceful jog-trot. A smaller ball than usual was utilised, but the strongest among them could propel it no further than a few yards. The most elementary rules of the game were unknown, and the referee, Mr. C. Squires, spent a most agonising time.

Not everyone who attended was so dismissive, however, and the topicality of the event ensured a wide success.

Nettie Honeyball did play in the early matches, but we remain not entirely sure of who she was. Some have suggested the name Honeyball was too apt a title to be her real surname and was probably an alias. This is probably the case as genealogical records show that a player, Jessie Allen, married Frederick Smith, whose brother, Arthur, lived at 27 Weston Park, Crouch End, which is where the BLFC was originally registered. This was the same address used by Nettie Honeyball at the time of the club's first appearance in 1894, and presumably where she spoke to journalists. There is also an interesting letter published on 9 December 1895 in which Jessie Allen, writing as Secretary of The British Ladies' Football Club, Ellesmere, living at 27 Weston Park, Crouch End, London, defends the efforts of the club from the criticism of the Archdeacon of Manchester. Were Jessie and Nettie one and the same person? And had she decided relatively early on to drop the pseudonym in favour of her own identity?

Certainly, in an interview given in November 1895, Jessie said she had taken over as temporary secretary of the club owing to Nettie Honeyball's illness. Perhaps she had just tired of using the pseudonym? Just as intriguingly, Arthur Smith married another of the women players, Hannah Oliphant, in 1896, and it may have been that one of the witnesses, Violet Heffernon, also played, although the spelling of her surname is not exactly the same. In April 1895 Arthur Smith was recorded as manager of the BLFC team in a dispute over a cancelled game, though whether that is due to his address being used for legal purposes or whether he was involved in the logistics of the enterprise remains unclear. There are also references to Nettie's brother being involved, so it may have begun as a family business, allied with increased women's rights. If this is the case, what prompted Jessie Smith to drop the pseudonym so soon after courting such extensive publicity? Probably because she had been too successful, and the enterprise took off rather quickly, so she may have needed a good back-office team to arrange the fixtures.

The publicity for BLFC fixtures came from posters and the press. On 6 April 1895 the BLFC participated in a Charity Festival of Football at Preston Park in Brighton. The event raised funds for local medical charities, on a rather blustery and wet afternoon, and around 5,000 spectators were happy to pay 3d per head. The scale of the undertaking was clearly challenging. On 13 April 1895 a planned match at Gigg Lane, Bury, saw only fourteen of the twenty-two players travel, and the patient

FEMALE FOOTBALLERS

An Unfeminine Exhibition Yesterday

Take it from one who wasted half-an-hour at the Athletic Grounds, Blackpool, yesterday, that where football is concerned the female sex is absolutely incapable. It is useless for the two gentlemen who have persuaded disengaged ballet-dancers to display their charms without the enhancing glare of the footlights to further attempt to convert us. He is a queer mortal who can spend three-quarters of an hour in watching 20 girls vainly attempting to kick a ball. If he pays a second visit, you may be assured he does not go to watch the football, but to admire the opulent figures outlined by the

THIN COTTON GARMENTS

most of the players wear. But the odds are considerable against a single member of yesterday's meagre audience turning up to watch to-day's game. For the girls are uninteresting. One would have thought that natural pride in appearance would have led to the costumes being smart. In their own way, it is true, they have gone one better than the original club, which included the immortal " Tommy." This troupe discards skirts altogether—a thin blouse, tight knickers, and black stockings is the general style of dress. One lady has suffered qualms of conscience, and therefore affects black " bloomers!" The best players are the youngest girls, the average age evidently being about 18. If one shoves another ever so lightly the latter rolls over, and after a mild protest stops to arrange the tresses which are hanging down her back. Another hitched up her knickers yesterday in the most approved masculine style.

THE ONLY EXCITING INCIDENT

of the game was when a tall girl in white suddenly stopped and plucked at her nether garments in a nervous sort of way. Then there were speculations as to what would have happened had not she caught them in time. The players were vigorous, too, on only one occasion. That was when the Whites upset the male goalkeeper in opposition, and sat upon him. Unlike the professional footballer who gets mad if his opponents thus molest him, this man seemed to like the treatment. Miss Dickson was supposed to captain one team, and Miss Duncan to have charge of the other. As a matter of fact they were all captains, and the referee was a very inconsequent person. It would have been fatal for him to enter into argument. Somebody said the Whites won. They may have done. It certainly did not concern any of the spectators, most of whom had had a surfeit of female footballing after the game had been going ten minutes.

Newspaper clipping of a BLFC match report, 'Female Footballers An Unfeminine Exhibition', at Blackpool.

5,000 crowd waited an hour to watch an eight-a-side game between the blues and the reds which ended in a 3–3 draw (two male players, Wally Holland and J.H. Edwards, were eventually to serve as goalkeepers).

In spite of an FA Council meeting at Crystal Palace on 20 April 1895, which advised Sheffield United that 'it was contrary to rules that the Lady Footballers should play on their ground in May' and thus prevented a match at Bramall Lane, the schedule was both ambitious and relentless. That month, teams played at the following grounds on the following dates: 6 April, Preston Park, Brighton; 13 April, Gigg Lane, Bury; 15 April, Caversham Ground, Reading (morning fixture) and Maidenhead (afternoon fixture); 16 April, Ashton Gate, Bristol; 17 April, Walsall; 20 April, St James's Park, Newcastle; 22 April, Barley Bank, Darwen; 24 April, Intake Ground, Doncaster; 25 April, Newark Town FC; 26 April, Harlaxton Road, Grantham; 27 April, Turf Moor, Burnley; 29 April, Maze Hill, Greenwich; and 30 April, St Mirren, Paisley. In May, at Murchiston Park, Falkirk, home of East Stirlingshire FC, a crowd of 3,000 spectators cheered as the South defeated the North 2–1. Maybe the England-Scotland rivalry was being exploited by the change of team names, though in Edinburgh the next day a crowd of 7,000 witnessed the Reds defeat the Blues 1–0 at Logie Green, home of St Bernard's FC. At Springvale Park in Glasgow, the home of Cowlairs FC, one of the founder members of the Scottish League, around 5,000 saw the Blues take their revenge 2–1. Then the tour returned to England for another eight games before returning to Scotland on 24 May and visiting Dundee, Aberdeen, Montrose, Perth and Arbroath before the end of the month.

Those interested in following the most comprehensive match by match account can access, the excellent website hosted by Patrick Brennan http://www.donmouth.co.uk/womens_football/blfc.html. For the purposes of the discussion in this chapter, though, we can see in those first three months that this was an enormous undertaking and crowds varied between 1,000–8,000 spectators.

There were many such penny entrepreneurs like Nettie Honeyball and her network in Victorian sport, from professional swimmers and pedestrians to cyclists, cricketers and balloonists who would enter races and create their own events to cater to a growing mass market for entertainment. Often a pseudonym or family name would be used, even by those who were not blood relatives. This was not an easy business model to develop, but for the most part it was an unregulated activity, away from the control of the Football League and Football Association. Unsurprisingly, rival players like Nellie Hudson, and later Mrs Helen Matthews, formed breakaway teams. Given that matches were played regularly, and at least once a fortnight for most of the first two seasons, we can imagine the logistical challenge of getting from one match to another by public transport in the late nineteenth century, let alone negotiating venues in which to play.

St James' Park in Newcastle was probably the most prestigious ground on which the club played after its first match at Crouch End, and the Reds won by four goals to three. In 1896 The British Ladies Football Club played at Wembley Park. Though Wembley stadium was not built until 1923 – to host the British Empire Exhibition of 1924–25 – this is probably the first time that women's football took place at Wembley. By now the sides were again playing as Reds versus Blues.

Emma Clarke and evidence to explore family history

One of the earliest BLFC players was Emma Clarke. The 1891 census gave her occupation as a nurse, and so the newspaper report was perhaps not entirely accurate. It has been claimed by a number of people that Emma was mixed heritage and so could be the first British-Asian woman football player. However, the paper-based evidence does not suggest this, and it may be that only family history sources could confirm one way or the other. So what do we know so far from the data? Emma's father, John William Clarke, aged twenty-eight, married Caroline Harriet Bogg, aged twenty-one, on 3 May 1863 in Plumstead. John's father, William, was a labourer, and Caroline's father was an overlocker. John was a labourer at the Royal Arsenal, where Emma's brother would later join him. Caroline's mother came from a long established Cornish family; her maiden name was Granville. The Boggs were of Irish-Scottish heritage going back to at least the eighteenth century.

Emma's birth certificate gave her date of birth as 2 December 1871, in Plumstead. The birth and marriage certificates going back to the grandparents do not show any mixed British-Asian heritage, but one aspect of her life has given rise to suggestions that Emma may have mixed heritage. Caroline Bogg's father served in the army for just over four years in Ceylon, where Caroline was born, just as her older sister, Mary Ann, had been born in Dublin when the family was living there. As both Caroline's mother and father were registered on the birth certificate and went on to have other children, there is no evidence from the paperwork to suggest that Caroline was illegitimate. Indeed, given the size of the British army patrolling the empire at the time, having a child while serving overseas was not that unusual.

A final case has been made for Emma being illegitimate, and this of course is just as difficult to prove as it is not recorded, for obvious reasons, on the birth certificate where both parents are listed. If this is the case, it would mean that even if either Caroline or John were unfaithful, the marriage seems to have been successful, with at least five children appearing after Emma, including her blonde sister Florence with whom she played football. As we know, families can have secrets, but for now the paper trail comes to an end.

As we know, women's football was very popular at the time, so the British Ladies Football Club matches were reported widely. There were also lots of photographs telling us quite a bit about the team, and in some of these photographs Emma appears to have darker skin and finer features than some other players, although this isn't always the case, depending on lighting and whether or not the photograph was taken indoors or outdoors. Some photographs were team portraits. There is one in the National Archives on which someone has written Emma Clarke on the reverse side. It is in good condition and seems to support the theory that one of the 1895 team was of mixed heritage. However, other surviving photographs are not so conclusive.

We do know that the newspapers often referred to the players by hair colour. *The Northern Whig* from Belfast has a piece written in 1895 about lady footballers, which includes Emma Clarke, who played right back. It calls her brunette, aged twenty-one, and says that she is a native of Plumstead. It also mentions her sister, Miss F. Clarke, who is seventeen, blonde and also of Plumstead. However, if we look at the census data our sisters are twenty-four and nineteen respectively at this time.

It also appears the sisters went on tour outside of London. *The Belfast Newsletter* of 20 June 1895 ran an article that was very celebratory of the women's teams, naming both Emma and Florence amongst the players, with 6,000 people in attendance. Emma's football career appears to have been short-lived, however. She was very active, and touring in 1895 and 1896, but a split in the team saw her appear less often in the newspapers. Florence and Emma played in a match against Preston North End Juniors male team at Cliftonville, Belfast, in June 1895, drawing 2–2, after which there was an exhibition women's match. Florence had enough energy left over to win a 120-yd race for a gold medal.

Emma Jane Clarke seems to have married Thomas Reginald, referred to as a navvy in the 1901 census, at Woolwich Register Office on 28 October 1899. Emma's father was listed here as John William Clarke deceased, formerly a foreman at the Royal Arsenal. Thomas' father, also Thomas, was a coachman. Witnesses were Charles Edward Clarke and Jemima Ann Clarke. Both were Emma's siblings. Thomas is shown as twenty-three years of age, and Emma was twenty-seven in the 1901 census when their first daughter, Ethel Lizzie, is listed. In the 1911 census a son, Charlie Reginald, had joined the family at 7 Rose Villa Station Road, Abbey Wood, Plumstead.

Emma died, aged fifty-three, in 1925, at 125 Abbey Road, Belvedere. The cause of death was carcinoma of uterus and asthenia. Thomas was present when she died and registered the death the same day. Emma's daughter died in adolescence and her son married but had no children, dying in 1977.

Finally, in exploring just one of the many mysteries about the BLFC, the newspapers often referred to a Dutch lady playing for the team. This has been interpreted by some historians to mean a woman who had mixed heritage. However, the term 'Dutch' may have several meanings. The popular Music Hall song of 1892 called 'My Old Dutch', performed by Albert Chevalier, implied that his wife was his best pal, thought to combine cockney rhyming slang for 'dutch plate' or mate, and 'duchess'. Similarly, Dutch was used to refer to objects and people of substantial build, and a Dutch wardrobe would therefore have been a well-built model. We know that Nettie Honeyball weighed about 10–11st so she would have been robust at a time when women were usually slighter than today. So, like references to hair colour, we have to be careful when using newspapers, photographs and genealogical sources.

Another British Ladies Football Club Mystery: Who Was Tommy?

In many of the newspaper reports of the British Ladies Football Club matches there is special praise for a player called 'Tommy', a name given by the spectators and who appears to have been amongst the more talented of the players. Many match reports state that Tommy was Daisy Allen, but some newspapers raised doubts about whether such a good player could actually be female, suggesting that Tommy may have been one of the players' sons. This was unlikely, though the age of the player is reported to be just eleven so it is conceivable that a young boy could have featured on more than one occasion. Daisy Allen, though, was a talented player who was consistently singled out in the press as a star. She regularly appeared for BLFC over several years and it is most likely that Tommy referred to her. Tommy appears to have been an affectionate nickname related to Tomboys, as women and girls who displayed male behavior were often called.

Although male professional football was being established at this time, the media coverage of women players who drew large crowds of paying spectators meant that the story of Tommy's true identity went around the world, inspiring other women to play globally.

The Victorian Railway and the Success of the BLFC

The Victorian railway system facilitated the success of the British Ladies Football Club as they travelled all over the UK. Ireland hosted fixtures in Cliftonville, Belfast, on 18 June 1895 as the Original Lady Footballers, drawing a crowd of 6,000. On 22 June 1895 the Original Lady Footballers first played against a team of men, North End Juniors, in front of a crowd of 3,000. Games were also recorded in Lurgan and Dublin in 1896. In Wales, matches were recorded in 1895 at Cardiff, in front of 7–8,000 spectators, before going on to Pontypridd, Aberdare, Newport, and Neath. In 1896 matches took place at Caernavon, Llandudno, Carmarthen, Vetch Field, home of Swansea FC, and Pembroke Dock. British Ladies Football Club games in Scotland in 1895 included Paisley, Falkirk, Kilmarnock, Glasgow, Dundee, Aberdeen, Arbroath, Greenock, Montrose and Edinburgh. In 1896 a match against men in Ayrshire resulted in the game being abandoned due to crowd trouble.

Cartoon by Mars,
Past and Present.

PAST AND PRESENT.

There were some groups of matches which show how challenging the logistics were, such as those played from 23 May 1896 onwards at Balhousie Park in Perth, Carolina Port in Dundee, Ochilview Park, home of Stenhousemuir FC, Brockville Park, Falkirk, Saracen Park, Glasgow, and Kinness Park, St Andrews. There were also matches at the City and Suburban grounds in Dublin held on 8 and 19 of May. In between these games a match against a men's team in Irvine, Ayrshire, terminated in a riot.

In October 1896 the team played a group of matches in Wales, increasingly using the format of Ladies v Men, at the Oval, Caernavon, followed by a Llandudno XI Ladies v Men match, a Flintshire Ladies v Men match played at Flint, a BLFC v Carmarthen Gentlemen at Morgan Arms Field, Carmarthen, a BLFC v Gentlemen match played at

Bierspool Football Ground, Pembroke Dock, and a BLFC 4 v Mr Jones's XI at the Vetch Field, Swansea FC. These tours could not have gone ahead without the existence of a scheduled railway service, but this was not perfect. On 30 July 1896 a planned match against men at Guernsey was cancelled because the women missed their train.

Men versus Women's Matches

While men versus women's matches had been tried before, in the 1896–7 season these were more widespread, beginning with The Susquehannahs at the Cardiff Exhibition Bicycle Track. Not all of the players were from the British Ladies' Football Club; some were the Original Ladies' Football Club, or other teams. Planned men v women matches at Wembley Park do not seem to have taken place, or at least match reports are scarce. What we do know is that these matches were immediately popular with a paying public – up to 2,000 spectators in Derbyshire – and increasingly so up to 1902.

On 25 October the Football Association Council held a meeting at 61 Chancery Lane and minuted a directive forbidding affiliated county associations from allowing male players to participate in matches against ladies teams. Biggleswade became an important site of resistance to FA power when the British Ladies' Football Club arranged a match in May 1903 against a local men's team, the Biggleswade Wesleys. The local county association, Bedfordshire FA, attempted to intervene, but it went ahead, even though three of the female players missed their train. Even so, British Ladies' FC were victorious by three goals to one. Miss Nellie Gilbert, one of the original members of the BLFC team which played at Crouch End, was the captain, and so evidently still enjoying her football, as was Hannah Oliphant, another of the early players. Oliphant by now declared herself to be the club's secretary in a letter published by the local press in which she complained about the FA's overbearing attitude to the BLFC. Although the issue of mixed football would be ignored during World War One and shortly after, the FA's 1902 ruling began a series of prohibitions on women playing football that would continue throughout the twentieth century.

Punch Cartoons depicting women playing football, 11 February 1914.

Would we judge the BLFC ultimately as a success or a failure?

As the saying goes, any new venture has to start somewhere. The Victorian women pioneers were therefore a mix of middle- and upper-class leaders and some working-class players, who proved that there was a demand for women's football and mixed football. Unlike the many men's professional clubs established at the time, Honeyball, Dixie and others were not able to establish permanent bases for women's football clubs. This was because the changes in the status of women in the eyes of the law – with successive Married Women's Property Acts allowing women to keep their own earnings in 1870 and then to own and manage their own property in 1882 – were gradual and recent. At a time when many male professional football clubs were being formed with directors owning a share, it was relatively new for women to have access to their own property, let alone to buy land and to establish sporting clubs. This peripatetic existence would define women's football as a sport with no permanent base. Even in our towns and cities today we know of our local football club, even if we are not interested in football, but women's football seems hidden from our everyday lives. The reason for this will become more evident in the next chapter as the FA literally went into turf war over women's use of football grounds.

Chapter 2

Banned

Before World War One a large proportion of young working-class women worked in service, meaning that they lived in the homes of other people as domestic servants. Think *Downton Abbey* and you will recollect that this meant many young women had little personal time or private space in which to enjoy themselves.

At the outbreak of war many young men volunteered to join up through their local football clubs, and formed what became known as Footballer's Battalions when on active service. It quickly became clear that the men would not be home by Christmas, as most people had forecast in 1914. Women moved increasingly into dangerous occupations such as munitions, manufacturing and mechanics, as well as traditionally female work like communications, nursing and factories.

There does seem to be a general consensus that after a relatively brief peak between 1917 and 1919, when women comprised perhaps half of the British labour force, the female proportion of workers outside the home remained somewhere between twenty-five and thirty per cent between 1911 and 1931. However, when we also factor in casual labour and piece-work inside the home, which were common in the clothing industries, the number of women who were economically active exceeded this by some margin.

After war broke out, and when compulsory conscription meant that most able-bodied young men had gone to war, women moved into traditionally male jobs and received better pay. The pay was often lower than that of the equivalent male workers, but it gave a chance of more independence. With these jobs, which were often dirty and dangerous, came camaraderie with other women, and men who had been left behind, as well as a right to leisure outside the home. As a game requiring team spirit, and a sign of normality on the home front, football proved to be popular and topical. It was a form of 'rational recreation' often encouraged by workplaces, meaning that it was considered preferential to other leisure pursuits that could distract young women, such as the pub, music hall or cinema.

However, women were not treated well for their war-service. World War One had emphasised the need for female physical fitness, courage, stamina and technological skill. Female labour was to be vital for Britain's industry and infrastructure during the war, but women workers were not so respected in peacetime. Half a million women who had paid their insurance contributions as munitions operatives from 1917 onwards were asked to give up those jobs by 1921, offered neither retraining nor government financial support, and many were forced into uninsured trades.

Many of the early 150 women's football clubs played games to raise funds for wounded soldiers, or for those suffering from trauma, and many matches were played against recovering male soldiers. There were also a growing number international matches from 1917 onwards. In 1920 the England v France game spread as a media event across the world.

Punch Cartoon 'Jane What is The Meaning of This Costume?' 19 April 1922.

When the two captains kissed in welcome and shook hands, the image was transmitted around the globe before a ball had even been kicked.

On 30 April 1920 25,000 spectators saw England beat France 2–0 at Preston North End's Deepdale Stadium, with goals from Florrie Redford and Jennie Harris. On 1 May 1920 15,000 spectators saw the rematch at Edgeley Park with England scoring five goals (Florrie Redford two, Jennie Harris, Jessie Walmsley and Alice Woods) to France's two (Genevieve Laloz and Madeline Braquemond).

This popularity threated the revenues of the professional male football establishment, which sought to expand the existing two divisions of the Football League in 1921 to include a division three north and a Division three south, thereby creating a need to protect income streams. Under pressure from these new league clubs, on 5 December 1921 the FA requested that the clubs affiliated to it withdrew their pitches from use by women's teams, on the understanding that it considered football 'unsuitable' for delicate female frames. The FA also ruled that too much money had been absorbed in expenses by players and clubs and there was a danger of professionalism. The precise FA Council wording was:

> Complaints having been made as to football being played by women, the council feel impelled to express their strong opinion that the game of football is quite unsuitable for females and ought not to be encouraged.
>
> Complaints have also been made as to the conditions under which some of these matches have been arranged and played, and the appropriation of receipts to other than charitable objects.
>
> The council are further of the opinion that an excessive proportion of the receipts are absorbed in expenses and an inadequate percentage devoted to charitable objects.

For these reasons the council request clubs belonging to the association to refuse the use of their grounds for such matches.

Although it lacked the resources, and inclination to police this ruling, the FA did pursue a spiteful policy of monitoring which of its affiliated clubs were complying, and then also asked other sports codes, such as rugby league and cricket, which initially allowed women to use their grounds, to support their policy. So, while some historians have criticised the use of the word 'ban' to describe the FA's prohibition of women playing on their grounds, the fact that it was reinforced regularly suggests that the idea was to forbid a female invasion of pitches. Following what was also effectively a ban on women playing in front of large paying crowds, the withdrawal of FA affiliated pitches for use by women's teams lasted for over fifty years.

The women's game effectively became a sport played on public land, without the ability to encircle a pitch in order to charge entry, and this initiated a belief, contrary to what had gone before, that women's football was unappealing and lacked the ability to draw paying spectators in their thousands. However, the rise of women's football could not be permanently stifled, even by prohibition. There had already been green shoots of interest around the world. Before returning to the story of how the success of women's football as a means of raising money for charity during World War One would lead to the FA's embargo, the next section considers briefly some examples of women's football around the world prior to this exclusion. Before we consider the FA ban as a seminal moment in shaping the history of women's football, it is important to remember that the BLFC had already sparked worldwide interest, and women had taken to the fields to claim their place in international football history.

Green Shoots

In the South American cone, according to *Futbolera*, written by Brenda Elsey and Josh Nadal, there is evidence that women played football in Chile by 1900, and possibly before. Photographs at the Museo Histórico Nacional de Chile (Chilean National Historical Museum) feature Team Talca from the town's school, dated c. 1900. Another photograph from the museum, dated eighteen years later, also shows *futboleras* from Team Santiago of Talca, although they are wearing formal schoolwear, not athletic clothing. Nevertheless, the women feature in a related press cutting that criticises them for entering traditional male spaces. However, Talca was not alone, In 1905 Badminton Football Club organised a match with a team of young women playing against one of men to raise money for a children's hospital. These seemingly isolated incidents could suggest a need for more research across the country.

Like the UK during World War One, Chile seemed to have experienced a boom in women's football, and Elsey and Nadal show how important

European women's physical education pioneers took team and ball games to Chile to encourage girls' physical development. On 11 May 1919 *El Mercurio* newspaper featured a match between two women's teams, Flor del Sport and Delicias del Sport, as the first event in a day's schedule of several football matches. Representatives of nine women's teams gathered in the offices of *El Mercurio* to form a women's football association. The teams included Flor de Chile, Progreso Femenino, Belgica Star, Compañía Chilena de Tabacos (Chilean Tobacco Company, most probably a team sponsored by the company, though it is not clear if they were employees). The newspaper also reported an exhibition match between Flor de Chile and Delicias del Sport as part of a sports festival sponsored by Club Motociclista Nacional (National Motorcycle Club), which included an aviation show and a motorcycle race. More coverage included the results of executive board elections of women's teams and announcing registration periods for the clubs, similar to what happened in men's football in Chile. Although politicians and dictators like Carlos Ibáñez sought to shut down women's teams, sport remained a hub of feminist struggle in Chile into the 1920s.

Prior to the First World War women's football games were also reported in Oceania, perhaps influenced by the links with the British Empire and the media. In New South Wales women's football teams were formed at the Clyde Engineering Sparta Club, overseen by works supervisor Mr A. Lennox of Parramatta in 1903. Of course, there may well be more, but the fusion, and perhaps confusion, of football to mean soccer, rugby and Australian Rules means that historians must be cautious. For instance, Peter Burke's work on women's workplace Australian Rules football between 1915 and 1918 indicated that a mix of company welfare, a reduced schedule for male matches, patriotic employers and improved public relations boosted female participation in team games generally. Female munitions workers also played football during World War One, as they did in New Zealand. In 1915 the first competition was staged in South Island, New Zealand, and played until 1918.

In the US, a women's football match between the Colleen Bawns and the Bonnie Lasses was recorded in San Francisco in 1893, attracting 2,500 spectators, with players set to earn $2 per match. Of course we need to be careful about which code this was. Newspapers reported that amongst the squad were two Algerian players and two Canadians who all

Page 489   The War Illustrated, 21st July, 1917.

War-time Football in Surrey Playing-Fields

"Open your mouth and shut your eyes."—Mdlle. Gina Palerme, the popular actress, helping to entertain wounded soldiers on the green of the Paddington Bowling Club.   The members of this club have during the past two years entertained several thousands of wounded men.

Smartly "saved" by the ladies' goalkeeper, and (right) an incident in the game.   The soldiers were handicapped by having their hands fastened behind them—all except the goalkeeper, who was allowed one hand free.

Ladies versus Soldiers in a "Soccer" match at Haslemere.   Watching the spin of the coin—and (left) one of the ladies has just missed a "header."   The ladies won.   The match took place in aid of the Red Cross funds.

'War-Time Football in Surrey Playing-Fields' featured in *The War*, 21 July 1917.

had experience of the sport. It was also reported that physical education instructor Lucille Hill had introduced soccer to Wellesley College, Massachusetts.

Although we are now aware of a growing number of early matches worldwide, it would seem that Europe was the main hub for women's football before World War One. However, the evidence is often patchy. In Russia two women's teams are recorded as playing on 3 August 1911 at Pouchkino Petrovsko-Rasoumovskoe. In Spain El 'Spanish Girls' Giralda versus Montserrat toured Catalonia and played at FC Barcelona's ground, Parc Brú Sanz, in 1914 before the outbreak of war. In Belgium in 1911 a match took place at the Convent L'Assumption à Huy between Namur and Liege L'ecole formation d'Uccle.

Besides the UK, the other main country for developing women's football at this time was France where, in 1910, Equipe Du Groupe Sportif de l'Ecole Supérieure des filles played a match against Pont-à-Mousson in Meurthe-et-Moselle. These appear to be sports students, and, unlike the factory workers of the British women's teams, the French players were often educated to secondary or college level and were also good, all-round athletes. In 1919 En Avant! played against Fémina in Paris, as referenced by André Isch in *La Gloire du Football Lorrain*. This was a kind of national championship. A third team, Academia, was founded in 1920, and a representative team to tour England formed later that year. This is covered later in the book but worth noting here that France would go on to have an important place in both women's football and Olympic history, with a thriving culture of teams during and shortly after World War One. Typically, Fémina had originally been a gymnastics club and had played amongst themselves and against youth men's teams before playing against other newly formed women's sides.

Munitionettes' Football

The term Munitionettes' football is widely used to describe women playing matches in front of crowds of up 55,000 in aid of charity between 1917 and 1921. But it is something of a misnomer in two senses. Firstly, once the Eastern front had collapsed, the demand for munitions decreased and demobilisation began before the Armistice in November 1918. Secondly, there were other work-based women's teams such as Horrockses' Ladies

288   LE MIROIR DES SPORTS

LE MATCH FÉMININ FRANCO-ANGLAIS DE FOOTBALL

LE PUBLIC, L'ENTRÉE ET LA PRÉSENTATION DES JOUEUSES, LE TIRAGE AU SORT ET QUELQUES PHASES DE LA PARTIE
1. Une partie des 10.000 spectateurs qui assistèrent au match du Stade   de Ricard procède au tirage au sort d...
Pershing ; en haut : le tableau d'affichage ; 2. L'équipe de France entre
sur le terrain ; 3. Les deux équipes ...

Detailed coverage of the France versus England internationals in *Le Miroir Des Sports*, 1920.

– named after the textile family known as the Cotton Kings of Preston
– and Atalanta of Hull, an affiliation of professional women such as
teachers and nurses. The Lancashire United Transport Company based
in Atherton had a women's team as early as 1915, and the women of the

Preston Army Pay Corps had already played at Deepdale, the home of Preston North End Football Club, in 1916.

As Alexander Jackson has shown, the Portsmouth Ladies FC, founded in 1916, had a diverse playing record, including games against male teams, and Councillor Tom Langdon was central to organising and promoting their activities. Photographic coverage afforded to the team, particularly by *The Portsmouth Evening News*, was extensive, especially the work of photographer Joseph Stephen Cribb. This increased coverage of teams such as Portsmouth shows not only an increasing interest in the women's game but also the changing nature of the newspaper industry as photographs became less expensive to print and therefore more space could be devoted to larger images, thus attracting the passing consumer. Women's teams were also being formed in other industries such as hospitality and entertainment. Lyons tearooms, for example, as ubiquitous in their day as fast food restaurants are now, had several women's football teams, more than one per branch in some cases.

It is quite wrong to say that the end of the First World War was the end of women's football. The ban on using FA grounds was not completely successful and it was contested. This chapter explores that nuanced picture. It is also wrong to argue, as several historians have done, that women's football was already in decline before the 1921 ban. Firstly, important clubs like Atalanta of Huddersfield and Bridgett's United of Stoke were formed after World War One had concluded. Secondly, if we explore both the match schedule of women's clubs, like the Dick, Kerr's Ladies team of Preston, and the establishment of new clubs after 1918, there were signs that women's football was growing, not declining. Thirdly, more international matches were being played after 1918, by teams claiming to be representative national sides, and also by clubs who were finding their opponents in the US and Europe.

Sport and politics have always mixed, and many women saw playing football as a sign of modernity, as we have already seen with Nettie Honeyball and Lady Florence Dixie. By the outset of World War One women played all kinds of sports, some as amateurs in more upper-class pursuits that were often played in clubs designed to exclude the lower classes; archery, tennis, croquet and golf, for example. Winners nevertheless often won prize money and took home 'fancy goods' as trophies. The first female Olympians were from this class base: golfers, tennis players and archers who could afford to travel to compete in the Paris Olympic Games in 1900, and London 1908 (although at the 1904 St Louis Olympics only US female archers competed). Swimming, cycling, equestrianism, ballooning, pedestrianism (running or walking) and women's cricket also had histories of professional female athletes. Team sports like hockey were also popular, and women also formed their own amateur associations such as the All England Hockey Association in 1894, mainly led by institutions of higher and further education and so quite unlike the social class associated with women's football. In middle-class homes with room for lawn games, mixed sports such as tennis and croquet became popular for socializing, while horse racing involved large crowds and dedicated 'ladies days' where the fashionable could see and be seen.

Many women who did not work in service, worked in mills and factories, often with long shifts, and then had a 'double day' of working when they got home; cleaning, cooking, washing and other manual jobs on top of looking after children. Leisure as we know it was extremely scarce; there were no 'white goods' like domestic washing machines, vacuum cleaners, tumble dryers, and dishwashers to make life easier. After 1914, however, women began to work on the land, in munitions

There were around 150 women's teams during World War One, about which much remains to be known.

factories and in communications, as well as more widely in nursing, and began to play football together.

The business model of women's football mirrored that of men's football: attracting large paying crowds through advance publicity and playing games in large stadiums, therefore maximizing the sums of earned. The main difference, though, was that women's games raised money for charitable good causes. Although some men's football matches also raised money for charity, and regional professional football continued, the point of women's football was that it was another kind of war work. Many of the early games during World War One were played to raise charitable funds for wounded soldiers, or for those suffering from trauma, and many mixed matches were played against recovering male soldiers, such as this match report:

> Ladies versus soldiers in a soccer match at Haslemere. Smartly saved by the ladies' goalkeeper. The soldiers were handicapped by having their hands fastened behind them, all except the goalkeeper, who was allowed one free hand. Watching the spin of the coin and (left picture) one of the ladies has just missed a header. The ladies won. The match took place in aid of Red Cross funds.
>
> Anon. 'War Time Football in Surrey Playing Fields',
> *The War Illustrated* (21 July 1917 p. 489)

Home Internationals

Initially, women's football followed the pattern of British teams playing 'Home' Internationals between Wales, England, Scotland and Ireland (which, after the partition of the country in 1920, became the Republic of Ireland and Northern Ireland). This was probably financially driven, and also down to existing networks. For instance, as Patrick Brennan has shown in his forensically researched book, *The Munitionettes*, published by Donmouth in 2007, in December 1917 the Munitionettes' Cup Committee in north-east England wished to stage an international match against an Ireland XI. Trials to select the teams from local sides included players from Jarrow, Sunderland, Blyth, Slipway, Birtley, Hood Haggie, North Eastern, West Hartlepool, Swan and Hunter and Willington Foundry. This alone gives an idea of the strength in depth at this time.

Managed by David Brooks of Rosehill and accompanied by welfare officer, Nurse Harrison, the team left Newcastle just after midnight on 24 December to attend a men's match, at which the captain Bella Carrott 'kicked off' to open proceedings, went to the cinema and visited a hospital, before spending Christmas Eve at the Belfast Hippodrome. It was a social whirl before the women's match took place on Boxing Day. The Irish team was mainly drawn from the Belfast Whites and the Lurgan Blues, and there was much ceremony, with the Lord Mayor of Belfast formally kicking off the match in front of 20,000 spectators. Bill McKracken, the Newcastle United professional and Ireland international, officiated, while the line was run by his Scottish club colleague Jimmie Lawrence, and Belfast-born Mickey Hamill, who would play for Belfast Celtic, Manchester United, Manchester City, Celtic, Boston, and the New York Giants in a professional career spanning twenty years. England won 4–1 with goals from Mary Dorrion, Ethel Jackson, Sarah Cornforth and Nellie Kirk, while Montgomery scored for Ireland, though was not dignified by a first name in the newspapers.

A charity ladies' football match was held at Celtic Park on 2 March 1918, and was billed as Scotland v England, in support of Sir Williams Beardmore's efforts to raise money for infirmaries. The match was actually between the works teams of Vickers-Maxim at Barrow-in-Furness and Beardmore's at Parkhead, or Beardmore's Munition Girls v Vickers' Munition Girls. Vickers, or 'England', won 4–0, but were defeated on the return fixture in Barrow a few weeks later.

St. James's Park, Newcastle, hosted another international against Scotland, specifically the West of Scotland, on 20 July 1918, in aid of St. Dunstan's home for Blinded Soldiers and Sailors. It is difficult to know whether the revised England team was drawn from a wider range of clubs because of footballing ability or because of who was available to travel. England's player were: Jennie Hodge (Middlesbrough); Hilda Weygood (Wallsend); Bella Reay and Nellie Fairless (Blyth Spartans); Bella Willis (Armstrong 60s Shop); Sarah Cornforth (Birtley and Pelton); Minnie Seed (Armstrong's Naval Yard); Mary Dorrian (Brown's, West Hartlepool); Winnie McKenna (Bolckow Vaughan); Bella Reay (Blyth Spartans); Mary Lyons (Palmer's, Jarrow), and Lizzie McConnell (Wallsend Slipway). Bella Reay was one of women's football's early superstars in the twentieth century, along with Winnie McKenna, who was captain of England and had featured strongly for her club in the Munitions Cup of 1918. Scotland drew their team from fewer clubs: Jean Brown (Cardonald, Govan); Dolly Cookson (Inchinnan, Paisley); Rosina Clark and Lizzie McWilliams (Clydesdale); Nellie McKenzie and Jean Wilson (Cardonald); Maggie Devlin and Agnes McConnell (Mossend, Carfin); Bella Renwick and Robina Murdock (Mossend).

St James's Park again hosted the return Ireland match on 21 September 1918 for the Lord Mayor's War Relief Fund. Hosted as part of a sports gala, this was far less spectacular than the first England versus Ireland match, as only 2,000 attended, possibly due to the influenza pandemic which was reaching more widely in the autumn of 1918. A 5–2 victory for England netted only £60 in gate receipts.

As this chapter will make clear, the FA still today does not recognise any of these matches as 'official' since it did not endorse them, even though they were played in major stadiums of professional clubs affiliated to the FA and the Football League. In effect, the FA has rewritten history to make these matches invisible. As an organisation that has been around for almost 160 years, this seems an immature attitude, possibly even arrogant and chauvinistic. The fact that pioneer women players and officials promoted the game of football with only very basic resources, largely for charity, and in their own time, without FA support can perhaps be understood in the context of its time, but it seems very begrudging now that the FA still cannot accept aspects of the history of women's football. The organisational history of the FA would partly be defined by the fifty-year ban in the twentieth century and into the twenty-first, though, fortunately, this meant that women's football would be in much better hands.

Early Stars: Dick, Kerr's and Fémina play as England v France

The most famous team, Dick, Kerr Ladies, had begun to play seriously in October 1917. They were based at the Strand Road tram building and light railway works, and originally founded by W.B. Dick and John Kerr of Kilmarnock. The production had by then moved to munitions but this would soon cease. It is important to remember that the team would play more in peacetime than during hostilities, therefore. Regional pride had, of course, been developing for a much longer period with a music hall song commemorating Preston North End as the first champions of the Football League and of the FA Challenge Cup in 1889.

The Dick, Kerr's women's team played first against male colleagues during tea breaks at the munitions factory, but the format developed into women's matches for charitable purposes, a pattern that lasted until the women's team disbanded in 1965. Minute books of Preston North End, held at the National Football Museum, indicate that those acting on behalf of the women used the existing connection with the Dick, Kerr men's football team in approaching 'Proud Preston' for the use of its ground. Dick, Kerr's male munitions workers used Deepdale for a match on 27 December 1915, after which they were entertained to tea at a cost of 2s 6d per head. Further applications were made for men's munitions games and Preston North End were also later to play against a team representing Dick, Kerr's men on 13 April 1918.

Deepdale ground was granted by the Preston committee on 30 October 1917 for a game against T. Coulthard and Co. Ltd munitions workers, to be played on Christmas Day. The board also offered their support in the forms of advertisements on Preston North End posters, to be jointly paid for by the club and Dick, Kerr's women. The game raised £488 and 7s for the Moor Park Hospital. The *Lancashire Daily Post* match report said of Dick, Kerr's 4–0 victory: 'Quite a number of their shots at goal would not have disgraced a regular professional except in direction, and even professionals have been known on occasion to be a trifle wide of the target. Their forward work, indeed was often surprisingly good.' Anon. 'Ladies at football', *Lancashire Daily Post*, 27 December 1917.

In the initial four-game season, Dick, Kerr Ladies Football Club played home fixtures against local rivals Lancaster (1–1 draw), Barrow (2–0 win) and Bolton (5–1 win). A ten-game second season for 1918–1919 followed and manager Alfred Frankland first wrote to other clubs via the newspapers to set up a Lancashire women's league. He seems to have abandoned the idea by the end of 1919.

By now, Dick, Kerr's rivalry had broadened to include Manchester, home of the British Westinghouse works team, Heywood Ladies, and by March 1919, Newcastle United Ladies, who played at St James' Park in front of crowds of 35,000. Their striker, Winnie McKenna, already had 130 goals to her name for Vaughan Ladies.

Dick, Kerr's Ladies FC of Preston.

There were also local women's leagues and cup competitions. While Blyth Spartans had played their first match against men, for instance, in 1917, with the male team billed the Jack Tars, a Munitionette's Cup focussed the attention of teams in the north east, including Palmer's Shipyard, Morpeth Post Office and Gosforth Aviation. Blyth would go on to win the cup in 1918, with Bolckow Vaughan Ladies as runners up. Both Blyth's star player, Bella Reay, and Bolckow's captain, Winnie McKenna, would go on to play for teams representing England, so local fame could spread to an international audience through such cup competitions.

As to league football, this was also largely working class and regionalised. For instance, in the 1920–21 season a Bradford Ladies' League had two divisions. In descending order from the top of the table, the first division teams were: College Ladies; Old Hansonians; Bradford; Odsal; Undercliffe; Grange; Tartan; Shipley; Frizinghall and Saltaire. The second division clubs were: Sion; Bowling; Cawthorns; Tetley Street; Phone Exchange; St Aidens; YWCA; Westgate; C.M. & M. Ladies and Eastbrook. There was also more than one cup or knockout competition, as in the week of the reference YWCA were due to meet Tetley Street in the second round of the Hospital Tournament (replay) to be refereed by Mr Millar. Not all of the above were work-based teams and some reflected other affiliations, such as the Bowling and YWCA teams, and geographical locations. With research in local newspapers, we could probably find more leagues and cup competitions like this.

It is unclear whether any or all of the matches were played for charity or whether players were awarded expenses. Most teams in the Bradford league had played nine or ten games, as opposed to almost sixty contested by the Dick, Kerr team in the 1920–21 season. There were also photographs of Lister's Ladies, Manningham and YWCA teams playing cricket in the summer and it would be good to know how many women played in these, and the hockey teams to which the article refers. A typical match was reported in *The Lancashire Daily Post* on 14 March 1921 with gate receipts of £210 followed by tea and a complimentary performance at the Hippodrome. It all sounded very convivial.

There were also an increasing number of international matches after World War One, implying that the media was important in making players aware of their counterparts in other countries. In 1920 Dick, Kerr invited Fémina over from France to play a series of games in Preston which received media attention in both France and England. England v France fixtures received national broadsheet recognition on both sides of the Channel, evidenced by the illustrated report of 'Ladies at Football England v France by a Special Correspondent' in *The Times* of 7 May 1920. A similar tie the next year at Longton Park, Stoke, with a crowd of 15,000 was titled 'England v France' and the *Daily Mirror* had two photographs of striker Lily Parr and a caption: 'Chairing Miss L Parr after the match. She scored all five goals.'

In France, the leading newspaper, *Le Miroir Des Sports*, also reported favourably,

> The match between a French team and an English team was played in front of ten thousand spectators and proved a real success. Each team scored a goal for their particular efforts; the English team showed their superiority for the most part by controlling possession. And the French used speed and stamina. Is it practical to expect women's football across all cities in France? The public on Sunday, who were equally passionate to meet at the Stade Pershing as they would be a male match, who encouraged, applauded, whistled and generally engaged, proves the interest in women's sport.
>
> (André Glarner 'Les Épreuves Et Les Vedettes De La Semaine',
> *Le Miroir Des Sports*, 4 November 1920, p.275.)

Dixième année. — N° 323.   Le numéro : **40** centimes.   Dimanche 1ᵉʳ Février 1920.

LE MIROIR

PUBLICATION HEBDOMADAIRE, 18, Rue d'Enghien, PARIS

LE MIROIR paie n'importe quel prix les documents photographiques d'un intérêt particulier.

UN MATCH DE FOOTBAAL ASSOCIATION ENTRE "FEMINA-SPORT" ET "ACADEMIA"

Une intéressante rencontre s'est produite à Paris, entre deux sociétés sportives féminines. On voit, ici, un dribling des avants de "Femina-Sport", pendant un match de football-association, fort savamment mené.

Front Page News, Academia versus Fémina, *Le Miroir*, 1 February 1920.

The four internationals, heavily featured around the world in print and on film, inspired many more internationals. It showed that women's football could capture the hearts, and finances, of tens of thousands of football fans in regular matches, often kicked off by the entertainment stars of the day, like the recently defeated French heavyweight world champion boxer 'Gorgeous' Georges Carpentier, captured on Pathé newreels.

For domestic matches, while eighty per cent of the gate receipts were given over to Dick, Kerr after expenses, there were also arrangements with Preston North End for practice matches at £12 for a Saturday fixture, £3 per week for training midweek nights and £20 for Christmas Day fixtures. It is now difficult to know whether the use of other large football league grounds such as Goodison Park, Old Trafford and Stamford Bridge, used by Dick, Kerr's from late 1920 and into 1921, was an ongoing attempt to win a larger audience or motivated by necessity as Deepdale became increasingly less available. Certainly by August 1920 relations were frosty.

Dick, Kerr were important as part of a growing change in women's football, as they drew in players from outside Preston who stayed for both short spells and longer careers. The playing personnel was certainly drawn from outside the immediate area, with Frenchwoman Louise Ourry, and later, Scottish player Nancy 'The Cannonball' Thomson moving to Preston and working while they played.

In early March 1921 *The Lancashire Daily Post* announced an international 9–0 win against a Scotland side at Celtic Park. Many of the England team were Dick, Kerr players and the Preston team had played again in an 8–1 win the previous Saturday at Coventry City in front of 27,000, with gate receipts of £1,622. The players reportedly travelled around on 'two special saloon cars put on without cost by the railway company' from Coventry to Leeds and then to a match in Hull.

Dick, Kerr won the game by four goals to nil and acquired a famous new admirer:

A crowd of 21,000 paid £1,160 towards the Hull Unemployed Fund at a ladies' football match on the Hull N.U. ground […] There was remarkable enthusiasm both in the city and on the ground, the teams being given a splendid reception. Georges Carpentier, the famous French boxer, who kicked off, created some amusement by kissing the rival captains before the game started […] At the Hull City Hall the same evening Carpentier presented the winning side with the Yorkshire Ladies' Premier Charity Cup. The French boxer obtained all the autographs of the Preston Ladies team.

An article appearing on 9 April 1921 in *The Football Favourite*, which was aimed at adolescent sports fans, reported ambitious tour plans:

LE MIROIR
DES SPORTS

Abonnements:
1 An . . 25 fr.
6 Mois . . 13 fr.

Abonnements:
1 An . . . 25 fr.
6 Mois . . 13 fr.

PUBLICATION HEBDOMADAIRE ILLUSTRÉE, 18, RUE D'ENGHIEN, PARIS

8/5,
ageux
r dans le
ettement et
en 11" 1/5, ce
après-midi de

DRÉ GLARNER.

UNE JOUEUSE ANGLAISE, LYONS, SHOOTE AU COURS DU MATCH FÉMININ FRANCO-ANGLAIS DE FOOTBALL

Front page news, *Le Miroir* reports on the France Versus England games in 1920.

Can Girls Play Football? Of Course!

To-day another very fine fixture is due to be played on the Elland Road ground, Leeds. The rival teams are Dick, Kerr's versus Yorkshire and Lancashire Ladies. Lucky Leeds! You are in for a real treat! I must mention that Dick, Kerr's have been invited to visit Canada. Indeed, letters have been received from all parts of the Empire imploring the famous Preston lassies to 'come over'. The matter of a world tour is under consideration but the state of the clubs finances will probably be a deciding factor […] A Ladies' Football Association is already an established fact. It flourishes under the title the Yorkshire Ladies' Football and Baseball FA. Moreover this association is offering a Ladies' Football Challenge Cup competition between all teams in England.

The magazine featured an ongoing fictionalized serial based on Dick, Kerr's dominance. It featured mill worker Meg Foster, who was captain and striker of Blake's Crusaders' football team. On the 16 April 1921 *The Football Favourite* ran a story entitled 'Football Island: A Splendid New Story of Meg Foster', which may have been influenced by the idea of Dick, Kerr's proposed world tour.

On 6 June 1921 *The Lancashire Daily Post* reported: 'Dick, Kerr's Most Successful Season. The team having won 58 out of 59 games, the other being drawn in Paris, with a total of 393 goals for, 16 against.' The report described the Crewe Cottage Hospital Cup and the Ex-service Men's Cup as, 'A handsome massive silver trophy given by Mr Hogge, MP for East Edinburgh worth about £100 […] Some £46,000 has been raised for charity so far.' A week later, at the Crewe Alexandra ground, Gresty Road, the concluding game of the 1920–21 football season saw an 8–0 win over a Welsh XI before Dick, Kerr's departed for a short tour of the Isle of Man. On 8 August 1921 *The Isle of Man Daily Times* announced:

> The visit of the famous Dick, Kerr International Ladies' Team has aroused widespread interest in the Island. They have been instrumental in raising vast sums of money for charitable objects in England […] Amongst the defeated teams are teams representing the France, Scotland, Ireland and Wales also teams representing the Rest of the United Kingdom […] It is pleasing to note that Manx charitable objects will benefit to some extent.

The column is next to one of the few newspaper advertisements for a women's game, announcing: 'Room has been made for ten thousand spectators,' at the racecourse at Ramsay, who were expected to pay, 'A Popular Price of One Shilling'. Bad weather beset the tour but games were played at Port Erin on the 10 August and concluded at Douglas three days later, where Dick, Kerr's won 4–0 at the Belle Vue ground.

In all of the coverage I have followed through the newspapers from 1917 to 1921 of Dick, Kerr's, there were no reports of serious injury, except a report that Florrie Redford had once been bitten on the ankle by a dog while playing football. Following the 1921 FA ban, exhibition games included Lyon's Ladies, who played in front of thirty members of the press at Sudbury on 13 December 1921. Alfred Frankland then invited twenty-plus doctors to watch a Dick, Kerr game on Boxing Day 1921 where the suitability of the sport was deemed by one reporter as no more taxing than a day's heavy washing.

After the ban, the celebrity of Dick, Kerr's took on a degree of notoriety; subsequent schedules became both more widespread in search of opposition but generally playing fewer games than the 1921 season. The Dick, Kerr factory became English Electric in 1926 and distanced themselves from Frankland and the women's team. Due to his contacts, several players like Lily Parr retrained as nurses to work at Whittingham hospital, a mental health facility. Dick, Kerr's fixture list developed outside of any formal league or association in order to claim to be 'the undefeated British Champions', and then 'World's Champions'. Although officially called Preston from 1926, the Dick, Kerr's name remains the one by which the team is best remembered today, effectively outlasting the company.

Atalanta of Huddersfield

The Atalanta Sports Club formed in November 1920 when a committee was established, led by Constance Waller. Their two main dilemmas were finding premises from which to base themselves and raising funds to play matches. At 32, Westgate Huddersfield on 8 December 1920, the club had been successful in securing the netball courts at Hillhouse Central, Birkby Council School and the Girls' High School. With netball as their primary focus in December, the club reported that a football would also be provided and there was an intention to obtain a football coach. Sandhouse football field at Crossland Moor would become the first base. The club was as enthusiastic about netball, cricket and water polo as football, and had about forty members. After a series of matches against themselves, Atalanta won their first competitive match against a rather robust Bath side on 25 March 1921 at the Huddersfield Town FC ground on Leeds Road in front of 15,000 spectators. In spite of winning 1–0, Atalanta's physical preparation was much needed, as was the football skill developed by Mr Street of the Huddersfield League. One of the four Harrison sisters playing for Bath upended the Atalanta goalkeeper, Ethel Lee, by grabbing her round the waist. Defender Hilda Clarke retaliated by taking on two attacking Bath players so comprehensively that their female trainer was required to tend to their wounds.

One month later, Atalanta travelled away to Thrum Hall, Halifax, to play a much more experienced team, St Helen's, and lost 3–1 with a consolation goal by Constance Waller. Then, in only their third competitive game, Atalanta would meet Dick, Kerr's, who had already played over fifty matches that season, at Hillsborough, Sheffield. Maybe Dick, Kerr were feeling charitable, or restrained themselves to make a better spectacle for the 25,000 people who attended, but the score was only 4–0. A few weeks later another experienced side, Hull Ladies, hosted Atalanta at White City, Hull, and treated them to a 2–0 defeat. When Atalanta met Dick, Kerr's again later in 1921, the more experienced team was not so generous and the result was a 10–0 drubbing.

In this respect, we cannot but admire the ambition of the new football team, which, less than six months after formation, would face a French

Atalanta FC.

XI mainly drawn from Fémina, at Fartown, in aid of the Mayor's Distress Fund, raising £424 and losing 1–0. Further matches against Dick, Kerr's, Hey's Brewery, Dewsbury and Hull followed. While Atalanta defied the FA ban to pursue its matches in 1922, these were mainly cup competitions which will be referenced elsewhere in the chapter. Their wooden pavilion was sold to a local cricket club in 1926.

Stoke United

Leonard Bridgett was a good footballer when young, but was outshone by his younger brother, Arthur, who was even better, totalling 321 appearances for Sunderland FC between 1902 and 1911 as a pacy left winger, scoring 112 goals and making many assists. Arthur's eleven caps for England came at a time when the team was travelling more widely to Europe and this would be useful experience for the women's football team that the brothers founded in 1921 (in defiance of the FA ban which came within a year of the formation of the new club.) Len became a wealthy man importing fish from nearby Grimsby. He also had a profound civic pride, and served in a number of offices in local politics for many years. Len must have been aware of the civic advantages of having a successful women's football team because Dick, Kerr's played in Stoke in March 1921 against a Cheshire side for whom his daughter, Eva, played on the left wing. A 10,000 crowd saw Dick, Kerr's win 12–0, and this undoubtedly set Len's mind to work.

Variously called Bridgett's XI and Stoke United the team had several encounters with the Dick, Kerr Ladies, who they seemed to particularly want to beat. On 28 March 1921, 4,000 spectators saw Dick, Kerr win 3–0. A week later, on 7 April, the rematch took place at the Old Recreation Ground in Hanley, in front of 13,000 spectators, and played in aid of the Royal Staffordshire Infirmary. Bridgett's team lost 2–0. This may have been progress but was also good entertainment as Dick, Kerr's Lily Parr and Stoke's Hilda Durbar were both sent off for fighting.

In April Stoke played just two fixtures, but ambitious ones. On 20 and 21 April they took on St Helen's, who were perhaps the second strongest side in England. The first game, in Birmingham, was a 2–2 draw. The following day saw a 1–1 draw at Port Vale in aid of the Stoke-on-Trent Police and Fire Brigade Charities. This was encouraging.

More ambitious matches followed. After the ban, Len Bridgett put up a 50 guinea challenge cup for his team to play any women's team in the world.

In September 1923 Len arranged for Stoke Ladies to visit Barcelona to play two games against a Paris-based team, for a trophy presented by the *Cooperativa de Casas Baratas* (an affordable housing scheme). The first match took place on Sunday, 8 September, on a ground which had been vacated the previous year by FC Barcelona. As well as Eva and Ida Bridgett, and captain Dolly Cooper, Stoke tried to play a ringer, one Florrie Redford of Dick, Kerr's who had moved to Paris to play her football. Listed as Bedford, deliberately or not, the French were not to be confused, mainly because Redford had been licensed in France as a player, and objected to her inclusion. This meant that Bedford was free to play in the first match, in which she scored a hat-trick, and was not eligible to play in the second which Stoke won by a single goal, thus winning the tournament outright.

The third fixture against Dick Kerr's came on 29 September 1923 at Colne, with Stoke declaring that they were holders not just of the cup from Barcelona but the English Ladies Football Association Cup (of which more in the next section). The programme featured Eva Bridgett and Dolly Cooper for Stoke, and Florrie Redford and Lily Parr for Dick, Kerr. On this historic occasion Stoke won 1–0, with individual brilliance

Stoke or Bridgett's FC.

from Daisy Bates. Having fulfilled their ambition, Arthur returned to men's professional football at Port Vale while his brother Len went on to more commercial and civic success.

Establishing the English Ladies Football Association in 1921: a Short-lived Experiment

Dick, Kerr's were not the only major women's football club: St Helens, Fleetwood, Chorley, Bath, Plymouth, Coventry, Stoke and Huddersfield Atalanta were also important teams. So why did the 150 existing teams not defy the FA ban by establishing their own association? The answer to this is threefold. Firstly women's war work was not treated with the respect it deserved, and many women found themselves unemployed by 1921, needing to retrain. It wasn't all bad news. Women's political and social progress in Britain included the 1918 Representation of the People Act, which gave the vote, in local elections, to women over the age of thirty who held property (or were married to householders), and those with a university degree.

In comparison, sport seemed trivial. But football was symbolically important, as 'the people's game.' The coal disputes of 1921 and 1926 saw more women's football sides develop in response to localised deprivation: teams included the Soup Canteen Ladies; Blaydon Ladies' FC and the Marley Hill Spankers.

The second reason was the internal politics of the existing teams. Thirdly, we should also remember that none of the women's teams at the time owned their own grounds (although as we have seen some had their own club houses), and so were dependent upon other sports organisations and providers to host them. This tells us as much about female ownership of land and property at the time as it does about football.

Many newspapers and local dignitaries, such as mayors, criticised the FA's attitude towards women. For instance, on 6 December 1921 *The Lancashire Daily Post* reported:

One of Dick, Kerr's best players is a nurse at the Whittingham Lunatic Asylum. Recently she was on duty all night in charge of refractory patients. When she came off duty she cycled seven miles in the wet to Preston, travelled by train to the Midlands, played a fine game in the afternoon before a record crowd and was back on duty at Whittingham late the same night.

Sportswriter Nomad, writing in *The Yorkshire Sports*, suggested that, 'If the lady players want to defeat the injunction of the FA all they need do is to popularise the game to such an extent in their own particular circles until they attain the power to snap their fingers at the present policy of the FA.'

The idea of establishing the English Ladies Football Association in 1921 came from the man who appointed himself the president, Len Bridgett, director of Stoke United Ladies FC. W. Henley of Grimsby was secretary, and there was talk of women's league football developing in Doncaster and the East Riding of Yorkshire, North Lincolnshire, where we have seen there were a number of strong teams, and as far south as Coventry. On the 10 December 1921 a meeting in Liverpool of around thirty women's teams formalised an English Ladies' Football Association, 'to popularise the game among girls and to assist charity […] and to deal with the receipts that there shall be no possible ground for complaint.' The twin accusations that not all money intended for charity had been donated previously by women's teams and that too much had been 'absorbed' in expenses clearly hurt. Chorley Ladies FC, who had about sixty players, let it be known that the club had so far raised over £3,000 for charity.

A second meeting in Blackburn brought almost sixty clubs, and had the following executive board, amongst whom eagle-eyed readers will note a prominent player: President – Leonard Bridgett (Stoke); Vice president– Fred Selman (Coventry); Vice president– Ted Foley (Darwen); Vice president– Harry Longworth (Fleetwood); Vice president– Thomas Ballham (Stoke); and Vice president– Mrs Barraclough (Huddersfield). Some of the ELFA rules were progressive: three married women were to be on the board of each club; the rules would not be changed to feminise the sport; and there would be regionalised competition to reduce travel. However, other rules were more restrictive: players could not be picked if they were further than fifteen miles from their clubs; and affiliated clubs could not play against non-affiliated clubs. The latter was clearly aimed at Stoke's rivals Dick, Kerr's. As well as an ELFA side to play a match at Grimsby, Len introduced a new ELFA challenge cup competition.

However, his influence can be gauged from the ELFA side featuring Stoke's captain, Dolly Cooper, as well as Daisy Bates and Eva Bridgett. While further meetings in London and Birmingham attempted to expand recruitment, this had limited success.

Though a reported sixty clubs did express an interest join the English Ladies Football Association, well known teams such as Dick, Kerr's, Bath, Hey's Brewery, Bradford, Chorley, Darwen, Lyons and St Helen's did not seem anxious to join. Stoke United, also known as Bridgett's United, got a bye in the inaugural English Ladies Football Association Challenge Cup of 1922, so joining would have meant that Alfred Frankland had to cooperate with a midlands and northern initiative led by a rival team who were looking to defeat Dick, Kerr Ladies.

The first round of fixtures gives an idea of the teams involved, though only twenty-three of the fifty-eight affiliated clubs entered.

Round One of the ELFA Challenge Cup

Stoke	v	Newcastle
Smallthorne	v	Chell
Birmingham	v	Dunlop
Coventry	v	Aston
Fleetwood	v	Manchester United
Mersey	v	Rochdale Amazons
Plymouth	v	Marazion
Ediswan	v	Osram
Grimsby	v	Doncaster Bentley
Huddersfield	v	Huddersfield Atalanta
Boston	v	Lincoln
Stoke United		initially given a bye, late entry Huddersfield Alexandria

What is interesting about this is the range of clubs involved, from as far south as Marazion, Penzance, up to Manchester and Newcastle. Eventually Stoke met Doncaster Bentley in the final, with Len Bridgett's side winning 3–1 at Cobridge on 24 June 1922; a fitting conclusion to the football at least. There appears to be evidence that Len tried to turn the ELFA into a company later in the year, but although there were about forty matches that we are aware of, played by affiliated teams in 1922, and some other cup competitions, it seems that the experiment fizzled out by the end of the year. Dick, Kerr's tours would continue, as would siging up the best players from the teams against which they played. So Alfred Frankland, having lost a match against Len Bridgett, eventually won the business war.

Alice Milliat

Alice Joséphine Marie Million (1884–1957) was a young rower from Nantes in France. Widowed relatively soon after her marriage, Alice worked as a translator and became president of the Fémina women's sports club three years after its formation by Pierre Payssé. In France, the exclusion of women from male sports federations had led to a rise in the number of sports clubs dedicated to their interests, such as En Avant. Another club, Académia, supported a range of physical activities, including natural movement dance (inspired by Isadora Duncan), bicycling, football and rugby (or *barette* to use its French term at the time). A French national track and field athletics meeting in 1917 showcased some of the leading all-round sportswomen like javelin and shot-put enthusiast Violette Gourard Morris (1895–1944). 'La Morris' was an imposing athlete who also boxed, swam, played football, and drove fast cars. Alice Milliat became President of the Fédération des Sociétés Féminines Sportives de France (FSFSF) in 1919, inaugurating a national coalition of female sports clubs.

Milliat first visited Preston in 1920 as a non-playing administrator with the Paris-based Fémina women's football team mentioned above, and was very impressed by the local hospitality and public support for the Dick, Kerr Ladies in Preston. Milliat devoted considerable energy to promoting women's sports, specifically international football, and Olympic track and field athletics. There were important differences, as women's football was an unregulated form of female leisure, or even casual work. Olympic track and field athletics tended towards an institutionalised, standardised bureaucracy and Milliat's attempts were part of an overall strategy of integration. While FIFA had been formed in 1904 as an international organisation for world football, it had no more idea of what its role should be towards women's football than the FA in England. Team games nevertheless featured strongly in Milliat's vision for more democratic sport.

The International Amateur Athletics Federation (IAAF) had been created in August 1913 with Sweden's Sigfried Edström elected as its president. The IAAF worked closely with the IOC because of the central role of athletics in the programme of Olympic sports. This enhanced Edström's ability to gain significant positions in international sport. In 1920 Edström was co-opted as a member of the International Olympic Committee (IOC), and one year later he joined the first IOC executive board.

While women's swimming, diving, skating, tennis and a mixed yachting event would feature at the Antwerp Olympic Games in 1920, female track and field athletics were not admitted. As a direct response Milliat broadened FSFSF's remit. In 1921 Monte Carlo hosted female representatives from France, Great Britain, Italy, Norway, Sweden and Switzerland at the first international athletics meeting, inaugurated by Milliat. By October 1921 the Fédération Sportive Féminine Internationale (FSFI) had begun to campaign on a worldwide scale for the advancement of women's sport, specifically targeting the inclusion of athletics in the Olympic programme. In 1922 the first Women's Olympic Games was staged as a separatist event with 101 competitors taking part in front of crowds of 20,000 spectators. This was a considerable success. At the 1920 Antwerp Olympic Games there had been only eighty female participants.

The French tour to Preston, Stockport, Manchester and Chelsea of 1920, was reciprocated in the autumn of that year by an England tour to France. Four matches attracted large crowds: firstly, at the Pershing Stadium in Paris, drawing 22,000 fans, and subsequent crowds of 10,000, 6,000 and 14,000 saw the matches at Roubaix, Le Havre and Rouen. In May 1921 France returned to England, losing initially 5–1 to Dick Kerr's, but then winning against Huddersfield Atalanta, Stoke and Plymouth Ladies. A team, mainly comprised of Plymouth players – although some reports have said it was entirely a Plymouth side – played two matches, in Paris and Le Havre in October 1921, and it seemed that, in spite of the FA ban, more regular internationals would follow. Could international games and tours defy the FA ban at home by playing abroad?

In March 1922 Olympique de Paris, which contained many top female athletes such as captain Gourard-Morris, and the three sisters Geneviève, Marguerite and Thérèse Laloz, played four matches against Dick, Kerr's in Cardiff, Preston, Liverpool and Hyde, and once against Hey's Brewery ladies at Bradford, losing all five matches. An FSFSF representative team which toured in April 1922 featured the two Darreau sisters, Carmen Pomiès, and Madeline Braquemond, all star players. Two of these matches were played against a British XI at Exeter and Plymouth, and there was a goalless draw against a Cornish XI at Falmouth in front of 1,500 spectators. After the Dick, Kerr's tour to the US in 1922, they increasingly played as England against visiting French teams, such as in 1925.

However, although these important steps had been pioneered by Alice Milliat, she increasingly chose to focus on getting women's track and field athletics into the IOC schedule of the Olympic Games. She was partially successful in 1928, getting five events included on the schedule: the 100m, the 4x100m relay, the high jump, the discus and the 800m. While track and field would remain on the schedule thereafter and expand all the time, Milliat was forced by poor health and limited finance in her campaign for women's football, as she was for hockey and basketball. All three sports would join the Olympic schedule, but it would not be until 1976 for basketball, 1980 for hockey and 1996 for football. Full suffrage was granted to women in France in 1944, so we can see how pioneering Milliat was, in a time when women could not vote to change their society.

The Legacy of the FA actions

After the 1921 ban the 'sporting tours' arranged by Alfred Frankland meant that Dick, Kerr Ladies Football Club could play more matches (and make more money for charity and expenses) than amateur leagues would allow. Lily Parr was to captain the 1922 Dick, Kerr Ladies tour to the United States. By the early 1920s women were playing soccer in the United States as part of intramural programmes and the sports had become sufficiently established to produce books like Frost and Cubberley's *Field Hockey and Soccer for Women* and the Smith book of Soccer in 1924. Yet college principals did not want their 'nice' girls to play against working-class factory operatives, nurses or shopworkers. This meant that the Dick, Kerr Ladies played against male professional and semi-professional teams in the US. The tour began with a 6–3 loss to Paterson Silk Sox, played at Olympic, Park, Clifton, New Jersey with 5,000 spectators in attendance. This was followed by a 4–4 draw against J. & P. Coats, at

Lyons Tea Rooms and Coffee Houses had several women's football teams as featured here in the company magazine, *Lyons Mail*, September 1925.

Lonsdale Avenue, Pawtucket, Rhode Island with a crowd of 8,500, many of whom were cotton workers displaced from the north of England who had migrated to the US. France's Carmen Pomiès had travelled with Dick, Kerr's, and her teammate Alice Kell, whose family would return to Pawtucket in 1922 in search of work in cotton mills, would go on to have children and settle in the US as a result of being part of the tour. I spoke to Alice's daughter, Winnie Bourke, about her mother's football career in early 1999 as part of my PhD research. Winnie's granddaughter was writing about her famous pioneering great-grandmother for a college assignment as well as playing college soccer. So there is much still to learn about migration and women's football at this time.

Dick, Kerr then moved on to New York City where they lost 7–5 to Centro-Hispano. They fared better in Washington DC, drawing 4–4 against Washington Stars. A narrow 5–4 victory followed against New Bedford Whalers in Massachusetts. The best result was an 8–4 victory against New York FC. Returning to Massachusetts, Dick, Kerr's drew 2–2 against the Fall River Marksmen, and concluded the tour with a 4–3 win against the Baltimore Soccer Club. In spite of the high point of President Warren Harding, 'kicking off' one of the matches in Washington in 1922, the tour had limited success. It had not begun as intended and would not be enough to sustain Dick, Kerr's abroad, as the lack of female opposition indicated. On their return to Britain in 1923 the impetus to form a coherent, nationwide response to the FA ban had been lost.

Sport, rather than leisure, is often called a 'peculiar business' because it relies on competitive cooperation rather than outright monopoly. If a given team or performer wins all the time without serious opposition then the spectacle of sport, which unfolds in real time and is unrehearsed, is lost. This is why it is difficult to translate sport to fiction films and the theatre. The whole entertainment relies upon spontaneity and surprise. Although there would be more matches, including in 1937 for the championship of the world against Edinburgh, these were inventions of the Dick, Kerr PR machine as they sought to devise new titles for themselves to draw audiences. Although there is now a blue plaque declaring Dick, Kerr's as world champions, it is a meaningless title, based on a single victory, as there was no world championship of which to speak. Although the scrapbooks of players indicate that friendships lasted between the England and French teams after World War Two, matches dwindled and, without ever really being stopped, women's football became very much a minority activity; not a school sport in the same way that netball and hockey were widely played.

Women continued to raise football teams and create playing opportunities, such as Woolworth versus Marks & Spencer in 1929, and the 1932 match between Quaker Ladies of Darlington and Terry's of York, made the news. Chipping Sodbury had a team, there were several iterations of Bath Ladies FC, and new clubs formed as far afield as Orkney. However, many had to play on local recreation grounds or on pitches meant primarily for other sports. For the next fifty years, despite a degree of civic support, such as we have seen here, most of these women would face derision and criticism for wanting to play a sport that they loved. It is no surprise that many stopped playing, though many more ignored the scorn and carried on.

Munitionette's football is therefore a rare and early case of selling women's team sport to a large paying public and creating spectacle. Football raised money for charity, but also paid expenses, enabling some performers like 'star' player Lily Parr to become the first person in her family to own their own home. Whether this was because of her income as a nurse, supplemented by the relatively steady income she reputedly earned from 'broken time' payments of ten shillings a game, is now difficult to say. Regardless of whether we see Parr as semi-professional or casually profiting from her football, from very local beginnings we can see a web of contacts develop across the United Kingdom, into Europe and the United States, bringing friendship, civic esteem and a moderately comfortable lifestyle for some physically gifted working women.

Judging by the newspaper reports of the time, and the programmes, Lily Parr was the next big star after Nettie Honeyball. She enjoyed widespread acclaim in the United States and Europe during the inter-war years, and became the first woman admitted to the inaugural Hall of Fame at the English National Football Museum in 2002. A long-time leading member of team, very little is known about her playing career over three decades, let alone her private life. Yet Parr achieved celebrity (a word used to describe her at the time) early in her career. Fame, in this case, meant civic, media and public recognition, sharing a sporting stage with some of the key entertainers of the time: for example, Harry Weldon's Team of Lady Internationals' competed in aid of unemployed ex-servicemen, Liverpool hospitals and the Variety Artistes Benevolent Funds. A reported crowd of 25,000 in Liverpool produced £1,500 in declared gate receipts, and more people saw the match in the cinema.

Hayes Women's FC versus Twyford Athletic Edinburgh, 16 April 1938, featured in *Strang's Pictorial*.

Lily Parr and her colleagues were received by a range of municipal and political dignitaries. Large audiences of mainly male football fans paid regularly to watch her play.

We also know that the US tour had a legacy, albeit indirectly, on early women's college soccer. An educator, Marian Knighton, published her soccer coaching manual in 1930, opining that it was a very good game for young women, provided it was carefully supervised. Knighton goes on to say:

> Soccer is estimated to be the national game of fifty different countries. It is compulsory in England for boys in the majority of preparatory schools. I feel very strongly that it should be compulsory in our physical education schools for women. Originally it was an endurance contest in dribbling and running. One team would always start on one side of the river and carry the ball with their feet to some nearby town. On the other side of the river another team and ball would race them. In this country soccer is a comparatively recent game for girls and any changes to the rules have been carefully considered and suggested solely as adaptations suited to sex differences. The spirit of the game is the same and, if precautions are taken the interest in a fast running exhilarating game is evident.
>
> Marian Knighton 'Introduction' in *Spaldings Athletic Library Soccer For Women: Official Soccer Guide of the National Section on Women's Athletics of the American Physical Education Association* (New York: American Sports Publishing company, 1930, p. 5).

This was aimed at a readership unlike the working-class male organisers and female players of the Dick, Kerr's tour, who were mainly drawn from a competitive industrial social context that suited small-scale entrepreneurialism. This was aimed at middle-class parents and their daughters, for whom soccer was less violent and physical than American Football: it was corporate, collegiate soccer for well-to-do young women.

Overseas tours were also an opportunity for like-minded individuals to take holidays and trips together, as well as receiving civic welcomes for their sporting prowess. These comprised dinners of several courses, a show, a singsong on the bus and an overnight stay. Lily Parr is photographed in scrapbook snapshots of her football career in a posh frock having a good time, cigarette and drink in hand, as frequently as she is in her football kit. She scored an estimated 1,000 goals during her career, so perhaps we can guess what an exciting social schedule football provided for a nurse who supported herself all her life. But what of the other teams and players who defied the FA ban over the next fifty years? The next chapter looks at some of the key events and people in the wilderness years for women's football.

Chapter 3

The Corinthians and Nomad Globe Trotters Ladies Football Club of Manchester

The Corinthians Song

We're Corinthians from Manchester
Football Ladies from Lancashire
Blue and Black for Corinthians
Boy! What a team!
Fa la la la la la
We'll beat anyone who we play
Makes no difference, home or away
We have the talent,
Our youngsters are gallant
Corinthians from Manchester
Ole!

The Nomads Song

The Northern Nomads are coming today
The Northern Nomads are on their way
The Corinthians they are playing
And everybody's been saying
That the crowd will be swaying
With excitement and glee
With excitement and glee.
The Northern Nomads are a very good team
They are the finest team the world's ever seen
And if they score a little goal
Just one, or two, or three, or four, or more
We'll call them the team of the year!

(To the tune of 'Me and My Gal', 1942)

F or almost fifty years women's football would remain an unregulated activity. It became routine to make fun of women playing football, even more so than girls, and the language of a 'ban' made their enthusiasm seem unusual and unfeminine. Using the case study of the Manchester Corinthians FC, this chapter shows how going 'on tour' overseas could counter these stereotypes, and continue to raise money for charity.

World War Two was not as significant as World War One for women's football, partly because of the lack of major stadiums in which to raise money for charity, and partly because petrol rationing and other shortages made wider travel more challenging. After 1945 women's role in the war and on wider British society began to change, and there were again advances in women's rights, such as the end of the marriage bar in teaching, clerical occupations and nursing, all of which had limited married women's right to work. Further Married Women's Property Act Revisions enabled women to keep half of the savings of a joint household, and equal pay campaigns slowly gained ground. Added to this, the introduction of the contraceptive pill in 1961, and the Abortion Act of 1967 gave women more birth control options.

So, with economic, contraceptive and financial independence, more women could make informed choices about their lives. The idea of a meritocracy also grew in popularity, based less on where and what class an individual was born into, and more on what a person could achieve through hard work. So the growth of the Welfare State, combining free state education for the majority of pupils, free healthcare at the point of access in the new National

Photograph of Percy Ashley, who founded Manchester Corinthians FC for his daughter, Doris.

Health Service, and help for those who were unemployed or incapacitated by ill-health, extended more people's lives and opportunities.

In the footballing world, the England men's national team entered their first ever World Cup in 1950, held in Brazil, and while other leisure pursuits drew crowds away from top-flight football, the increasingly global nature of rivalry in the sport would be reflected in the more regularly organised European club championships after UEFA was formed in 1954. One of the main draws away from football grounds for spectators was television, which increasingly took over from the radio as a way of consuming the game, first in black and white and then in colour, just in time for England to win the World Cup in 1966.

In women's football, an unofficial European Championship in 1957 was organised by Lotte Specht and German businessmen from Essen, in West Germany. The tournament was won by an English team, Manchester Corinthians, which had formed in 1949, led by Percy Ashley, whose daughter, Doris, was profoundly deaf and had a cleft palate. It is this globetrotting team that this chapter focuses upon.

Manchester Corinthians Ladies Football Club was able to organise a varied range of overseas tours and domestic matches in spite of the FA ban. It has often been said that 'Where Manchester leads others will follow,' but this has seldom been applied to the relatively neglected topic of women's football in the city and its surrounding area. Manchester Corinthians were able to take part in tours to the European Cup in Berlin in 1957, winning against Germany 4–0 and reportedly singing 'Land of Hope and Glory' on their victory lap, before going on tour to Portugal for a month the same year. The Corinthians' interpreter in Stuttgart earlier that year had been Manchester City keeper, Bert Trautmann, so there were clearly two trips. Some players remember that Trautmann had phoned Percy Ashley, the Corinthians manager, to quickly arrange the second trip to Berlin, and they had to leave directly from work to travel to the Continent.

More overseas trips followed, including six weeks to Portugal/Madeira, and, in 1959, two weeks to The Netherlands. The most ambitious schedule was twelve weeks in South America and the Caribbean in 1960, followed by one month to Italy in 1961, playing on the grounds of Juventus, Milan and other major clubs. During their existence, both Nomads (see below) and Corinthians toured extensively, including to Ireland in 1962, Morocco in 1966, and France in 1970, in all winning more than fifty trophies.

Nomads, or Northern Nomads, were Corinthians' second team, and players often moved between the squads. Using a range of methods, including oral history, family history interviews, a reunion of the surviving players and player memorabilia, this chapter provides a history of Corinthians and Nomads from 1949 onwards. The chapter also looks at some individual players, concentrating on how each felt about playing for the club, and particularly its overseas tours, and charity work. Not all of the players are represented due to constraints of space, but this is an introduction to a larger ongoing project to reclaim the teams' history.

The short songs at the beginning of the chapter are those that the players would sing on tour, along with others celebrating their victories. The sources for the club history of Manchester Corinthians draw on the scrapbooks of long-time goalkeeper, Carol Aiken, and oral testimony of the players, many of whom survive and were reunited at the National Football Museum on 30 September 2018. The eldest of these was eighty-four years of age, having started playing when aged fourteen in 1949. Carol Aiken's mother Gladys and father George also managed the club after Percy Ashley died and an interim manager, William Oldfield, resigned.

Corinthians and Nomads were two of the most significant women's teams before the formation of the Women's Football Association (WFA) in 1969, of which they were founding members along with forty-two other clubs. In 1969 the world governing body, FIFA, had decided to take control of women's football through its member national associations. Gladys Aiken of Manchester Corinthians was the membership secretary of the WFA from 1972 to 1974, which gives an insight into women managing their own teams, as well as working as volunteers in the development of the wider football industry. Interestingly,

Photograph of Bert Traumann, the German-born Manchester City FC goalkeeper who travelled with Corinthians to their match in Stuttgart.

Pat Dunn, the Corinthians' trainer on many overseas tours, was the first woman to qualify as a referee in 1967 and was a vocal critic of the FA's attitude to women. Dunn was briefly the first chair of the WFA in 1969, before the FA requested that she be replaced by a man less than a year into her tenure (a male referee, Pat Gwynne took over). Defiant, Dunn went on to referee an international men's match in 1969. She would later travel to the unofficial World Cup in Mexico with Harry Batt's team in 1971 as their trainer. So the links between unofficial women's football teams and an emergent WFA, affiliated to the FA on the same basis as a county association, are also pertinent to the Corinthians as a case study club. What was to be 'official' and 'unofficial' in women's football would remain a thorny issue.

Manchester Corinthians: A History

Corinthians was to be one of the most important post-war women's clubs to pioneer women's football as socially acceptable, benevolent, and by the late 1950s, internationally as a celebration of civic pride in Manchester. By the time of the formation of the WFA in 1969, the club already had a twenty-year history and an international reputation as an outstanding team. Percy Ashley formed Corinthian Ladies in 1949, mainly so that his daughter, Doris, could play in a team. Doris was an outstanding player, and from these humble beginnings in Manchester, Corinthians' subsequent trips included a three-month tour of South America, and more European international tournaments such as Reims 1970, raising in all £275,000, mainly for the International Red Cross. Percy was a scout for Bolton Wanderers and a well-known local referee. All the players I have spoken to remembered Doris as an outstanding footballer, so it would seem that building a team around her was Percy's way of combining her sporting and social interests.

Manchester Corinthians LFC were not at all like the upper-class amateur male team, the Corinthian Casuals formed in 1882 and from whom they took their name. Corinthian Casuals, an amateur team mainly comprised of university and public school graduates, had beaten professionals Manchester United 11–3, still one of their worst defeats to this day. Perhaps naming a women's side after the amateur giant killers was a way of reclaiming the name for Manchester, as well as emphasising that players were amateurs.

Their home ground was on Fog Lane Park, Didsbury, and facilities were sparse. Players had to be both very determined to play football and resilient: several reminisced washing after matches in the duck pond as there was no running water in the changing rooms, which were also unheated. There were very few other women's teams in the region and teams that had been once great, such as Dick, Kerr's Ladies of Preston, were in decline. In 1957 a second team linked to Manchester Corinthians was formed by Percy Ashley under the name 'The Nomads', or less frequently 'All Stars', to enable them to play against each other in international charity matches. These exhibition matches were hard fought, and each side badly wanted to win. There is so far no evidence of women's football league activity in the 1950s and 1960s. The Corinthians were entirely self-funded, combining domestic competition with overseas tours.

Presenting the teams as pioneering, altruistic and humanitarian gave the club a niche in the market for football which Percy Ashley astutely amplified. In an increasingly meritocratic society, the Corinthians earned their right to play football by doing good. Even for an organisation so chauvinistic as the FA in the 1950s and 1960s, it would have seemed crass to try and ban the Corinthians, and so they flourished. This gave the players, and Ashley, life experiences way beyond the realms of most of the people they worked with during the week.

As amateurs the team was perhaps appealing for generosity in social attitudes, and also emphasising it was a 'ladies' football club in the terminology used at the time. The team was made up of career women, from typists and civil servants to machinists and self-employed small business owners; all of whom trained and played at Fog Lane Park every Sunday whatever the weather. Missing training or being late were sure to result in the player being dropped for at least one match. The players tried to make washing after matches more pleasant than the dreaded duck pond, and there are also snapshots in the scrapbooks of players trailing buckets of water to the changing rooms nearby as there was no running water, let alone hot water. Percy Ashley was assisted by Derek Ingham as trainer. If any players were injured Ingham would use his motorbike as a means of conveying them to Mr Beardo, the osteopath. Players reported being more fearful of the well-intentioned cure than any injury caused through football.

It is clear that Percy Ashley wanted to contest the FA ban as well as provide top level coaching for his team. Individual players remembered specific coaching sessions on using defenders as attacking wingbacks, and Percy's many blackboard sessions on team tactics. There were also individual coaching sessions, from how to send a goalkick down the field to attacking teammates to defensive drills. Percy was a serious disciplinarian: no boyfriends or relatives were allowed on the team coach, and he emphasised the sporting aspects of Corinthians, at the cost of social niceties if needs be. In other words, the players and management were absolutely serious.

Between 1949 and 1956 most of the Corinthian's matches were domestic, and this is perhaps unsurprising. By 1951 they were acclaiming themselves the 'premier' team in Britain, having won (in the order listed in the 1951 Festival of Britain Trophy programme): the Southern Cup; Manchester Area Cup; Sports Magazine Cup; Roses Trophy; Midland Trophy; Cresswell Trophy; Odeon Championship Trophy; Belle Vue Trophy; and the Festival of Britain Championship Trophy. Having travelled a reported 9,000 miles by 1951, Corinthians had reportedly raised £8,000 for aid organisations, varying from local causes such as the Multiple Sclerosis Society Salford and District Branch to national and international health charities, including the British Limbless Ex-Servicemen's Association, and the British Empire Leprosy Relief Association. While programme notes report twenty-six teams entering tournaments across the UK, evidence of a basic level of competition, the scale of Corinthians' ambitions was about to change.

In 1957 they were invited to tour Portugal on behalf of the International Red Cross. No expense was spared and the logistics were arranged on behalf of the players, who were then free then to concentrate on playing entertaining football. Next they were invited by the International Ladies Football Association, a German-based organisation, to represent England in a European championship against Austria, Luxembourg, The Netherlands and West Germany. In the final, held in Berlin, Corinthians beat Germany 4–0 in front of a crowd of 40,000. Here players' memories become a little hazy. Bert Trautmann, who was the Manchester City goalkeeper, and had presented the team with the Festival of Britain Trophy in 1951, travelled in 1957 as their interpreter. But it seems there may have been two trips to Germany in 1957, rather than one. There is a Pathé newsreel of him in the crowd at Stuttgart, but not in Berlin.

Quite how Trautmann was funded to interpret, and why he specifically joined a women's football team for a trip to West Germany remains unclear as no paperwork has emerged from these early tours. The trip took place within a year of his heroics in helping Manchester City win the FA Cup Final in 1956, playing the last quarter of an hour with a seriously injury. The Corinthians players have many snapshots of Trautmann and remembered him as being very supportive. For the Berlin game, which seems to have come after Stuttgart, several remember that he asked Ashley to get a team together to play in Germany, with very short notice, so it may be that he was contacted and knew of the legendary Corinthians.

This European victory seemed to change Percy Ashley's ambitions and business model. Overseas tours became annual events for a period of time before his ill health prevented them. In 1958 the International Red Cross invited Corinthians and Nomads to play against each other in Portugal and Madeira, drawing huge crowds in the

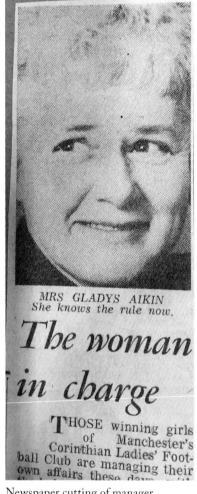

MRS GLADYS AIKIN
She knows the rule now.

The woman in charge

THOSE winning girls of Manchester's Corinthian Ladies' Football Club are managing their own affairs these days

Newspaper cutting of manager Gladys Aiken, 'The Woman in Charge'.

stadiums of major men's professional clubs, such as Benfica in Lisbon. In 1959 the team went to The Netherlands, playing teams from Haarlem and Utrecht. The International Red Cross then invited both teams for a three-month tour South America and the Caribbean in 1960. While some of the young women could afford to go because they were still at school, others gave up their office jobs to take the opportunity to play abroad in front of large crowds.

The displeasure of the FA spilled over into sexist sourness, but could not extend to outright prohibition since women's football was unregulated. The *Daily Express* featured a team photo in smart travelling suits accompanied by a quotation from an amused Nat Lofthouse, 'Let the girls go abroad'. Meanwhile, the England coach Walter Winterbottom was quoted as saying: 'Well, one cannot quite take it seriously can one? The experts say that Football is not suitable game for women anyway. And they certainly can't look attractive playing it. Still, I'm quite sure that their tour to South America will cause quite a stir, even if the spectators aren't exactly concentrating on the finer points of the game.'

In contrast, the seriousness of both the International Red Cross and the Corinthians can be evidenced by the schedule, which involved some twenty-nine flights, compiled here in Table 1.

Table 1. Corinthians and Nomad Tour to South America May-August 1960

Destination	Length of stay	Hotel name
Brussels	10 hours (connecting flight)	
New York	1 night	Hotel Sheraton
New York	3 nights	Hotel Sheraton
Caracas	10 days	Humboldt
Maracaibo	3 nights	Granada
Valera	1 night	Guadalupa
Barquisimeto	1 night	La Francia
Puerto Cabello	3 nights	Balnerrio
Valencia	2 nights	La Paris
Caracas	11 days	Pinar/Humboldt
Aruba	2 nights	Strand
Curaçao	2 nights	Park
Baranquilla	1 night	Victoria
Santa Marta	2 nights	Park
Baranquilla	2 nights	Victoria
Bogotá	6 nights	San Francisco
Manizales	2 nights	Escorial
Medellín	2 nights	Veracruz
Bucaramanga	2 nights	Bucarica
Cali	4 nights	Aristi
Aruba	4 nights	Strand
British Guyana	3 nights	Woodbine
Suriname	5 nights	Rosedale Guest House

Port of Spain (Trinidad)	1 night	Bretton Hall
Kingston (Jamaica)	12 nights	Flamingo
New York	connecting flight	
London	connecting flight	
Manchester		

Some readers may think the listing of the New York nights early on in the trip is an error, but *en route* to Caracas first time around an engine on the plane failed two hours into the flight and the team had to return to New York to stay an additional three nights before completing the flight to Venezuela. Perhaps unsurprisingly, the 1961 tour to Italy – which was then becoming an important locus for women's football – was an easier event to arrange in Italy, followed by an even more manageable trip to Ireland, and in 1963 a modest tour of the Isle of Man. While domestic football continued, it was the international reputation of being invited by global charities that gave Corinthians an added gloss that most women's domestic teams in Europe did not have.

Not all the tours were equally successful and there was evidence of experiments going wrong. The tour to the Tunisia Mediterranean Games was really a flop from a football perspective with poor crowds as a result of cultural values unused to the idea of women's football. It turned more into a holiday than a sports tour, with players quite content to be in the sun for three weeks. In 1966 the major overseas tour was three weeks in Morocco. First the team flew to Gibraltar, sailing from Gibraltar to Tangiers, and then travelling 3,000 miles by coach through Casablanca, Fes, Marrakech, Oujah and Rabat. Kath Davis (née Moxon) remembered: 'We played in a floodlit stadium in Casablanca with a crowd of 22,000!' A programme for a match at Brighouse in West Yorkshire in 1967 reported that the Morocco tour had raised £8,500 for the Red Cross, and that at the Oujah match 3,000 spectators had been unable to get into the stadium due to the popularity of the fixture.

It is difficult to know whether these comments were hyperbole to entertain the spectators or whether the novelty of women's football in Morocco at the time drew large crowds. It may well have been a bit of both. Like Dick, Kerr's before them, the Manchester Corinthians were not afraid to claim their place in history in programme notes, and said they were: 'Unbeaten by any foreign team at home or abroad and had one run of 141 matches unbeaten' in the full knowledge that most of their opposition was effectively their own second team. A 1965 programme recorded: Corinthians played 394, won 353, lost twenty, drawn twenty-one, goals for 2,122, goals against 473 and Nomads played sixty-eight, won forty-seven, lost eleven, drawn ten, goals for 368, and goals against 121.

Percy Ashley died in October 1967, and his legacy proved difficult to maintain. Doris was, understandably, bereft and wanted to end the team, but it continued. Ashley had developed a particular business model in order to raise large sums. Firstly, the main problem in staging women's football was that many matches had to be played on open parkland. However, playing for a local or international charity combined entertainment spectacle with altruism. Programme notes emphasised that the women gave their time and effort for free, benefitting only from 'a coach ride and a little supper' in reward. Percy Ashley's preferred style of play, and one for which he would swap players between Corinthians and Nomads/All Stars, was attacking football with a high score, even though the sides were balanced. So, even if it was a bit chillier in Brighouse in May 1967 than it had been in Morocco in 1966, the spectators could cheerfully expect their 2s admission at the gate (1s 6d with programme advance purchase) to buy them a lively game, and to make a charitable donation to local good causes.

Behind this sporting philanthropy, however, lay an enormous logistical task. Gladys Aiken took charge of the team in 1968, and kept a series of scrapbooks to trace the journey of the Corinthians. They give a personal account of the activity of the team, featuring newspaper cuttings glued alongside match day programmes, as well as photographs of the team during matches, and enjoying themselves afterwards. There was a lot of post-match time in which to enjoy themselves, and they did. Their major achievement of 1968 was to win the inaugural Deal Ladies tournament, in which fifty other teams competed, with Nomads reaching the quarter-finals. Corinthians won all their fifteen domestic matches in 1968, scoring 170 goals and conceding just five.

In 1970 Manchester Corinthians flew to Reims, France to play in a two-day knockout competition against women's teams from the Italian club Juventus, the Czech club Kaplice, and the home club Stade de Reims. The print media casually referred to the teams as England, France, Italy and Czechoslovakia, but there seemed no direct attempt on behalf of the organisers to identify teams as representative sides. This would prove to be significant. Arrangements were left to manager Gladys Aiken and trainer John Rule.

In an interesting letter from Pierre Geoffroy, the manager of Stade de Reims FC, on 20 April 1970, he suggested that this would be an annual tournament comprising AFC Roma, champions of Italy, Czech champions Slavia Pramen Kaplice, and Stade de Reims FC. Then, in a letter dated 11 May 1970, the line-up was changed to Corinthians, Nomad, Juventus, Kaplice and Reims. It is worth briefly covering the tournament before discussing why an invitation from Geoffroy was particularly significant in 1970.

Another letter, dated 22 May 1970, from Pierre Geoffroy suggested Corinthians fly Air France and get return tickets for sixteen people, and Reims would fund the airfare, accommodation and rail transport. Interestingly, the contract itself bears the letterhead 'The Corinthians and Nomad Globe Trotters Ladies Football Club of Manchester'. The scrapbook contains telegrams from well-wishers Pat and Alf Dunn of Weymouth, and others. Corinthians flew from Ringway to Orly on 25 June, flight BEA 77-10-76. Games took place at Châlon sur Marne and at Épernay, with the price of entry 6Fr and no concessions. Juventus beat Reims to get to the final against Corinthians. The Juventus team was: 1 Amari; 2 Rossero; 3 Grisorio; 4 Fillipeto; 5 Coda; 6 Losito; 7 Cum; 8 Gianotti;9 Abate; 10 Bertolo; 11 Germena; and the reserves were 12 Branca, 13 Cum, and 14 Petronillo. Perhaps there were two sisters or relatives in the side? For Stade de Reims the squad was not numbered but the programme included the following names which I have copied as they were recorded and may or may not be accurately spelled: Marie-Louise Butzig, Régine Pourveux, Ghislaine Royer, Chantal Lebrun, Nicole Mangas, Marie-Claire Harant, Michèle Darbre, Michelle Monier, Nadine Juillard, Maryse Leisieur, Marie-Bernadette Thomas. Many of these players would later be recognised as playing in the first international match retrospectively recognised by FIFA as the first women's international. On 17 April 1971, Stade de Reims, playing as France, defeated the Netherlands, 4–0 at Stade Auguste Damette in a qualifying round for the unofficial women's World Cup in Mexico.

In the final match, newspaper reports commended the speed of Manchester Corinthians and their combination play, which was able

A snapshot from a player scrapbook showing spartan conditions at Fog Lane Park, where Corinthians trained.

to outdo the *catenaccio*, the tight defensive system of Juventus for a 1–0 victory. Although I have been unable to name the Juventus line-up, either through programme notes or press coverage, the Corinthians players were: Christine Miller, Pauline Quayle, Janice Lyons, Margaret Wilde, Margaret Taylor, Margaret Temple, Margaret Whitworth, Patricia Quayle, plus Eileen Gay, Sheila Isherwood, Sue Kelly, and Linda Hallam, who all received a winner's reception at Hotel de la Ville on 6 July. One journalist reported in *l'Union* newspaper that Margaret 'Whitty' Whitworth made a big impression in the final, winning player of the game. Since at one point there were seven players with Margaret as a first name in the team, nicknames were to prove vital.

This seems to have been the last big Corinthians international tournament win, and perhaps the Pierre Geoffroy connection explains why. Stade de Reims went to the unofficial women's World Cup in Mexico in 1971 representing France. In 1971 The British Independents Football Club, led by Harry Batt, represented England, although the WFA insisted that they could not, and did not, carry that title. Batt and the players were then 'banned' from WFA activities on their return. Although Batt initially ignored this and took another England team to Italy in 1972, he was later banned for life by a WFA committee and gave up on women's football altogether.

Batt had previously been a member of the WFA committee and attitudes clearly differed over how best to develop women's football. Having seen how 'unofficial' internationals were handled by the WFA, maybe Gladys Aiken decided that official channels provided better options. Maybe too, she agreed with WFA policy. By not explicitly calling themselves England, but representing England in the 1970 tournament as a club side, Corinthians were able to tread a fine line which evaded WFA sanction. The Women's Football Association invitational tournament for the Teddy Gray Memorial Challenge Trophy featured both Corinthians and Nomads, with the former victorious in 1968 and 1969, losing to Southampton in 1970. As the 1970s progressed, trainer Ray Vaughan continued to put his team through their paces at Woodley Sports Club on Sundays and Brinnington Leisure Centre on Tuesdays. Affiliated to the WFA, Corinthians and Nomads played in the Three Counties League, becoming winners of the Women's Football Association Mitre Cup. With less frequent fixtures, the club splintered into different teams such as Veronica Bailey's Benfica Beechams and Red Star Manchester, which would become Manchester City women's team sometime in the mid-1980s.

The following oral histories are from players who played for Corinthians between 1948 and 1973.

Oral histories of Corinthians on Tour

Dorothy Barnett

'I always wanted to play football. I used to play with my brother, Bill, who was a good footballer and played semi-pro. When I was fifteen I heard about a man in Bardsley, Mr Ashley, who was organising football teams (his daughter, Doris, also played with us). Bardsley was a community not far from Ashton-under-Lyne where I lived so I went to see Mr Ashley and ended up playing on the first team as left full-back. We travelled all over England and a bonus was that my parents got to travel with us. They would never have had this opportunity otherwise.

'I started playing for Corinthians when I was fifteen, and I think the first European trips were around 1956–57. We played in

Germany, in Berlin, and beat all the European teams we played. We were on the international news in the cinema, about a two-minute clip, and kept returning to see ourselves. We played under the charity the Red Cross. When I was seventeen we travelled to Portugal. We went to Portugal twice, and met the great player, Eusebio, who I think was younger than us at the time! We travelled there by flying boat, *The Sunderland*, as at that time there was no airport in Lisbon. We stayed right on the beach and were there for five weeks. We also went to the Madeira Islands for one week. I have fond memories of rocking and rolling with the locals in the mountains.

'When you are young you take so much for granted but as I look back I remember how well we all got along, and how fortunate I was to be part of this. I think of it as the best times of my life. The team later disbanded as there was an issue about money. We should have been receiving spending money and it was not forthcoming.'

Annie Grimes

'Winning in Germany in 1957 was a big achievement and gave us a taste for the major stadiums. When we played in Portugal, we filled the Estádio José Alvalade in Lisbon with 50,000 people and also played at Benfica stadium. Playing on Fog Lane Park did not necessarily prepare you for this, but Percy Ashley did. He would coach individuals and took the science of the game very seriously. There would always be a blackboard and he would expect individuals to do a specific job on each match. Between him and Eddie, the two of them taught us tactics, like what they call today wing-back, those overlapping runs. Well we were doing that in the 1950s! Our keeper could not send a dead ball sixty yards when she started but they taught her, and that was a huge advantage. In spite of being deaf in one ear, Doris was a very good player. Her mother was the welfare officer and Doris would be very strict. We sometimes called her the De Stefano of our team. Again, in the Netherlands we played in Haarlem and Utrecht, in front of very large crowds, and the International Red Cross appreciated our efforts for their charity.

'When we left New York for Venezuela and the engine caught fire, Percy would not allow us to fly that airline again. He insisted that we go with Lufthansa. When we arrived in in Caracas, to get to the Humboldt Hotel you could only use the cable car to get up the mountain, so up we went! There was some kind of protest or revolt in the town lasting a while, so we couldn't go down for a couple of days. From the luxury of our rooms, though, we could see poverty and rats as big as cats. It was very humbling and travelling made a big impression on me. We played against Costa Rica and shared rooms; three women to a bedroom.

'After Percy died, the breakaway group was Babs Large, her mother, Mrs Large, and Veronica Bailey, but they didn't have the organisation that Percy had. Babs' sister, Stella, took on some of the management. I remember Percy being absolutely serious and insisting we were taken seriously. One time at an airport, I think it was in Brussels, we came across Walter Winterbottom and Sir Stanley Rous who asked if we were a gymnastics team and Percy said no we were a women's football team. When they laughed, he had a right go at them. He was such a nice man. Very kind. But absolutely serious about what he did.'

Marlene Goddard/Cook

'I played for Corinthians for a relatively short time between 1958 and 1963, but I played hockey for South Manchester for fourteen years until I was about thirty-six or thirty-seven. For Corinthians, I started out as a forward. In my time with Corinthians I went on tour to Holland, Portugal, Madeira, and three months in South America. They wanted us to stay longer, but we had been away from home so long and some of us were quite young, so we wanted to go home. Margaret 'Titch' Wilde was only twelve after all. So Percy spoke to everyone who was of age, and for those who were not he spoke to their parents. South America was my last big tour because I got married in 1961 and didn't go on tour then. My maiden name was Goddard and my married name was Cook, so I didn't really have a nickname before marriage as there was only one Marlene. After, we had two Cooks so I became 'Cookie'.

'What I remember most about the tours were the crowds, twenty to thirty thousand people regularly watching us play in large stadia and staying in top class hotels, where the wealthy people would stay, with different foods and entertainment and different cultures. There were various media responsibilities, such as in Surinam we had to ride around on a big fire engine through the streets to promote the game, with advertising all over it.

'The split came after Portugal and some of the team had an argument with Percy, and then formed Benfica Ladies FC, where I was moved from up front to left full-back. I don't know what the argument was about but Babs Large, who was a brilliant left-winger, was part of Benfica and I think her mum and sister helped organise the team, but they didn't play for long after. They liked the name while we were on tour in Portugal and formed their own team. It wasn't that there were too many in the squad for Corinthians and Nomads, it was something else.

'After marriage and giving up with the Corinthians I have always continued my love of travel. My aunt lived in America and I took the children over to see her several times. I have four sisters who live in Australia so we regularly visited when my husband was alive, and after he died I went on my own. Now, I love all sport on television, if there is sport on, Marlene will be watching! I support both City and United, both Manchester teams, but I support United a bit more.'

Margaret 'Whitty' Whitworth

'I joined Corinthians when I was eleven and I was fourteen when I joined the main teams, which was inspiring because there were so many good players. My first flight was the tournament to the Netherlands, and I found it really well organised, and thrilling to be doing something I couldn't have afforded back home like staying in hotels, going on planes and so on. The hotels were always top quality.

'For me, the stand-out tour was to South America, which should initially have been six weeks, but went so well that the management wanted to stay on, when we previously had planned to return and play in Holland. This caused a bit of bad feeling with the Dutch organisers but, as players, we were delighted.

'It wasn't all glamorous; the flights in South America included a late-night trip on a cargo plane. Before I could go my parents had to get the permission of the school education authority, who agreed to the six weeks because it might be educational. When the tour was prolonged to three months my parents had to go back and ask for an extension. All my dad kept saying was, "Bring me lizards back". He was a curator at Manchester Museum and always on the lookout for new specimens.

'But mostly it was very glamorous. I felt like a star staying in top-class hotels, where wealthy people stayed, lots of media attention, people gave us gifts at airports and at hotels and sent us telegrams of good luck. Even a proposal of marriage! I was only fourteen. We went to a lot of receptions, with politicians and the well to do. It was non-stop really.

'Being part of the younger group, we got into some scrapes the manager didn't know about, and so we also had to keep quiet when Doris was around. For example, we formed a plan to go midnight swimming at the hotel Humboldt in Caracas, which had two lifts, one for the guests and one for the maids. We went down in the maids' lift and were swimming around when one of the girls couldn't resist diving in, causing a big splash. Someone came to investigate and we all had to hide around the pool. We thought we would be locked in until morning. But fortunately we climbed the steps back to bed.

'Percy was very proper, "My Girls Are Ladies" he used to say. So another time in Paramaribo, in Surinam, the hotel was right on the beach, right by palm trees and the sea. Although we were told not to go out unless supervised, a few of us went onto the beach and one girl was sitting with a lad, when a woman from the hotel saw us. She began shouting, "he's got a knife, he's got a knife!" Of course he had nothing of the kind, but we were made to apologise to the older players and the management because they were afraid for our safety. Percy was very kind but very correct in that respect.

'We played to full stadiums of people with 50–60,000 spectators. Having previously played at sports grounds in England, when we went abroad it was completely different and felt very professional. Sometimes I was a bit intimidated at the age of fourteen. I played teams in South America such as Odica and Caracas. We kicked off at 10pm because of the heat, and once the president arrived by helicopter after a big parade. It could be a little bit frightening, as I hadn't experienced anything like this. We played exhibition matches, of course too, and even on our nights off, when we went to the cinema, on the newsreel it was us!

'Percy used an agent, called Virriato Kavachio, who I think was quite wealthy himself, and put money up front to organise the tour, then he would donate the money to the International Red Cross, minus our expenses. In Venezuela alone we handed over a cheque at a reception for £12,000. There would be sixteen players and maybe four managers/agents, so it was a huge undertaking. While we were in one place, Kavachio would go on ahead and organise the next matches and venue. This meant that when Pauline Fairweather got appendicitis in Aruba, one of the other girls had to stay with her, and an agent. They had a nice holiday but Pauline had to go home to recuperate and so they had to go with her and missed the rest of the tour.

'Compared with this, the tour to Italy in 1961 was a bit of a flop crowd-wise, although we played in Turin, Milan and Bologna. The Ireland tour of 1962 was just a couple of matches in Ballymena and followed by a tour of the Isle of Man. I couldn't go to Morocco as I couldn't get the time off work. We were an amateur side who worked.

'I now think, "what if people had taken women's football seriously because we had some really very good players who could have been in any England side?" I was so lucky to go. When I got back my outlook on life totally changed. When you've been to a place and then see it in a geography lesson, you know what that place was like and who was rich and who was poor in that country and how they lived. Since then I have travelled widely and love travel, especially to Canada, and America.

'We worked hard and were a good side. One time, against a Coventry side, at Dunlop sports ground I think, I had already scored seven and because we were so far ahead, we swapped the defence with the attack to liven things up, and I scored my best goal ever! A diving header; the only time I scored with my head. I was a right-winger.

'Margaret Wilde was an unbelievably good player, powerful and brilliant with her feet. I played until I was twenty-seven when a knee injury ended my career. There wasn't the surgery available then that there is for ACL injury now. I never played for any team other than Corinthians, but was once loaned to Benfica, who were a team created after some of the players had a row with Percy and formed a breakaway side. I was terrified and couldn't wait to go back. My last tournament was 1970 in France where we played the French, managed by Pierre and his wife, Christine. It was very well organised and we beat Juventus in the final by a single goal. They were very Italian in their play; very defensive. Four of us went back in 1971 camping, and met up with some of the French players. My memory of the winning reception in 1970 at the Lord Mayor's offices was us all standing round in two-piece suits, with little handbags and all the other players from other countries looking very professional in tracksuits. Meeting the Lord Mayor, lined up in little two-piece jackets and skirts! But that was Percy, very correct.

Sylvia Gore

Sylvia 'Margaret' Gore joined Corinthians as a twelve-year-old, which, as we have seen from player testimonies, was not that unusual. Sylvia was born in Prescot, Lancashire on 25 November 1944. Her father, Jack, and uncle both played for British Insulated Calender Cables in Prescot and encouraged Sylvia to take up the game of football.

At secondary school Sylvia was not allowed to play football, which did not deter her, and she joined Manchester Corinthians in 1961, spending six years with them. This means she misremembered in an interview she gave to women's football historian John Carrier shortly before her death:

You know things were tough back then, when I was playing for Corinthians back in the 50's we had an agent based in Portugal, the International Red Cross would sponsor our trips abroad, and he would pay for our trips and donate to charity after our expenses were paid. We played all over the world. As a youngster I played in front of 80,000 in South America and at the San Siro Stadium in Milan. This was because of the ban on women playing in England. It was hard to find grounds to play on, that's why we played abroad such a lot. While with the Corinthians we raised over £250,000 and would be away from home at 3 months at a time.

As John Carrier – who was kind enough to share his interview with Sylvia – pointed out, *The Liverpool Echo* reported on 13 June 1962 that seventeen-year-old Sylvia was to tour South America with the Corinthians, but unfortunately that second tour South American tour did not take place. It may have been a misunderstanding. However, it does seem that Sylvia joined a trip to Italy trip and scored several important goals.

Sylvia signed for Fodens in 1967, a great opponent of Corinthians, as were the more recently formed Southampton side for which Sue Lopez played. Gore would see great changes by the time she played in the first official England team in 1972 against Scotland, at the age of twenty-eight, while Jean Wilson, with whom Sylvia had played at Corinthians, was twenty-three. Wilson was a very good striker, who started the first international in the first eleven, but her England career was more short-lived and she remained a Corinthians player. This meant that when the WFA did form the first official England side to play Scotland in 1972, Gore had over fifteen years of expertise on which to draw to score the first goal in a 3–2 victory. Wilson was less experienced, although she also started as a striker in the Scotland match.

'Whitty' as one of the forty-five women players invited for the trials for the official WFA England side, but was injured and so could not attend to make the cut to twenty-five players who were invited to Loughborough

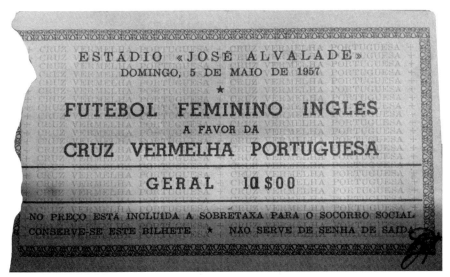

A ticket stub to a match in Portugal at the stadium José Alvalade, 5 May 1957.

University for a final squad selection. Perhaps her best years were to be for Corinthians rather than England, which came too late. Sylvia had a distinguished career as a national coach for the Wales women's national team, as well as being an advocate for women's football in the community, and as an administrator. She received many accolades over her sixty years in football, none more so than her M.B.E. awarded to her in 2000 for her services to women's and girls' football in England.

Margaret Vaughan 'Griff'

'I was born Margaret Griffiths, and when we were young football was a big part of our lives. I was born in Ancotes. We did the Pools and Dad took us down to watch City and United once. When I was two-and-a-half we moved to Clayton, but I still went to school in Ancotes. I played football in the street with the boys and had one younger brother. There weren't girls' teams and yet I loved football from a very young age. Mother said that in a photograph taken when I was very young, about one-and-a-half, I sat on a table and there was a prop ball, a beach ball, and I wouldn't settle for the photograph until I got the ball. I left school at fifteen and worked as a sewing machinist in the rag trade, as we called it. I was not particularly academic; I was the physical one. In the end I worked in the office and then my own business.

'Like everyone else, I saw an advertisement in the paper and went down to Fog Lane for a trial. Our formation was an attacking style with five at the back, so the wingers could get forward. Percy was technically strict about how we should play and overlap. He would give us individual instruction on our role.

'I have photographs with no dates on them, many featuring aeroplanes because I hadn't flown until then. We went to Portugal and Madeira by sea-plane. We took a coach down south and didn't have an airport as such. We were not warned about the plane, we just sort of got on with it, and next stop Portugal. As well as visiting Portugal twice, I did the South American tour, Belfast, the Isle of Man and Italy. Obviously the cable car and the military coup in Venezuela at Caracas stood out as memories, and the Humboldt Hotel was fantastic.

'When I came back, not only was it the first time I had been on a jumbo jet, I was the only person in the street who had been on a plane, except for men who had fought in the war, so for working-class people we had once-in-a-lifetime opportunities. In South America we travelled on one of those planes with single seats and parachute wires, you just got on to find a bucket behind a curtain at one end. We didn't know until we got on. On another occasion we were on a coach going through the desert, and all there was the whole trip was a caravan selling drinks of orange, coca cola or water. That was it. All these were new experiences, and you couldn't lose face, you just got on with it.

We did so much flying. When we went to the Isle of Man I thought we were crashing because we had no sooner took off than we were coming down, and were only minutes in the air. I thought, "what's going on?" Plus after the game it was a normal scheduled flight, so we had to rush to get back on the plane, as they wouldn't wait for anyone.

'In New York I had fallen asleep on the plane going to South America after we had changed planes at JFK, and the propeller had flames coming out of it so we had to turn back. I had to be woken up or I'd have slept through it. There was a big bar like you saw in the films at the airport and we had something to eat and drink. A Mexican family, I think they were, had a baby at the airport. When we took off again we sort of ran out of runway and went on the grass and had to walk back and Mr Ashley was not very happy with that. We stayed over a few days and I didn't really like it. I remember the sun did not reach the street. I was shocked. I knew skyscrapers were high, but not that high. We went to the top of the Empire State. We didn't go in but we saw where Audrey Hepburn had breakfast at Tiffany's. There were a lot of rough sleepers, which we had not seen in Manchester. We had tramps but they moved around, not sleeping on the streets. One girl, I remember, at the hotel in New York, could not get over the televisions in the rooms and she watched twenty-four hours of Elvis on television as she didn't have a set at home.

'I played for Corinthians until 1965 but I didn't go on the Tunisia tour because on New Year's Day 1966 I went to Australia as a £10 Pom. I had always wanted to go because when at school we had done topics like geography, I had looked at Australia on the map and wanted to go. When I was out there, I played for a team in Perth, organised by English and Irish girls, but it wasn't very competitive. There were five English players, a South African, a German, Italian. I think it changed to something else later. In 1967 I played netball too and had by then moved to Sydney. There was the Metropolitan Soccer Association in Sydney and I have quite a few programmes. I lived the outdoor life all right. The name of the club, Sydney Prague, came from the players who had originally come from Prague. My friend Pat Redmond, as she was called then, chose to stay, and settled there but I came back.

In December 1969 I came back because I either had to stay or become Australian, and my parents were getting older. I went down to see the Corinthians, but I wasn't really interested by 1970 as the magic of the old days had gone.

Carol Aiken

'I was always sporty, played boys' games and loved football. I also played badminton, hockey, netball, and did trampolining. I am not sure how I heard about the Corinthians, but my parents went for an interview with Percy Ashley off Fog Lane, in Didsbury, and I remember that they were looking for a goalie. Although I was really an outfield player, I accepted. I had to be fitted for football boots. We were not a particularly well-off family and my sister was not sporty, so my mum and dad said, "You had better be serious about this" as they stretched their finances to buy my boots. They were not regular season ticket holders or football fans either, although my dad took me to Maine Road to see some top-class football to encourage me, and to see what to aspire to. I was serious! I would practice for hours; angles of shots and passes and returns with a tennis ball against a wall. I started playing for Corinthians aged fourteen when Doris Ashley was still playing. We always played for charity and it was usually a charity match against Nomads.

'Funnily enough, I don't remember the games as such. Maybe while I was playing I was one of those people who were "glad to be there". I can't remember the scores and such. I became an outfield player at Corinthians and played centre half, although I wasn't as skilful as in goal.

A snapshot of Bert Trautmann, centre of picture, with his arm around the shoulders of Percy Ashley, second from right, and other friends on their trip to Germany 1957.

'I went on the tours to Morocco and Tunisia in 1966, my first time on a plane, and I was allowed by my school to go during term time. It felt very prestigious, and quite important playing exhibition matches. I was fifteen at the time and had been on one foreign holiday to Switzerland. I was amongst the first at school to get a passport and I took the photos from the football tour to school to show my friends. The names of the places seemed exotic: Casablanca, which people had heard about because of the film, Rabat, Hammamet; in all about five cities where we played in proper stadiums, with large crowds and we were chaperoned to the grounds. I remember the dry heat and the drums, and the International Red Cross crescent [sic]. Then we prepared for the Reims tour. My mum led the tour and she managed the team, which we won against Juventus. I remember most playing in major stadiums, large crowds and the generous hospitality. My brother-in-law then coached at Corinthians after Mum gave up as manager.

'I trained as a PE/French teacher at Coventry College of Education between 1969 and 1972 so training was difficult because I was also trying to do athletics, hockey, netball, rounders and volleyball. I've always been sporty and always loved travel, doing as much as I can now I am retired. In 1973–74 season I moved to

Fodens, aged twenty-two, as I felt that it would help with my ability and played in an WFA Cup Final then ended playing in 1975–76 season. I travelled to Sandbach by train. I played alongside England internationals like Sheila Parker and Sylvia Gore at Fodens. Sylvia had previously played at Corinthians, and had moved to Fodens, so it seemed like a good move.'

Margaret Shepherd

'I joined Corinthians, aged nineteen, in 1966 or 1967. I had not really heard of women's football in my little Lancashire town, although I used to play football and cricket with the boys. Not long after I started work, I got picked for the civil service netball team in my area. Going along to practice, I kicked the ball as it ran along the ground to me as I would kick any ball. Another girl the other end kicked it back! She said, 'Do you play football?' I said, 'Girls don't play football but I play with lads on the local field.' She said, 'You've not heard of women's football then? I play in a women football team, do you want to come and train?'

'It was Sheila 'Isshy' Isherwood and she was a really good player. It was just by chance. She lived in next town and invited me to go with her on the bus to train on Sunday at Fog Lane Park. I came from a mining town so even going to Manchester on the bus was an experience. We were both in the civil service on £5 a week. The changing rooms were dingy and if you wanted a wash you had to break the ice on the duck pond if you didn't want to go home on the bus with muddy knees. But it was freedom, and from then we were never in. We would work in the beer keller [sic] on a Friday and Saturday night, pack a bag of food for the bus and be off out playing football.

'I was part of the team who won in Reims, France, when Corinthians won against the Italians in the final. It was very professionally organised and I remember we were treated very nicely. There were plans to go to South Africa following the tour that Chelsea had just completed, but trouble in Mozambique meant that we had to cancel and we were bitterly disappointed.

'We had to be resilient! We went down to Deal every year to play in WFA cup, returning after matches on Sunday night by coach. We used to return in the early hours and have to go to work first thing. Then, if you got through to the later rounds in Deal you had to go back and do the whole thing again the next weekend. However, increasingly from 1968 we started to play Fodens, Doncaster Rovers Belles, and Southampton, those kinds of teams.

'I gave up playing for Corinthians in my late twenties when my daughter was born. In her early teens I set up a girls' team because there were a lot of youngsters just roaming the streets. So I got a group of girls to play football and they were changed kids! So I did my bit for women's football in the modern era, starting about 1992–93, for about three years until commitments like looking after my parents meant I had to give up.'

Jan Lyons

'I fell in love with football as a young kid and fostered an interest in anything football related. My dad, Thomas Lyons, was a good player, but not as good as his brother Alf, who had trials with Everton. Dad played for Princess Road School and Manchester Boys. Someone said that Denis Violet was related to us but we never really got to the bottom of it, so I am not sure. My mum, Avis Lyons, played netball when she was younger. She wasn't really that sporty, but she was a very clever woman, very supportive of me, more so even than my dad in many ways. There wasn't really any street football for me, just the school playground or shooting practice on my own.

'I used to pester my mum to send off the Typhoo tea vouchers so I could collect them. The first football card I received was Denis Law. My dad took me once to Old Trafford once before 1966, and he used to take me and Judy to the reserves at Manchester United to get us out of the house while Mum was cleaning or something. So Denis Law was the first player I remember being excited by. He was exciting in the box, a tricky player, and I loved it if he flicked the ball up or did a back heel. Tricks came so easy to him.

'I couldn't contain my excitement as England hosted the 1966 World Cup. The Portuguese team stayed at the Stanneylands Hotel in Handforth. I lived on the Spath Lane Council Estate and nothing could have been better at that stage of my life. I spent many a day camped outside the hotel waiting for a glimpse of one of the greatest footballers of all time, my hero Eusebio (the Black Pearl). I suppose I'd have been about eleven or twelve, and bear in mind people didn't go abroad on holiday as they do now, so to see overseas players in real life was very exciting. I didn't get to see him in real life though, just on the telly. He was such an exciting player, technical, with superb technique, and I loved that style of play. He also seemed like a smashing, genuinely nice man off the field.

'The Aberfan Disaster on 21 October 1966 was a catastrophic collapse of a colliery tip; a disaster that shook the nation. Many children died in their school. It was my first football game as captain of the girl's team of the Spath Lane Estate versus the boys. Mr Adge Jupp, a local man off the estate, organised it and played me at full-back. So he knew what he was doing. The match was played on my school playing fields, Handforth Hall County Primary School. All the donations raised went to the Aberfan Disaster Fund in November 1966. We raised £125. We lost, I think 6–4, or so the newspaper said, and I scored a penalty and made the other three goals, the journalist reported.

'I was the best player on the day and I was chaired off the field by the organisers and spectators. At the presentation evening I was awarded with a shield for the match. It was engraved with my nickname, as I was affectionately known as 'Tiger'. I also got awarded with a Toby jug and a sports voucher. I remember feeling very confident on the day, and I enjoyed the crowd, showboating a bit, and being a bit cocky. For example, instead of kicking the ball forwards from a free kick, I back-heeled it to the goalkeeper. I wouldn't do it now, but I thought I was a star then!

'My mother saw an advertisement in the local newspaper, I think it was the *Manchester Evening News*, in late 1967 or early 1968. We wrote in and were offered trials by Bill Oldfield, as Mr Ashley had died by then. I have the letters of both trial games, and I know the pitches on Fog Lane Park were bad so it must have been midwinter. Gladys Aiken had not yet taken over as manager. The letter of selection came and Mr Oldfield said, 'I have been impressed with Janice, even in bad conditions,' and so on, but also stressing that I would have to work hard to progress. I hadn't been sure in the trials that I would be selected as there were very good footballers, and

I was only thirteen and didn't turn fourteen until that September, whereas some were grown women. It was a big step up but I was speedy and had spirit.

'I joined on 6 February 1968. I knew the club's reputation. I still wanted to be a forward but I could see others were better than me at that position, and when they played me at full-back very little got past. Sheila Isherwood would say to me, "Jan, if you can't stop them, drop them". I was like a little rat! I was a great tackler. I played all over in my time, but mainly for Corinthians as full-back.

'I was influenced by Whitty too, and to try and play like she did. She also loved players like Eusebio, and the other continental players. She liked the South American style, and idolised Pele, Garrincha, Ronaldinho, Rivaldo and Jiarzinho. Players with magical technique. She was great at using the same techniques, like looking one way and shooting the other. I tried to be a forward, because I wanted to score, but I could see that others were better going forwards.

'I was very fortunate to be able to travel round the country playing football and visiting so many interesting places and people with the same ambitions and hopes as myself. I played locally with the Corinthians and Nomads teams. I also had the opportunity to play around the country at Scunthorpe, Maidenhead, Blackpool, Prestatyn, Worcester, and a favourite of mine, the annual Deal Tournament in Kent. I remember playing and winning The Deal Tournament in 1968 and the Deal International Tournament in 1969.

'The Reims International Football Tournament July 1970 was my first memory of travelling abroad and my first trip by Air France to Paris and the city of Reims. Our team was Margaret Temple, Eileen Gay (Joker), Margaret Taylor (Tiny), Chris Millar, Margaret Wilde, Jan Lyons, Pauline Quayle (Captain), Jackie Thornton, Margaret Whitworth (Whitty), Pat Quayle, Sheila Isherwood (Isshy), Sue Kelly, and Linda Hallam.

'Corinthians played against Juventus (Italy), Stade De Reims (France), and Entente Kaplice (Czechoslovakia). It was so interesting to meet these foreign footballing ladies. We shared a dormitory with the Juventus team, they were on one side of the room and we were on the other. We shared stories as best we could, we also sang together and just had a great time.

'The first game was an exciting match between Manchester Corinthians and Entente, which we won 5–2. In the other game Juventus beat Stade De Reims 2–1, which meant it was a Manchester versus Juventus Final at Stade De Reims stadium. First half, a very tough match, both teams cancelling each other out and both playing cautiously. At half time it was 0–0. The second half was similar, everyone playing with caution. Eventually we scored. A cross came over from the wing and Linda Hallam slotted it in with her left foot. We all went wild but we knew Juventus then had to come out and attack us. With ten minutes to go I was carried off with bad cramp, a substitute defender was brought on and we managed to hang on till the final whistle. We had done it! I then went on holiday with an Italian friend to Turin the next year and that set me off to play in Italy.

'In 1973 I travelled to Paris by plane. My parents said their farewells at the airport, and I caught an overnight train from Paris Gare Du Nord to Torino (Porta Nuova). In Torino, my Italian friend Valeria met me at the train station. We immediately went to visit the president of Juventus at his home, where I met some of my new teammates.

'After a short time, I was moved to a Pension Hostel in the centre of Turin, Casa Fraterna, on Via San Dominico. I absolutely loved this place. A hostel run by nuns, and a place for young women to stay whilst working in Turin. They came from all over Italy. It was so vibrant especially the girls from the southern areas of Italy, such as Sicily and Naples. Meal times were amazing. The pace was buzzing with life, full of noise and chatter. This is where I

Poster for the Reims International Tournament in 1970.

learned to speak Italian plus many swear words! I shared my room with what turned out to be one of my best Italian friends, Carla Pivotto.

'I must admit, football was so professional in Italy. The training was so intense but enjoyable. The amazing difference between playing in England and Italy was the Italians had a great emphasis on the importance of diet and healthy eating. The correct nutrition was necessary for stamina, health and growth. Football training was Tuesday evening and Saturday morning as we played our games on a Sunday. The club had its own house in Turin, with its own meeting room. It was furnished with clipboards regarding tactics and awareness. There were bedrooms for the teams to sleep or relax in. We met here before we travelled to the games.

'Places I visited and played football in Italy, Milan, Piacenza, Bologna, Pescara, Rome and Naples. I loved Sicily; the team spent journeys looking for Mafia gangsters wearing white suits in the city of Palermo. I remember the team spending the weekend at a seaside resort at San Benedetto Del Tronto, in the province of Ascoli. It was an ancient fishing village turned into a seaside retreat. We won the game quite easily 4–0.

'We also played against Lazio in Naples, where I played against Dorothy Cassels, an ex-Southampton player who also played in England at the Deal Tournament. After the game we talked about our life in Italy and mainly about where we lived, our lifestyles and the food we liked or disliked. I ate Mortadella sandwiches a lot. I remember at that time in England we didn't really appreciate the different flavours, spices and herbs of foreign food; this came much later than 1973. I spent two years playing football in Italy before coming home for family reasons in 1975.'

This chapter has shown how Percy Ashley encouraged goodwill for his players during the time of the FA ban by consistently telling a story of female amateurism at a time when football's retain and transfer systems, and maximum wage caps were being challenged. From the 1950s, stars like Billy Wright, and later in the 1960s, George Best, were pioneering new kinds of male professionalism and links with the entertainment and media industries, for ever higher personal gain. Of course, many women's teams had used charitable fund raising to host women's matches in major stadiums during, and more successfully still, shortly after World War One, before the 1921 ban. However, the Corinthians case study suggests a need to examine how similar tactics were used after 1945 in peacetime. Amplifying this example with other local studies can help to contextualise the gradual acceptance of women's football as officially sanctioned by governing bodies, and the forty-four clubs of the inaugural WFA season seem like a good place to start.

The Corinthians and Nomads players may have life experiences that they otherwise would not have had without their enthusiasm for football, but by raising vast sums of money for a range of charities, the wider societal disapproval of women playing the sport could be offset by presenting a kind of robust, plucky sporting altruism, typical of Manchester's reputation for busy worker bees. Ashley was not just an astute football tactician, but wise in public relations and in networking.

Newspaper clipping of the match in French, headline translates as 'The Speed of Manchester Prevails over the tight "catennacio" defence of Juventus'.

Percy Ashley had already pioneered complex and ambitious overseas tours twelve years before the WFA were in a position to have domestic trials for an England team. He understood that businessmen and philanthropists could make women's football spectacular, if ambitiously staged and sold to a paying public as exciting entertainment. Harry Batt agreed. The WFA and the FA did not, and have continued to perceive women's football as an economic drain on resources rather than as a financial asset today.

There is still much to know. Brenda Elsey and Josh Nadal, in their book *Futbolera*, recently indicated that the South American tour was intended to include Brazil and that businessman José da Gama supported the intention, only to have it blocked by the government who had at that time banned women's football by law. It would also seem that the tour to Tunisia was not as successful as some of the other overseas trips, and the players were not encouraged to speak about it upon their return other than as a nice holiday. So there is a lot more to do to understand both the full extent of plans for the tours and exactly how each was organised, as well as the other Corinthians internationals.

The chapter has shown the processes by which the Corinthian and Nomads players became mediated as ambassadors for respected international charities. In this, there is perhaps something new that had not been tried before in promoting women's football, even by big name clubs such as Dick, Kerr Ladies. This ambassadorial role, now very fashionable amongst movie stars and celebrities today, also gave Corinthians a gloss of international approval, which helped their image domestically. Most of the charities I have seen in the Manchester Corinthians source material so far were large and complex aid agencies, like Oxfam or the International Red Cross, or health charities for serious and complicated conditions. There was an absolutely serious approach to women's play and an ambitiously professional level of organisation, combined with a committed social conscience.

Given this, we may well look back on feminist fathers like Percy Ashley as well ahead of their time. Not that he would probably have used those terms himself. But in practice, what he did for his daughter, his local community, many charities and for women's sports undoubtedly merits more recognition than he has so far received. Similarly, the players who gave up so much of their time for charity, and who challenged convention to play a sport that they loved, even when the prevailing conditions were

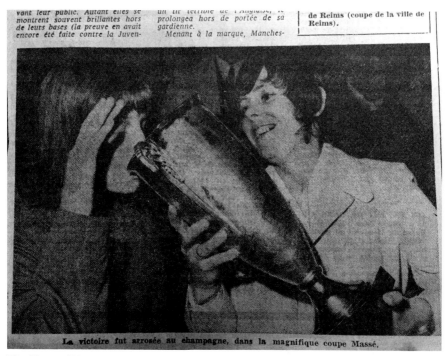

The Taste of Victory – Corinthians drink from the Reims Cup.

against them and it would have been easier to go off and do something else instead, deserve recognition and respect. We get a sense of how fragile the good fortune of a young woman to be geographically close to clubs like Corinthians could be from an aspiring Anne Day, who began to play football aged eight and wrote to Manchester Corinthians aged twelve in 1970 to ask to play, only to be told by her parents that she was too young to travel with the team. Undaunted, she formed her own team, and went on to have a career in coaching. But it could have been so easily different. It is satisfying to know from the oral histories that at least all involved had a lot of fun and some fame, if short lived.

In Corinthians, not only did Percy Ashley create a team that then grew to a club with three sides, he also used overseas tours to develop a level of technical playing ability that the women's domestic game at the time could not sustain. If Manchester Corinthians were defeating opponents like Coventry 36–0, with individual players like Whitty scoring seven goals and using such matches as experiments between their defensive and attacking players, then only going abroad could provide more rigorous tests of opposition. Even the exhibition matches, where the Corinthians and Nomads players were evenly spread across both teams in order to provide high scoring, open matches, must inevitably have raised the quality of play, as did regular practice. It is intriguing to know why Benfica Ladies FC broke away from Percy Ashley's organisation, but it does seem to have been a short-lived team thereafter. It would be useful to extend the player evidence with views of those charities involved to know why and how women's football was used in this way. Much remains to be done.

The Corinthians at our reunion at the National Football Museum, 1 October 2018.

Chapter 4

Harry Batt's Touring Teams 1968–1972

This chapter concerns the teams formed by Harry Batt, who went on overseas tours to Italy and Mexico just when the term world championship or World Cup was being used to describe growing international tournaments for women. Held outside the auspices of FIFA, there was a successful Women's World Championship in Italy in 1970 which amplified the business case for women's football as a lucrative draw. In 1971, only one year after Mexico hosted the men's World Cup, an even larger tournament became a key moment in the history of women's football because it proved that there was a large commercial market for women-only tournaments. The opening games in Mexico were played in front of crowds of 80,000 people. England played against Argentina and hosts Mexico in the group stages, losing to France in the fifth- and sixth-place play-offs. But England were hugely popular with the Mexican fans, and spent a full month appearing on television, in the newspapers, socialising at swanky dinners and being hosted at numerous receptions.

The chapter starts with a discussion of how a European organisation, the Federation of Independent European Female Football (FIEFF), was formed and invited Harry Batt to manage an England team to attend a representative tournament in Turin in November 1969. Soon after, FIEFF's ambitions grew and it dropped European from its title to become a more ambitious organisation called International Federation of Feminin Football (FIFF). This expanded administration staged two women's world championships, in Italy in 1970 and Mexico in 1971, sponsored by Martini & Rossi, the Italian drinks company. A third tournament in 1972 was less successful, and marked the end of the FIFF control of women's internationals.

The chapter moves on to consider the career of Harry Batt, and how he came to form the teams that played under his management. Finally, the chapter considers the memories of players, some of whom were as young as thirteen, to provide a lived experience of the tournaments, and pulls together a collective biography of the England team. Harry's ambitions for women's football did not end well. As the historical aspects of the chapter will explain, he and his players travelled as the British Independents, many of whom were banned from women's football on their return from Mexico. Harry and his wife, June, were banned for life.

The formation of a Federation of Independent European Female Football in 1969

When FIFA, the world governing body of football, announced that its national associations should take control of the women's game in 1969, change was glacially slow. In the same year in England the Women's Football Association was formed (WFA) and affiliated to the Football Association (FA) on the same basis as a County FA, as we have seen in a previous chapter. However, outside of official FIFA- or FA-sanctioned competitions, women's football had become attractive to business interests. Charity games, such as those covered in the previous chapter on Corinthians FC, proved that women's football could draw large crowds.

During 1969 a Federation of Independent European Female Football (FIEFF) was formed and invited Harry Batt to put together an England team to attend a four-team representative tournament called the Coppa Europa per Nazioni (women) in Novara, Aosta and Turin during November that year. It is important to remember that at the same time Harry was a member of the WFA Committee, and so well placed to understand what was happening domestically and internationally in women's football. He had formed Chiltern Valley in 1968–69 season because his wife, June, had begun playing football and he wanted to support her interests. Things grew quickly from there.

As well as Manchester Corinthians, Southampton were a strong team, and Harry always scouted for the best players for his overseas tours. Southampton striker Sue Lopez was selected, along with her colleagues, goalkeeper Sue Buckett, defenders Jill Long and Barbara Birkett, and forward Dot Cassell. England lost to Denmark 4–3 in their first game on 1 November in Aosta, and won the third-place play-off against France in Turin on 2 November. Sue Lopez is credited with scoring a hat-trick against Denmark and a goal against France, with Sue Tungate providing the other England strike.

As a direct result of her high profile in the Turin event, Lopez was signed to Roma in the Italian professional leagues, though to observe WFA rules that players must be amateurs, she was careful to play without pay. This is because the FA did not fund the WFA at this time, and the Central Council for Physical Recreation (CCPR), who did provide some modest financial help, only supported amateur athletes. Nevertheless, Sue remembered in her 1997 book, *Women on the Ball: A Guide to Women's Football*, that the 1969 tournament in Italy was ground-breaking in scope and ambition:

> It was a thrill to play foreign opponents on some of the best pitches in Italy. All the grounds were excellent and the same ones used by the professional men's teams. The crowds of 10,000 plus were beyond anything we had experienced. We felt elated to have been part of such an exciting tournament, after the small-scale events in England, to find everything taken more seriously. It was how we imagined that male professional players were treated, with nice hotels, beautiful venues and respect, especially from the press.

The English team, Lopez reported, shared hotel rooms with the Danish squad, represented by club side Boldklubben Femina (also known as BK Femina or Femina) from Gladsaxe. Formed in 1959, this was perhaps the most experienced side that had consistently played together in the Italian tournament. Biographer Hans Krabbe has recently published a collective biography of the Danish team – who would later go on to win women's world championships in Italy in 1970, and in Mexico in 1971 – called *Den Glemte Triumph* and it is a valuable work.

Krabbe includes the intriguing detail that, as a result of the 1968 Femina tour to Czechoslovakia, two leading Czech players defected from the Communist regime to join the Danish team. Newspapers support this, listing Maria Scevikcova, aged twenty-three and originally from Lobey in Czechoslovakia, and Jana Menschicova, aged twenty-five of Comutov, as players for Denmark in the 1970 Italian women's world championship. This took place in the context of the Prague Spring, a period of political liberalisation in the Czechoslovak Socialist Republic. On 5 January 1968 reformist Alexander Dubček was elected First Secretary of the Communist Party of Czechoslovakia (KSČ), and mass protests continued until 21 August 1968, when the Soviet Union and other Warsaw Pact allies invaded the country to prevent change. Towards the end of these reforms, and particularly after, Czechoslovakian women's teams tried to play in international tournaments, but were often denied visas to leave the country.

The Formation of the International Federation of Feminin Football in 1970

The four-team FIEFF European tournament paved the way for an expanded enterprise, and with South American participation, a more ambitious organisation evolved called International Federation of Feminin Football (FIFF), or in English the International Federation of Women's Football. In February 1970 the FIFF organising committee included Dr Vinicio Lucci, Dr Marco Rambauddi, Dr Domenico Rambauddi, Giuseppe Constantino and Claudio Seroco. They planned for a world championship, called the Coppa del Mondo, to be held in Italy in July 1970 and sponsored by the Italian drinks manufacturer Martini & Rossi. This was a crucial part in the success of both the 1970 and 1971 women's world championships and it is worth briefly covering Martini & Rossi's sports sponsorship history up to this.

In 1863 Alessandro Martini and Luigi Rossi took over the National Wine & Spirits Distillery in a small village near Turin. In the twentieth century, the four Rossi di Montelera cousins (owners of the Martini & Rossi company) were all keen sportsmen. This family passion became a company policy, to use sport, be it professional or amateur, as a base on which to build a dynamic and modern company image. Theo was a real sportsman: he had been world speedboat champion and taken part in Olympic bob, while Metello founded the Martini International Club in London in 1958, established to support 'all areas of culture, science, art and sport, particularly car and motorbike racing, all winter sports, nautical sports, horse riding, golf, tennis and fencing'.

Firstly, Martini & Rossi understood the communicative force of cycling and motor sport and decided to sponsor leading events from 1914 onwards. The First World War soon interrupted this, but in 1925 in Turin the Gran Coppa Martini & Rossi cycling race was launched. This sponsorship reached its peak with the tours of Italy in 1934 and 1936. In the first race, the company sponsored the cup awarded to the rider who was considered *Gran Premi della Montagna*, or King of the Mountains, and had two bespoke advertising cars designed specially for their brands Elixir China and Martini Vermouth to follow the race. In 1936 Martini had a luxury eight-cyclinder Isotta Fraschini with an enormous cardboard bottle of Elixir China mounted on the bonnet. It must have been some sight for dry throated and thirsty cyclists on the dusty roads of the peninsula.

Martini & Rossi entered the world of car racing after the Second World War, and the name appeared on bridges over racing tracks or along guardrails. The was soon changed to Martini Racing and the distinctive livery of pale and dark blue and orange became a feature for over thirty years, especially at events like the Le Mans 24 Hours. The legendary Martini Racing Team was founded in December 1970 as an offshoot of the Martini International Club. Martini then moved increasingly into sponsoring women's sport, including the Martini Fencing Trophy, the first women's football World Cup, the Women's Himalayan expedition and the women's golf open.

They initially focussed on amateur sports, where economic gain was not the most important goal, but as we have seen with the staging of the women's World Cup in Italy, this was a dynamic and modern tournament that also drew large crowds and promoted the Martini & Rossi brand widely. In addition to their economic support, the company decided to award a special trophy called Trofeo Martini & Rossi. The golden cup was inspired by the famous sculpture Nike of Samothrace, or Winged Victory, displayed in the Louvre Museum. The players of the tournament team would be given a copy of the trophy while the original was kept by FIFF. We do not currently know the whereabouts of this trophy today.

The 1970 Coppa del Mondo, in Italy

In 1970 FIFF invited teams from Austria, Denmark, Czechoslovakia, England, Italy, West Germany and Switzerland to compete. Mexico also received a special invitation to attend, though it remains unclear how, or when, the contacts were made. France had to retire from the tournament and Czechoslovakia were also not able to attend due to visa problems.

There were two groups: in Group A, played on the 7 July in Bari, Mexico beat Austria 9–0, with goals from Alicia Vargas (four), Maria

Sopra: finale Italia-Danimarca. Azione della capitana azzurra osta-
colata dalla difesa danese. Sotto: due Trofei messi in palio per
la prima edizione della Coppa del Mondo del calcio femminile

1970 World Cup trophies sponsored by Martini & Rossi.

Eugenia Rubio (two), Patricia Hernández (two), and Elsa Huerta. On 8 July Italy beat Switzerland 2–1 in Salerno, and went on to top the group by defeating Mexico 2–1 on 11 July in Naples, both goals scored by Elena Schiavo. Group games averaged about 24,000 spectators and were widely reported in newspapers such as *Tuttosport* and *Stampa*. In Group B England beat Germany 5–1 in Genoa on 7 July, while Denmark defeated Germany 6–1 on 8 July in Bologna. On 10 July Denmark beat England 2–0 in Milan. This left England in a play-off with Mexico for third and fourth place, which they lost 3–2. Denmark won the final 2–0 against the hosts in front of a crowd of 40,000 at the Stadio Communale in Turin. A reception at the Martini & Rossi headquarters followed, although it was not quite as celebratory as if the host country had been victorious.

The 1970 Harry Batt squad, referred to as England throughout the Italian media, combined Chiltern Valley players with Louise Cross, Jill Long and Dot Cassell from Southampton. This may have been pragmatic, and though Batt appears to have looked at players from other teams it is unclear why Fodens or Manchester Corinthians players were not invited to a trial. Perhaps it was just down to logistics. The England squad were: Paula Rayner, Val Reid, Kath Everitt, Angela King, June Foulke, Joan Briggs, Jill Stockley, Sue Knowles, Trudy McCaffery, Valerie Cheshire, Louise Cross, Dot Cassell, Janice Seymour, Jill Long, Marion Crook and, playing at number ten, striker Barbara Dolling. Wikipedia currently lists Sue Lopez as scoring the fifth of England's goals against Germany, but as she was not playing, this should be treated with some caution. Neither Lopez nor Sue Buckett travelled in 1970 due to pressure from the WFA, and by extension the FA.

As well as the two Czech players, the Denmark team were mainly from Copenhagen and included Inge Kristensen, Jytta Termansen, Love Yvonne Hansen, Joan Nielsen, Kirsten Evans, Irene Christenden, Kirsten Schaefer, and Kara Jacobsen and Inge Kristensen. The press did not list all of the victorious squad. The Italian side comprised: Wilma Seghetti, aged just fourteen, and her teammate from AFC Verona, Adriana Canepa; student Orietta Bonanni, who was nineteen and played alongside the great striker, Elena Schiavo, who, aged twenty-one, played her club football in Torino, as did her teammates Rosanna Cerutti, Claudia Avon, Caterina Molino, Anna Castelli, Marisa Mondo and Derna Isoline. Cone Riva played her club football in Juventus, and combined well with Schiavo for Italy's goals. Giuliana Mella, Adriana Cella and Ketty Rampon also featured. The press had not expected such a large or enthusiastic crowd. The tournament was a huge success and the organisers looked to build upon the business model they had developed for an even larger tournament.

Later that year, a two-day conference on 5 and 6 December, in the Ambassador's Hotel, Torino, convened the first world congress of the FIFF and plans were made to host another tournament. In the minutes that I have seen, the participants were often just referred to by surname, but were led by Jaime de Haro, a dynamic entrepreneur and sports enthusiast. From the available information to date, other members included Helmuth Goldsmieth of Austria, Korsuize of The Netherlands, Mazzoni of Italy, Harry Batt of England, Hans Gunther Hansen of Germany, Stuby of Switzerland, Fernando Quevedo of Spain, Manelich Quintero of Mexico, Franco Talanco, who represented Martini & Rossi International, and also the organising committee of the Second World Championship of Feminin

Football from Mexico. So it is clear that sponsorship arrangements were already in place for Mexico. Also assisting was Madame Christiane Geoffrey of France, who, with her husband, Pierre, had been so instrumental in establishing the Reims team that sought out international club rivals like Manchester Corinthians in 1970.

Medal from the 1971 World Championship in Mexico, held from 15 August to 5 September.

The directors of the Mexico congress included the president of the organising committee, Dr Lucci, the vice-president, Mr Zamparelli, Professor Marisa Bachet, Dr Piero Boero, Dr Ferraro, Dr Saraco, Mr Rambauddi, Mrs Canceron, and the secretary, Mr Alfredo di Stadio. Again, it is interesting that women were part of these senior administrative functions, whereas at this stage FIFA was an almost entirely male workforce. Professor Efrain Perez and Manelich Quintera also joined the central committee. Accountancy was led by Gustavo Rubio Alcalde, and renowned sports journalist Raoul Sanchez Hidalgo provided media advice, along with Teadoro Cario and Juan García Vasquez. Much remains to be known about these individuals.

The 1971 Campeonato de Fútbol Femenil in Mexico

Germany, Spain and Switzerland were all prepared to host the 1971 Campeonato de Fútbol Femenil, or Women's Football Championship, but the decision was made in favour of Mexico. The discussion had centred on the effects of altitude, and medical opinion had been divided previously on the best way to cope with this and the heat at both the 1968 Olympic Games and the 1970 men's World Cup. The England men's national team, for instance, had toured Central and South America in 1969 to prepare for Mexico.

Although the amateurs of women's football could not fund expensive medical preparations, or overseas tours, the Italian women's squad visited Mexico in October 1970 to assess the effects of altitude and heat on the players, and also to assess the degree of public interest in women's football.

The Italian players had no clear side effects of playing at altitude but it was decided to play matches in the early evening. More promisingly still, the two friendly games drew crowds of 30,000 and 70,000 respectively, thus proving a viable commercial market. So Mexico 1971 was a carefully arranged business enterprise, designed to produce good football, as a result of the test matches in 1970.

After choosing Mexico as hosts, FIFF agreed to allocate four European berths and two South American places, leaving one spot available for the hosts as automatic qualifiers. Eleven European countries applied for the elimination competition: Austria, Belgium, Czechoslovakia, Denmark, England, France, Italy, The Netherlands, West Germany, Sweden and Switzerland. In South America, Brazil, Chile and Peru applied for funds to play the qualifiers. Not all of the European sides made it to Sicily for the early round matches in June 1971 and so dropped out. Denmark eliminated Sweden 5–0 to qualify, while France despatched Netherlands 4–0 and England equalled this score to end Austria's hopes. Czechoslovakia again suffered from visa problems and the club sides from Belgium, West Germany and Switzerland struggled to find funds. Argentina defeated Costa Rica to qualify as one of the two Latin America nations, alongside the hosts Mexico.

There are several oddities about the way that these games have subsequently been perceived as 'firsts'. The France-Netherlands fixture is one such example. Pierre Geoffroy was a journalist at the *L'Union* newspaper, and the instigator in July 1968 of an exhibition match scheduled for the publication's annual carnival. The one-off experiment turned into a real team because of the seriousness of the young women who responded to the call for players. Also writing for *L'Equipe* and *France Football*, Geoffroy had plenty of opportunity to promote the women's game. Like Harry Batt, Geoffroy toured with his teams to the US and Canada in 1970, the West Indies in 1974, Chinese Taipei in 1978, and Indonesia in 1984. Along with his assistant trainer, Louis Petitot, Geoffroy then became the coach of Reims, and in 1971 the coach of the first official women's French team.

However, this was only recognised as such latterly by the French Football Federation (FFF) and FIFA. The FFF had officially recognised women's football just over a year earlier, on 29 March 1970. As we have seen, Reims had fulfilled this function before and after that date as a representative team, but these games are now not considered 'official' but as friendlies. This included fixtures against England in 1969 and two Italian fixtures in 1969 and 1970. Thereafter, when FIFA began researching early women's football matches as part of its efforts to create the FIFA/Coca-Cola Women's World Ranking, the France-Netherlands match was confirmed as the first-ever official women's international. This is a bizarre rewriting of history which sought to erase what had gone before, and provides a much less interesting story.

The Azteca stadium in Mexico City and the Jalisco Stadium in Guadalajara staged the 1971 games. The ambition was grand in scale. It is important to remember that the men's World Cup in Mexico 1970 had been broadcast in some regions in colour – a first – and had new merchandising deals like Panini sticker books for collectibles. Following the use of an official mascot, World Cup Willie, for the first time in the men's World Cup in England 1966, thereafter sporting tournaments of all kinds used a mascot to promote their event, including unofficially in the form of Schluss, a little abstract man on skis, at the 1968 Winter Olympics in Grenoble. However, Mexico played a key role in promoting mascots as emblems of various tournaments: there was an unofficial dove and jaguar mascot at the 1968 Mexico Olympic Games, and, officially, Juanito, a little boy in football boots and a sombrero, for the FIFA men's World Cup tournament of 1970.

FIFF learned very quickly from these technologies, and also had the first international women's football mascot, Xochitel, or flower, replicated across many formats. Xochitl was widely used and merchandise included ticket stubs, enamel pin badges, pennants, paper collectibles. It was further endorsed by the diet and soft drinks industries, as well as Martini & Rossi. Each national side, with the British Independents listed merely as England, had their own set of dedicated memorabilia and players who travelled with very little spending money reported being so overwhelmed with their collection of gifts that some were unsure as to whether it would be accepted through customs, and so abandoned suitcase loads at the airport. This was another first for women's football in marketing terms, as those who could into make it into the stadium could buy a piece of memorabilia, or find out about the matches through television broadcasts, with each team having a dedicated publicist.

The FIFF 1971 tournament trophy *Angel de Oro*, or Angel of Gold, was also sponsored by Martini & Rossi. There was an elaborate opening ceremony led by the Band of the City of Mexico, and followed by several others bands and speeches. Festivities went on throughout the tournament: firework displays, groups of children from local schools and colleges processed, groups of motor cyclists from the Department of Transport performed, songs were sung in traditional costume and recitals performed on regional instruments. The closing ceremony was no less lavish, led principally by Tony Aguilar and his horse, accompanied by dancers and gymnasts, and lit by a host of torches. The cheapest seats,

Cover of *Futbol* magazine covering the tournament, 29 August 1971.

Azul Popular, were 30 Mexican pesos, the next category *Amarilla* (yellow) were $100 pesos, while the discerning could sit in covered *Verde* (green) seats for $200 pesos, and the wealthy could enjoy *Naranja* (orange) hospitality for $330.16 pesos.

What, though, of the matches themselves? Group A, played between 15 and 22 August in Mexico City, comprised Argentina, England and Mexico. One programme records the players for Argentina as: Martha Soler, Carmen Brucoli, Ofelia Feito, Teresa Suárez, Zumilda Troncoso, Zulma Gómez, Eva Senbezis, Angélica Cardozo, Bety García, Elba Selvo, Bianca Brucoli, Dora Gutiérrez, Mariá Esther Ponce, Mariá Fiorelli, Virginia Cattaneo, Mariá Bowes and Virginia Andrada. However, we must be careful as these were often printed before players travelled to the competition so are not always accurate. The England squad in the same programme was made up of: Louise Cross, Trudy McCaffery, Jill Stockley, Leah Caleb, Paula Rayner, Valerie Cheshire, Jean Breckon, Carol Wilson, Lillian Harris, Janice Barton, Christine Lockwood, Yvonne Farr, Marlene Collins, Gillian Sayell, Maureen

Dawson and trainer Pat Dunn. As we saw in the previous paragraph, Pat was also a big supporter of the Corinthians overseas tours. Accompanying Harry and June Batt was their son, Keith, who became the England team 'mascot'.

In the same programme, the large Mexican squad was represented by: Yolanda Ramírez Gutíerrez, Elvira Aracen Sánchez, Irma Chávez Barrera, Martha Coronado Díaz, Bertha Orduña Padierna, Paula Pérez, Rebecca Lara Pérez Tejada, Mariá de la Luz Cruz Martínez, Guadalupe Tovar Ugalde, Elsa Huerta Mendez, Sandra Tapia Montoya, Irma Mancilla, Alicia Vargas, Mariá Hernández Montoya, Patricia Hernández Montoya, Teresa Aguilar Alvarado, Silvia Zaragoza Herrera, Mariá Eugenia Rubio Ríos, Erendira Rangel and Esther Mora.

In Group B, played between 18 and 22 August in Guadalajara, the French team were: Marie Luise Butzing, Monique Hilaire, Regine Pourveux, Marie Bernadette Thomas, Nicole Mangas, Chantal Serre, Colette Guyard, Aline Meyer, Marie Christine Tschopp, Betty Goret, Michele Monier, Ghislane Royer, Claudine Die, Maryse Lesieur, Joselyne Henry, Joselyne Ratignier, and Armelle Binard. They were managed by Pierre and Christiane Geoffroy, who also ran the Stade de Reims female teams in Epernay. The Denmark line-up was: Ann Andreasen, Susanne Augustesen, Annette Frederiksen, Ingrid Hansen, Helen Hansen, Solveig Hansen, Bente Jensen, Mona Lisa Jensen, Marianne Kamp, Birte Kjems, Lis Lene Nielsen, Lone Grete Nielsen. Asta Vig Nielsen, Lis Westberg Pedersen, Inger Pedersen, Lena Schelfe, Kristiane Jensen, Jorgen Andreasen and Inge Kristensen. The Italian side comprised: Wilma Schetti, Anna Stopar, Mariá Fabris, Paola Cardia, Manuela Pinardi, Elena Schiavo, Silvana Mammina, Manola Conter, Maurizia Ciceri, Claudia Avon, Elisabetta Vignotto, Derna Isoline, Daniela Sogliani, Aurora Giubertoni, Rosetta Cunzolo, Mariá Rosaria Castelli and Carmela Varone, managed and coached by Giuseppe Cavicchi, Piero Boero, Andrea Patomo and Giuseppe Cosetina.

In Group A England were defeated in each of their games, scoring a single goal in a 4–1 defeat by Argentina. Mexico then beat Argentina 3–1, and England 4–0 to top the group. But they played in front of crowds of 80,000 and were no less popular as a losing team for being expelled in the group stages. In Group B France had a goalless tournament and were also expelled in the group stages, losing to both Italy and Denmark. Italy and

Denmark drew 1–1 in their group game. France then beat England 3–2 in a subsequent friendly fixture.

In the semi-finals Denmark defeated Argentina 5–0, and in a surprise win, Mexico defeated Italy 2–1. So Mexico met Denmark in the final. The star players included Elena Schiavo, the captain of Italy, who played her club football at Astro, and her compatriots Wilma Seghetti (Verona), Manuela Pinardi (Parma), Maurizia Ciceri, Claudia Averi and Maria Castelli (Real Torino). Unsurprisingly though, perhaps the most famous star in 1971 was Alicia 'Pele' Vargas for Mexico, along with Carmen Alacanter, Silvia Zaragoza, María Eugenia Rubio, Irma Mancilla and Erendira Rangel. The Mexican players, especially Vargas, have spoken about the pressure they felt to win on home soil. But it was not to be, as Denmark defeated the hosts 3–0 in the final, with fifteen-year old Susanne Augustesen scoring a hat-trick. Augustesen, therefore, shared the golden boot with Argentina's Selva, with four goals in total. She then went on to a professional career in Italy.

The England players, having travelled by Aeronaves airlines via New York, were the first to arrive in Mexico. Carol Wilson, the captain and a defender as in Italy, was aged nineteen and popular with the press, along with the England star forward Janice Barton. What is striking is how young most of the England team were. Lilian Harris, the goalkeeper, was nineteen, as was defender Evonne Farr. Midfielder Christine Lockwood was aged fifteen, Trudy McCaffery was seventeen, and Marlene Collins twenty years old. Forwards Leah Caleb and Gillian Sayle were fourteen, ad Paula Rayner was sixteen, as was Lois Cross. The oldest player was twenty-four. Being a Beatles fan singled out McCaffrey for media attention, and Jean Brecken, who lost a finger in an accident with a goal net, was also popular with the press. But what were the personal experiences of the England players, and how do they now view those experiences?

Yvonne Bradley (née Farr)

Family and early football

'I was one of eight children, born in 1955 in Luton. I am the third eldest in a family of six girls and two boys, bought up by my mum. She brought us up really well. School-based sport was mainly athletics, but there was a one-off occasion when there was a girls v boys game. At about the age of fourteen or fifteen I went to play for Yellow Scorpions in Stopsley, who, unsurprisingly, played in an all yellow kit, although I cannot now remember how they came about the name. Really, it was playing for fun, and we didn't even look the part, but Mr Toyer, the manager was really encouraging. Most of the other girls were there to socialize, and were not competitive like me. At senior level, Jean Bentley, the manager of Daytels football team, asked me to go to Germany and play for them. Then Harry Batt asked me to play for Chiltern Valley and then in the England team for Mexico. I was still quite young, and it was exciting to be in a more competitive and serious environment.'

Harry Batt and Overseas Tours

'I first went to Germany in 1969–70 with Daytels and not long after, Mexico. I didn't initially want to go, as I was quite shy and did not know any of the girls very well. But when I said I didn't want to go, Mum said, 'You're going!' I was a bit apprehensive because of the scale of the trip but I also wanted to play football.

'A couple of times, I had been away from home with athletics meetings for one or two nights and I didn't really enjoy that. However, Mum packed me off! Luckily, I was strictly a jeans and T-shirts person, so that was easy enough, and we were provided with some sort of uniform for going out at night and a tracksuit. Shorts, boots and so on, were my own.

'My mum had never met Harry Batt before, and his wife, June, was also involved as a chaperone, and the trainer was Pat Dunn. So anyway, Harry came to meet my mum and the next thing I know she was sending off for a passport, and we went to Peterborough to pick it up, so looking back, it must have been an urgent trip. I also remember Mum persuading the school to let me go for a month, as I would miss some of term, and the local authority also had to be persuaded. It wasn't easy but she was very determined. Looking back, I can see it was touch and go. Because I joined late, I was not listed in the programme notes or photos and I do not remember training with the team until we got to Mexico.'

Futbol magazine back cover advertising the championship; needless to say the models used in this image did not reflect the players.

Mexico 1971

'Firstly, I had never flown before, and it was a very long flight. I remember getting off the plane a bit relieved and then the heat hit me in Mexico. Then there were the reporters surrounding us on the coach, and again I was a bit apprehensive as we came down the steps. The reception was unbelievable! When we were in the coach people were tooting and cheering and we hadn't kicked a ball yet. The food generally was an experience not to be repeated, though the hotel, Hotel Royal Plaza, had the best of everything. We had many exciting trips out, to the grand Xochimilco canals with a festival, and here we could see how poor people were, to the Mariachis singing for us. We walked to many of these events, where I remember the fumes and the deprivation were a bit overwhelming. At the reception at the British Embassy I felt so privileged to be involved and, of course, I was very grateful to my mum!

'The food I remember most was not even Mexican. There was this lovely cheesecake baked in the hotel and you could just go up and request some as you wished. I think we all ate too much of it, as after a while I remember them saying cut down a bit. My room was a suite, and I had not really stayed in a hotel of that quality before, with a separate lounge area, and a bathroom. I shared with Leah.

'We trained early because of the heat. Being young, the altitude didn't really affect us. I really enjoyed the training, as I was young and enthusiastic and made good progress with Harry. I could play right or left wing or centre forward, but I generally stood at the back and let Harry decide where I should play.

'The games themselves I don't really remember that much because my leg got broken in the game against Mexico. I remember being excited about the atmosphere going to the match on our coach, as there were lots of supporters, and then in the changing room you could hear the crowd shouting and chanting in the stadium before kick-off. The Mexicans had some semi-professional players and they stood out. I came on 10–15 minutes before the end as a sub, and although I went in for the tackle, I came out with the injury. But the Mexicans were really professional and we had played all our subs, so I sort of just hopped about and hoped no one passed the ball to me. I asked to come off, but what could we do?

'Back at the hotel, I was just coming down stairs as Harry was taking some of the other girls to a private hospital and I was still hopping so he said, 'You'd better come with us.' I ended up in a cast, as did Carol. It didn't spoil it though. It couldn't, although I couldn't go in the swimming pool with the others, obviously. No, it was just one of those things. My knee hit her leg.

'For the return flight we panicked a bit because we had so much memorabilia given to us that we were frightened we would not get it through customs. Someone had a walking stick with a sword in it, someone else a sombrero. There were so many local gifts given to us. We left a lot of it on the side, though I remember the walking stick making it back, so we would probably have been alright anyway. But it you had never been that far before it was hard to know what customs would accept. Probably none of it had great value other than to us. I wished I had kept it now.'

Afterwards

'Given my personality, you will understand that when I heard about the reunion, I thought "Shall I go?" It was such a long time ago. But I made myself go. Funnily enough, it was like we were all young again. It has been lovely. I am glad I did go. I suppose when we were out there for four or five weeks we became very close and you don't lose that. It is really quite unreal. Talking to Keith about what happened to his mum and dad is (was) such a shame. Harry did what he did for women's football and it was pretty rotten how he was treated. I have memorabilia, like photos our newspaper reporter out there gave us. I have the letter Mum had to write, and one from the Justice of the Peace saying I could go. I got quite homesick at one point and threw stuff out of drawers in the hotel in my anxiety. We were very young. But I remember the extreme kindness, such as the hotel owner inviting us to the christening of his daughter, and going to his house, which was very fancy, and the gardens overlooking a volcano.'

Leah Caleb

Family and Early Football

'My parents were May and Dermot Caleb and my older siblings, Mary and Derry. I was born in 1958 in Dublin, Ireland, and came to Luton in 1961, aged three. My parents throughout my life were always very supportive of my sporting interests. My football connection started at Hitchin Road Infants School. The playground was rather small and the boys always played football. Rather than stand watching, many of the girls joined in. I quickly realised I enjoyed playing and at such a young age could compete with the boys so it was a natural progression to continue playing. At my next school, St Matthews Junior School, my headmaster tried to get the local authority to agree for me to play in the boy's school football team. Unfortunately, as was the case at that time, football was not 'for girls' and they would not agree for me to play. Hours were spent in the garden practicing keeping the ball up, dribbling all becoming part of my natural sporting psyche. I developed my football growing up at school in the playground and in the park with the boys. Alongside my football I did other sports: hockey, netball, swimming, cross-country, and athletics all being an important part of my early and later life.'

Harry Batt and Overseas Tours

'My mother was made aware of a women's football club and at the age of eleven I joined Chiltern Valley Ladies Football Club in Luton. Chiltern Valley was a successful team and managed by Harry and June Batt who, following a discussion with my parents, chose me, at the age of thirteen, for the Sicily and Mexico '71 England squads.

'Sicily hosted the qualifiers in June 1971 for the Women's World Cup in Mexico, both exciting but very different experiences. We travelled on an overnight train to Sicily and were taken by coach to our destinations which entailed a triangular trip to Trapani, Catania and Syracuse. Both events were sponsored by Martini and Rossi. We qualified for the World Cup.'

Mexico 1971

'For a thirteen-year-old girl the Mexico trip was life changing, an experience beyond comprehension. Crowds up to 100,000 in the Aztec Stadium watched this Women's World Cup. We didn't win the tournament but the interest in us, both as individuals and as a squad, alongside the warmth of the Mexican people towards us, was incredible. The Mexico experience included my first long haul flight; staying at the Hotel Royal Plaza; TV experiences; autograph requests; police escorts to games; evening engagements; attending a reception at the British Ambassador's residency for a cocktail evening; theatre; going to the Piccadilly Pub, and during the daytime, visiting *The Herald* newspaper offices; a toy department store; sightseeing trips to the Teotihuacan Pyramids; going to the Xochimilco canals, and during several of these events, sometimes being serenaded by the Mariachi musicians.

'After training we were taken to a sports club to relax, enjoying swimming and tennis. So much of this was captured in the daily newspapers. These are now an important part of our memorabilia.

This was such a surreal time with many treasured memories. I was sometimes referred to as Xochitl (flower), which was the name of the tournament mascot; I assume this was due to my youth and long dark hair. To play in the Aztec Stadium, where the year before the men's World Cup had been played, in itself was unbelievable. England men and Pele had walked through the same tunnel and played on the same turf! It was such an honour and a privilege.'

Afterwards

'On returning from Mexico there was a short period when the WFA banned us from playing and Harry and June Batt were ostracised. Chiltern Valley Ladies Football Club eventually folded. Christine Lockwood and I continued to play football with the boys in the park and then, with Valerie Cheshire, joined Luton Daytels Ladies Football Club in 1972 where my passion for football continued until I finished playing in 1991. Now, revisiting my football career and recognising my achievements within the sport has been extremely rewarding.

'Having played competitive football all over Britain with four very successful clubs, winning fifty-plus trophies in eleven years and five-a-side leagues and tournaments, and also making lifelong friends demonstrates the strength of ladies football as a team sport. There was no financial support during this time and our passion for football was funded by the players themselves. I have played for Chiltern Valley Ladies 1969–1972, Luton Daytels Ladies 1972–1978, Aylesbury Ladies 1978–1983 (reuniting me with Gill Sayell from the Mexico 1971 squad), and Biggleswade United Ladies 1983–1989.

'I feel Harry and June Batt should be recognised for their contribution to Women's football, not only in England but abroad, taking teams to Italy, Sicily and Mexico. These are historic milestones. My parents always supported my sporting passion and gave their blessing for me to play football abroad in 1971 at such a young age – first in Sicily, then the Women's World Cup in Mexico – for which I am eternally grateful.'

The branding, included the Angel de Oro trophy and the mascot, Xochitel, or 'Flower'.

Chris Lockwood

Family and Early Football

'I was born in1956 in Bolton upon Dearne, Yorkshire. My nan and grandad had a farm so I had just the most fantastic childhood. Although my sisters were not into sport, my cousins were all boys, who, like myself, loved football. We used to play football and cricket in the farmyard with my uncles, usually with a burst plastic ball or a cut up piece of wood and a bald tennis ball!

'My family moved south to Luton in the early 1960s as my dad got a job at Vauxhall Motors. My mum and dad were not really into sport, although dad and I loved watching wrestling on *ITV Sport* and he occasionally took me to watch Luton Town play. I carried on loving playing football. I was always up waiting for my dad to come home from night shift and I would be at the infant and junior school gates with my ball waiting for the caretaker to unlock the gate so I could play on the football pitch. At the end of school, me and the boys who played were there until the headmaster, Mr Best, left and locked the gate.

'When I went to senior school I was not allowed to play football and was often banned from PE for kicking the ball. Once school was finished it was up to the local sports ground to play football with the lads. We were always there, and when dark, we played under the lamppost.

'One day a girl at school asked me if I wanted to join a girls' football team. I didn't even know there were any other girls that played football. I turned up and joined but I was the only one who could really play so we joined a league and I went in goal just to keep the score down really.'

Harry Batt and Overseas Tours

'I could actually play almost any position, but although I was quite a natural goalkeeper, I hated it really. Chiltern Valley Ladies found out about me and after a bit of a rift eventually my club let me go. Chiltern Valley had really fantastic players and I felt very honoured to play for them. I was quite shy at that time and my first game was in goal at a five-a-side tournament in Buckingham. While I was sitting about. knowing nobody, a skinny little girl with a ponytail came up to me and said, 'Do you want a kick about?' That girl was Leah Caleb who became a teammate for club and country and a lifelong friend. We also won the tournament!

'I managed to get games playing outfield as well as in goal and I was very happy to be playing in such a great team. We often won the league championship, and also various cups and tournaments. Sundays were just fantastic with great football, camaraderie and visits to different parts of the country.

'Chiltern Valley manager Harry Batt was a very astute man and very supportive of the game. He had contacts within the international circuit. He had taken a team abroad before I had joined. In 1971, when I was fifteen years of age, Harry and his wife, June, asked my parents if I could represent England unofficial team in Sicily for the World Cup qualifiers. My parents agreed and I went there for about three weeks, and we qualified. Upon returning Harry and June told my parents the Italians were interested in me playing goalkeeper semi-professionally. I was too young and I remember I wasn't really bothered about it, maybe as I wasn't comfortable with being a goalkeeper.

'Later in the year I was picked for the England unofficial squad for 1971 Women's World Cup in Mexico City, by which time I was playing up front, but also back up goalkeeper if required.'

Mexico 1971

'Upon arrival in Mexico it was instant stardom. We were in the newspapers every day, invited to many functions at embassies and theatres, and guests on TV. We were staying in a beautiful hotel with people waiting outside for autographs. We had police escorts to the training ground and games at the Aztec Stadium in front of crowds of 80,000 and 100,000. Our group games were against Argentina and Mexico and we lost both matches.'

Afterwards

'Upon returning to England I recall we played for a while with Chiltern Valley, but Harry and the club were to be banned by the WFA, so the team disbanded. Leah and I eventually joined Luton Daytels. I also started work in computer systems at Vauxhall Motors.

'For some time I had been carrying an injury in my left knee. It wouldn't take much for it to start bleeding and it was always painful and there was a burning sensation. I had been to the doctor, who said it was scar tissue and I should stop playing such a rough game. The ex-chairman of Chiltern Valley, Mr Impey, took me for a second opinion at Manor House Hospital in London. It turned out I had an ulcer embedded in my knee. I had an operation and was told I was not going to play again. I was heartbroken. The specialist agreed with me that if I didn't play at all for a year he would see how things were. It was a very long year! Thankfully David Bowie had come into my life.

'I returned to football after the all-clear and could still play to a high standard. After a while Tina Oliver, Leah and I signed for Aylesbury United where Leah and I reunited with Gill Sayell from the unofficial England squad. I was now playing centre-back in front of a sweeper, which suited me very well by then. Aylesbury were a very successful team and we had many great achievements.

'After a few years I eventually gave up playing in my late twenties. I was by then doing twelve-hour shifts on Unix support team and often wasn't turning up for training so it all went to pot really. I worked for thirty-nine years with transitions from Vauxhall Motors to EDS to Hewlett Packard.

'Yes, I regret packing up so early but that's how it was. I would always say to anyone, play as long as you can as football is fantastic. Leah, Gill and I have recently got together again to reminisce. It is interesting to know all three of us were at different schools. I asked Leah and Gill if their school announced their achievement when they returned from Mexico. Their answer was the same as mine – "no".

'I wouldn't swap my experience for anything as it was so unique and will never be repeated again. I do, however, wish that Harry Batt's knowledge and contacts could have been utilised upon our return to help pave the way for women's football.'

Gill Sayell

Family and Early Football

'My immediate family were my parents, Bob and Popsy, two sisters and four brothers. Dad worked as a self-employed plasterer, and, later, was a proprietor of a fishing tackle shop called "Coarse Angler" in Aylesbury town centre. He is living in Menorca aged ninety, where he has been for the last thirty years. Mum worked evenings cleaning until we were older, and then was a lab technician in a bakery named DCA, the Donut Company of America. I grew up on a council estate, one of the oldest estates in Aylesbury called Southcourt. It was a great place, and we knew all the families around locally. We lived in Elm Green, which, as the name suggests, was a large "green" that all the houses surrounded, so was a perfect place to practice my football. There were always kickabouts arranged with the other kids.

'Football did play quite a big part of our family life. My dad played and captained a local village team. All of my brothers played locally for various Aylesbury teams. I have two older sisters and two older brothers, and then it's me, and two younger brothers. I did support Chelsea when I was younger, and was number seven – Charlie Cooke! My elder brother supports Arsenal, as I do now. Two of my brothers support Newcastle United, and my eldest sister supports West Ham, so there was always a bit of banter going on. The only hobbies I had were all sport related, but football was always top of the list. As long as I can remember I have always played football. I was very much a tomboy, and having four brothers there was always a ball and a brother to kick a ball about with! Sport has always been a big part of my life and if there was any team or sport I would be there; but football was always my first love.

'I first joined a boys' football team called the Cougars in 1965–66, aged nine or ten. They all called me Billy as girls were not allowed to play then. There were no girls teams around that I knew of, so just to be able to play was all I wanted to do. It soon became apparent I was a girl, and the opposing boys didn't want to play against me as I was better than them!'

Harry Batt and Overseas Tours

'My sister-in-law lived in Thame and knew of a women's football team there, Thame Ladies. My parents were very instrumental in my playing career, and at the age of twelve helped me join and play for the reserve side, Thame Wanderers. They would drive me the ten miles each way for training on a Tuesday, and playing matches home and away on Sunday. This was typical of my parents: they supported all of us if we showed an interest in something. My brother, Dave, was mainly into boxing, which, as with me, involved Dad driving us to training a few times a week, and also to boxing matches and football matches, wherever they were. Mum did not drive, but was nonetheless involved and as enthusiastic as Dad. He also bought, and drove, the team coach for the Aylesbury Ladies football team.

He also got onto the Board of Directors at Aylesbury United FC, so we could use their pitch for training and home games.

'After a season playing for the reserves I was promoted to the first team, and was the youngest player in the squad. We were one of the top teams in the country at this time. It was while I was playing for Thame LFC that I was picked to play for Harry Batt in an unofficial England team in Mexico. I was fourteen years old!'

Mexico 1971

'I played in the Women's World Cup in Mexico City 1971. The things I remember most of Mexico '71 were the crowds, the hospitality, the Aztec stadium and the excitement of this massive occasion. We had television appearances, a cocktail party at the British Embassy and so many more events. I was in awe of it all.

'The games were physical and fast-paced, as you would expect. We did not fare too well on the pitch, but we did gain a lot of respect from the other teams and supporters. What an experience for a fourteen-year-old schoolgirl! The crowds were amazing, topping 100,000; something I don't think had or has been seen since in women's football. I don't really remember too much about the games unfortunately as it all seems so surreal now. I played outside right as I had speed.

'The training sessions were usually 7–7.30am and we were bussed there and back with a police escort. At training there were crowds watching us, even though it was early in the morning. I can remember being in the changing rooms of the Aztec Stadium, and then walking up the steps and out onto the pitch: breathtaking! The noise of the crowds was deafening!

'We had quite a lot of free time, which we spent swimming and generally chilling out. I remember going to an Advocaat factory, and a newspaper office, a large toy shop, and a floating flower market on the canal boats. We were guests at the house of the owner of our hotel, which was amazing. We went swimming in their pool and had a buffet lunch. We went to a cocktail party at the British Embassy and were invited to an "English" pub. We were invited to a theatre to see a play called *Sleuth*.'

COMPRE AQUI SUS SERIES

SECCION		
	NARANJA	$330.00
	VERDE	$200.00
	AMARILLA	$100.00
	AZUL POPULAR	$30.00

Y SUS SOUVENIRS

VERMOUHT   IDENTIFIQUELA AGUA MINERAL

MARTINI   *Peñafiel*

CALIDAD Y PUREZA

Arte e Impresión: Editora Nac. Agropecuaria, S.A. Bacoari 1

The prices for tickets ranged from economic to aspirational, and well to do.

Afterwards

'After Mexico I carried on playing for Thame Ladies, and we became one of the top teams in the country. In 1976, along with many of the Thame team, I started Aylesbury Ladies. My Dad was manager. We were also very successful and attracted players from a wide area.

'I had some time out from playing in 1986–87 to have my daughter. By July 1987 I pulled on my first Arsenal shirt, with my daughter sitting on the touchline! In 1987 one of our players was working at Arsenal FC and was told they wanted to start a women's football team there. She suggested Aylesbury and that's how it all started. My parents were moving to Menorca so my dad said it would be a fantastic opportunity for us all that Arsenal would be taking up the mantle. This is how Arsenal Women's Football Club was founded. I think my football skills and knowledge were taken to another level while playing under coach Vic Akers. He changed my position to centre-back, and I loved it. I was a good reader of the game so that position suited me perfectly. This is where I finished my playing career at the age of thirty-six.

'I did manage the Arsenal reserve side for a season, but found it quite frustrating as all I wanted to do was play. I did a bit of coaching, on and off, with youth club teams. I moved to Eire in 2007 and in 2008 was involved with the Football Association of Ireland (FAI) in a programme called Soccer Sisters, in Donegal Town. The scheme was to increase the number of girls playing football from the ages of seven to twelve. There was a huge turnout of enthusiastic girls, which was great to see.

'I am proud of my football career, and I like to think I was one of the pioneers for the game it is today. We had to face a lot of adversity towards women and girls playing football, but we were determined, and pushed forward in doing a sport we all loved.

'And looking back? I was so fortunate to have kept my memorabilia, and also how it survived. My brother recently told me he took my Martini & Rossi kit bag to use as his football bag, unbeknown to me! I didn't realise until I started going through it that I had so much. I did get it out and look at it from time to time and it is quite precious to me. It's amazing it managed to stay intact as I have moved many times over the years, but I'm so glad it has. My family were a major part of every aspect of my football career, and I know I wouldn't have achieved as much as I did without their help and support. It was their life too! I have many paper cuttings and photographs to tell my football story.'

Carol Wilson

Family and Early Football

'I am the eldest of three children, and my mam used to say that I kicked a ball as soon as I could walk. My mum and dad encouraged all of us in everything we did, but it was my dad who nurtured my interest in playing football. When I was around six years old we moved to a larger house. It was a few streets away from St James' Park, which was home to Newcastle United. Me and my dad used to walk past the ground on match days, and I remember the perimeter – a huge, beige corrugated fence. We used to kick my football against the fence while listening to the roar from inside. I was always curious to know how it looked in there, but it was to be a good few years before I ever got the chance to find out.

'Throughout the rest of my childhood I loved playing football but I was always the only girl on the field. By the time I went to secondary school I'd grown to love all sports, and was part of most of the sports teams at my school. It was always a disappointment to me that football never featured for girls. As time went on, I knew I wanted to be a PE teacher. My school work was pretty good, and my reports, but exams made me really nervous. After much consideration we all agreed I was to leave school and get a job.

'I began working at Winthrop Laboratories in their accounts department, and soon found out I didn't enjoy office work. I then looked into the RAF, who seemed keen and interested in me, finding out about my likes, dislikes and skills, etc. During this informal assessment they uncovered my love and aptitude for all things sport related. The flight sergeant told me that one of the jobs on offer was a PT Instructor. I nearly took his hand off there and then, but he said I would have to go to RAF St Athan in South Wales to be formally assessed. This involved being far away from home for three days and felt like quite a big deal for me at the time. Having got through the assessment processes the next step was for me to officially start to train to be an RAF Physical Training Instructor (PTI). Once I qualified, in 1971, I left St Athan for my first official posting to RAF Henlow in Bedfordshire. This is where I met Harry Batt.'

Harry Batt and Overseas Tours

'There I was, at nineteen, at RAF Henlow. There was a small gym where we played five-a-side. The gym was also rented out to the local community and one day I noticed two women's five-a-side teams. I had never seen organised women's football teams before, so it attracted my attention straight away. The organiser of the games turned out to be Harry Batt who, along with a scout, was watching our game. I confess to feeling slightly irritated as I thought he should be concentrating on his own teams' games. Three days later my PT officer called me in to say Harry had asked if I would be interested in playing for his team as a guest player. I went down, met the team, played as a guest, and was later invited to join the Chiltern Valley Ladies team.

'I played centre half every week in the ladies Sunday league. One day, we were having a team meeting on the field and Harry told us he had been invited by FIEFF to get a team together to represent England in a World Cup in Mexico. Harry said he was doubtful it would all come together as he felt the politics could make it difficult, but it would be worth a try. I couldn't believe it! I had always loved playing but never thought I would get a chance like this.

'Harry and the scout then travelled all over the country recruiting the best talent to represent England. Harry didn't really mention the struggle he was having with the FA, but we did get the sense that things were difficult. In the meantime Chiltern Ladies carried on training as usual, then one of the team, Jean Breckon, had an awful accident. She had been in goal and caught her engagement ring on the hook attachment for the goal net and took her finger clean off.

'Following that incident I think Harry wanted our sessions to be more formal and asked that I use my PTI experience to take on the fitness training of the team. Harry gave us the news that FIEFF had recognised us as an international team and that Martini & Rossi were going to sponsor us to go to the qualifiers in Sicily. We had around two months to prepare.

'We left for Sicily in early summer, which meant me taking a week's leave. We travelled by train through France and Italy and took a ferry across to Palermo in Sicily. We toured around quite a bit and were treated with respect everywhere we went. I felt absolutely blessed to be having all of these amazing experiences. It was all down to Harry having seen me play in the gym that day.

'Having qualified comfortably, we headed home, having all had a great time. Once home, we found out that Martini & Rossi were also going to sponsor the final leg of the competition. We were going to Mexico! I remember struggling to get more leave from the RAF, but was then told that as I was going to represent my country it would be sanctioned. We were all set and I was so excited.'

Mexico 1971

'The excitement I felt the day before going to Mexico was mixed with nervous anticipation. There were lots of things for me to think about: I had never flown before, I was already thinking ahead about whether I had I got our training programme right, and was conscious of the big responsibility lying ahead of us. I so wanted to get everything right.

'The day passed quickly and Harry had arranged for us to go and see Manchester United v Luton in an evening friendly. I got to see players such as Bobby Charlton, Dennis Law, Nobby Styles and George Best, who seemed to float over the ground. It was the first time I had ever seen George Best play live and it was amazing! The experience of watching elite players such as these inspired me. It was an amazing start to the trip.

'After a long flight we eventually touched down in Mexico. It was late evening as far as I remember, and the most vivid image I have in my head is of all the flashlights going off as we came down the steps

A Mexican $25 dollar ticket to the final in the Azteca Stadium, 5 September 1971.

of the aircraft. They were blinding, and we were totally unprepared for that level of press attention. As far as I'm aware there was not one single journalist present when we left the UK.

'Once through customs, Harry asked me to give an interview to the press. Of course I agreed, but this was another thing I was totally unprepared for and didn't feel totally confident that I was going to be saying the right thing. It turned out that we would all be getting plenty of practice at this type of thing: during the following five weeks it would become the norm to speak to the press.

'I will never forget the coach journey from the airport to our hotel, The Royal Plaza. Our coach had an impressive police escort, consisting of a car at the front and back and also outriders to each side. They would be a constant sight through the competition. The crowds were huge: they lined the roads, filled the verges, hung off bridges and seemingly any other vantage point they could find. The windows of the coach were open as it was so hot, and the sound of the screaming crowds was deafening. They were throwing things at the coach and at first we were unsure about their intentions. We weren't actually sure if even the press attention was positive at that time. It turned out that the crowds were throwing small gifts to us. It was so sweet, and it was an indication of the positive reception we would experience throughout our trip.

'We stayed at a lovely family run hotel and found out fairly soon after arriving there that there would a photographer assigned to the team throughout the whole tour. The hotel was only a few miles away from where we trained every day. Our training sessions needed to start at 6am to enable us to cope with the intense heat; we also needed to acclimatise ourselves to the altitude. Once training sessions were finished our days were pretty much organised for us. We attended other teams' matches, took part in public relations events (opened supermarkets, appeared on TV and radio). In addition to that, each country's embassy hosted an evening reception for all the teams.

'One evening Harry asked me to go with him to meet Franz Beckenbauer who had captained the German side that played England in the final of the 1966 World Cup. I was ecstatic! I remember shaking like a leaf all the time we were talking as he was one of Germany's elite. He was actually a really nice man who I would love to meet again. Any other free time we had was spent in the Cuban swimming pool or back at the hotel just relaxing and watching games.

'Our first match seemed to come around really quickly. We visited the Aztec stadium the night before the game to get a feel for the pitch. There seemed to be fans everywhere. The stadium looked absolutely huge once we got inside. We were told it seated 110,000 people. Walking out onto the pitch for a kick around, it struck me that here we were, about to play on a perfectly flat pitch in front of a potentially huge crowd as opposed to playing in front of twenty spectators, if we were lucky, on the sloping, uneven pitch we were used to.

The journey to the stadium the next day was extremely slow due to the extraordinary amount of fans blocking the route. Once we arrived we were ushered straight to the changing rooms and even from there we could hear the roar from the crowds inside the stadium. Nothing could have prepared us, however, for the noise that hit us coming out of the tunnel. The crowd went absolutely wild. I thought my heart was going to burst out of my chest and I definitely had jelly legs.

'Our first match was against Argentina, and as soon as we kicked off, the noise, the heat, and the occasion became background factors. Five minutes in, my nerves had evaporated and I started to relax into the game. However, it quickly became obvious that we were playing totally different styles and that the game didn't flow. I was involved in a clash that I remember causing me some discomfort in my foot but I managed to play on until the final whistle when Argentina won 4–1.

'Our second game against Mexico was a totally different experience. The stadium was packed to capacity and we were going into it with a different mindset having lost the first game. There was also pressure on us to win in order to be placed and continue in the competition .We had always known that it was going to be a tough call playing Mexico. They were used to playing together as a national team: they were used to the heat and the altitude, kick-off was under the searing midday sun, and, added to that, they were the home team. Mexico scored quite early on in the game and went on to win 4–0. Even so, I was really proud of the way we performed, feeling that we had given the Mexican team a run for their money. I had felt some pain in my foot during the game, but thought it was probably just bruising from the clash in the game against Argentina the day before. Another player, Yvonne Farr, had also been suffering pain during the game and so we were both taken to hospital to be checked out.

'It turned out that I had broken a bone in my foot, and Yvonne had broken her leg! Both of us ended up in plaster. This meant that we were unable to take part in the play-off against France that would determine the fifth and sixth places. We ended up being placed sixth, however, I felt really proud and privileged to have been a part of the whole event. Being placed sixth would normally have ended our stay in Mexico, but Harry told us that the Mexican people had taken us into their hearts and our accommodation had been paid for right through to the end of the tournament. We were then invited to go and watch the final between Mexico and Denmark. I was really impressed at the standard of football I was watching. The game was fast and exciting and the girls displayed a lot of technical ability. I honestly felt that it was on a par with men's football.

'During our last week in the hotel we were presented with a huge cake that said "You may have lost the game but you have won the hearts of the Mexican people". That sentiment was really humbling and has to this day left me with gratitude and warmth for Mexico and its people.'

Afterwards

'One of the biggest thrills for me on my return was telling my dad about Mexico and all that had happened there. I told him about the trip in great detail and he was open mouthed on hearing about all the fabulous experiences I'd had. I described how devoted and obsessive the fans were over there and how huge crowds had come to see us play. It was like telling about dreams coming true.

'It was during one of these conversations that the phone rang with an invitation for me and a plus one to attend an event being held by Newcastle United FC. It was at the Gosforth Park Hotel, which at the time was somewhere you would definitely accept an invitation to. It was to be an evening of talks on football and the invitation involved me speaking about my experiences in Mexico. Of course, I took my dad as my plus one.

'Sad to say, the evening didn't turn out as I had expected. Various people gave talks and speeches, then it was my turn. I had assumed (despite my misgivings about some negative press coverage we had attracted on our return) that the evening was going to be enjoyable and something great for my dad and I to remember. I was told that the compere would be asking me questions about my experiences in Mexico. However, what actually happened was that he consistently put words into my mouth, which seemed designed to make a mockery, not only of the competition but women's football in general. I think I even remember one of his questions being, "So it was a bit of a bun fight then?" When I went back to sit with my dad feeling humiliated, I thought back to the amazing final I had witnessed and wanted to scream at his ignorance.'

Jill Brader

Family and Early Football

'I was given my first football boots at the age of four for my birthday. They were black and shiny, and I was told later that I was so excited that I slept in them; wouldn't take them off as I thought they were beautiful. I grew up in Nuneaton, and where we lived there was a big football pitch on a piece of land just past the bottom of our garden, and I was always on it. I loved football. I lived on that piece of land, dribbling. A lot of our games were jumpers for goalposts. I was into all sports, swimming especially, running, hockey, so I was pretty fit and had good stamina. Hence, when I played in proper teams, I played as an attacking centre half, and, though I say it myself, I scored a few.

'Dad was a big sportsman in the Midlands, and for Warwickshire. He was chair of the Aston Villa Supporter's Club. I used to have a kickabout with him, as did my sister, and one day Fred Crump, the Nuneaton Town goalkeeper, saw me and told my dad I could be special. So, at about the age of thirteen or fourteen I went to play for a women's team, which I hadn't previously heard about in Stockley. There were more teams in the Midlands and it opened a new world to me, and we eventually moved to a larger club at Nuneaton Wanderers. Our manager, Fred Gibson, and our trainer, Derek Giggs, are unsung heroes of women's football at that time. They were very serious and dedicated a lot of their time to support the women's game, yet you very rarely hear about women's football in the Midlands at this time. Three of us played for Warwickshire regional squad – myself, Sue Knowles and Cathie Everett – and this must be where Harry Batt saw me play, but it's hard to know exactly.'

Harry Batt and Overseas Tours

'I had already been abroad with Nuneaton before I met Harry. We played in Reims, France, in 1969 and 1970, Calais, Dresden, and Braum FC in Belgium in 1971. So this was already very exciting, and of course I loved it. It was such an education. In France we stayed with families in Normandy, and we were out in the sticks on a farm. I would have been about fourteen or fifteen, and in the evening there were little kids half my age running around, and after dinner they all sat and had a glass of wine and lit a cigarette! I just sat there, not knowing quite what to do.

'Don't forget, I was about fifteen and football mad, so I wasn't paying much attention to how it all got organised. The first I knew of it was when someone came to the door to talk to my dad. I don't think he had met Harry before. My grandfather was so disgusted that my dad was thinking of allowing me to go with Harry to Italy that he offered to pay for me to go to boarding school so I could get this "football nonsense" out of my system. I remember my uncle storming out of the house when he came to "reason" with my dad. I am so grateful that my mum and dad let me go in the face of this from their own families. I hope they know today how grateful I am.

'Ahead of the Italy tour, my dad dropped me off at Crawley service station where the rest of squad picked me up to play at a gala at Brighouse on 20 and 21 of May or June. I know some England players were due to come along, such as Sue Buckett and Sue Lopez, but I don't know what happened to them. I think we flew out of

Luton? So within a couple of weeks I was off to Italy. I know my mum had to write a letter for this one, for the school, and I scored, I think, against West Germany.

'My dad made a trolley out of wood so I could pull my sports bag along, ahead of its time like a suitcase on wheels now. In Italy we played in Turin at the old Juventus stadium, which was fantastic, then on by train to Sicily, and all the time we were treated so well. We were taken to places for eating and entertainment, stayed in Milan and saw the sights, playing in their stadium also where the pitches were just fabulous!

'We won the qualifiers in Italy against a lot of good sides like Austria, Demark, Czechoslovakia and Switzerland, as well as the hosts. The dates I have for this are 6 July 1970, and some people played who didn't go to Mexico. Angela King, Joan Biggs, and Cathy Everett. Paula Rayner did go to Mexico, as did Jan Bing. Italy was like a dream for me, and I would have loved to make a professional career out of football. I will never forget being under the Juventus stadium and listening to the noise of the spectators. We made good friends, especially Paula, Louise and myself.

When we came back from Italy, I carried on playing for my club side in Nuneaton, and the Midlands. I was sort of in touch with Harry and the others but not very much. I remember going down for a trial by train and stayed with Harry and Paula Rayner, so that was maybe it.

Mexico 1971

'I was sixteen when we went to Mexico, so I had already left school. I already had a passport for my trips with Nuneaton, but my mum had to get a visa for Mexico, so we went to London for an overnight stay, and visited my uncle who was a Beefeater at the Tower of London at the time. My parents put me on a train at Nuneaton, and I met the rest of the team at Heathrow. I had never been on a jumbo jet before so that was very exciting. You will have seen the uniform for smart clothing, those white jackets, white shoes and socks. I nearly died. My mum had bought the latest thing, she thought; a pair of those stay pressed trousers for travelling and some extra kit, which I have to say

I do not remember washing at all while we were in Mexico. My mum's parents were dead set against it, and I was not to get a "well done" from either of my grandparents.

'There were so many amazing "pinch-me" moments that it is hard to summarise what it meant to me to go to Mexico. I still ask myself, "Did I do that?" You know, Nuneaton is quite a

A Snapshot of Leah Caleb in Mexico.

small town, so stopping off at JFK to change planes for Mexico, me and Paula were in awe really. Again, getting off the plane and all the crowds and the sense that someone famous was on this jumbo jet, looking to see and it turned out it was for us! In the hotel, I shared with Louise and Paula, and, like before, we just got on. None of us can remember feeling any conflict. Pat Dunn would come round at night to make sure you were tucked up. I had my seventeenth birthday in Mexico so that was very special. I had loads of cards and was treated all round: what an amazing experience.

'I actually got booked in the Azteca stadium; I think for dissent. I had always put myself about a bit and would often nobble the best player early on to make a point. Both games were very, very physical, because Mexico were under pressure as the home side and Argentina just played like that. But I was not a player to be intimidated. There is a photo of my nose being broken in the goalmouth, where I am going for the ball and you can clearly see in the photo this woman punch me in the nose.

'We trained very early to avoid the heat and had to take salt tablets. Other than that we just got on with it. I was just glad to be there, and though we lost, we sang "Walk On" by Gerry and the Pacemakers to keep our spirits up. We were very humble. They just took to us, and we took to them."

Afterwards

'My mum thought I needed to settle down and get a career. Then I did my nurse teacher training. Years later, I had my old teacher from school translate the seventeen postcards I had in Spanish, and we are in touch with the Argentine team on Facebook. Betty Garcia came over with us for a while to improve her English but had to then go back to Mexico.'

Lillian Taylor (née Harris)

Family and Early Football

'I had a sister and a brother growing up. I didn't get to play football properly in a team until I was seventeen or eighteen and spotted an ad in the paper for ladies football. I had loved to play football with the boys in my little village in the middle of nowhere when I was younger. The ad said "are you available Sunday?" I didn't know how to get there from my little village in Northampton to Brixworth, but my uncle gave me a lift in his car. We were living with my nan at that time. When I was only eleven my dad, who worked on the motorway, was killed, one of two workers who died. He would have been proud as punch. The lady who ran the team, Gwen, was very supportive, and I started off in goal. Frank Barker was boss of the shoe factory football team, Brixworth-Norvic, so we amalgamated, then became Town and County, playing against the likes of Painton, Brooke, Yardley-Hastings, connected to works teams. I think we had one match in Coventry.

Harry Batt and Overseas Tours

'Then we played against Chiltern Valley, and I was in goal (I normally played in defence or in goal). I played a game for Chiltern Valley as a defender and they were against good opposition, so I signed forms. They wanted to win because the opposing team were very cocky. I went straight from work with two pals. I got injured, and driving back my knee swelled up, so I went to the docs. He said he usually saw this in hockey players where the stick had gone above the shin pads.

'I loved my tackles, so there were injuries. Harry Batt asked my manager if he could invite me to play, and invited me to Sicily as the qualifier for Mexico and played me in goal or as a defender. I jumped at the chance. Just before, I got a phone call from Harry saying he wasn't sure if we could catch that flight, and that we might have to get an earlier one. This would mean I couldn't go, but work kindly drove me home, as I didn't have my own car then, to see what the arrangements were. It turned out that we could keep the original arrangements, so Harry said I might as well join them in my uniform. The place I worked, Manfield Shoes, let me go, but without pay.

'I had never been abroad before, but I had been away once with the school. I hadn't really played full team football with Chiltern Valley for very long, just that one match. What really sticks out is that, as a full-back, I got tackle after tackle in, including my sliding tackles, which I loved. It gave me a skin complaint as it took all the skin off my thigh, which wouldn't heal. Someone then suggested I had to have an injection, I suppose antibiotics. All the others went out and I was left at the hotel on my own to have this injection. Not a word of Italian. The chef could speak a bit of English and he told me to lie down and a man gave me three injections in my bottom! Half an hour apart. One in each buttock, and then another one in the first buttock. He was not a doctor, he was a barber, so he wasn't qualified. The manageress of the England team went mad when she returned. Alone in my bedroom, there was not a lot I could do.

'We played three matches. The crowds in Sicily were absolutely brilliant. They loved us and absolutely supported us. I took my football really seriously. I was playing defence against Italy, and Chris was in goal. She came out to get the ball but missed it and I cleared it off the goal line. When everyone saw me running back, I think they thought, "oh no!" but I cushioned it on my chest and cleared it upfield.'

Mexico 1971

'Mexico was totally hectic; we went from one place to another. We had no idea really what we were up against. Before Argentina, I played in goal in training, and got injured so used my hand as little as I could. I thought I had better get my eye in for the proper match, as my little finger got twisted out of joint. I had to go to the hospital with the interpreter, and it was spotless. They were brilliant. After three or four injections it was twisted back in and then strapped up. I couldn't swim with the others, but I hid it behind my back so the press couldn't see I was injured, Against Mexico I had another injury, this time my knee, but I didn't come off until the match finished. We couldn't afford to. Several of us had injuries, like Yvonne's broken leg. Others, like Carol, had injuries like a broken bone in their foot, but played on. We had two games in less than twenty-four hours, with a small squad, playing Argentina on Saturday, and Mexico on Sunday. It's no wonder we got so many injuries. They wanted us to play, though, including a friendly against France. For that we had to borrow two Mexican players, and lost 3–2. I remember because I was in goal. We came back and there was no one to greet us. This was downheartening, but we had had an amazing experience. One newspaper, the *Daily Express*, had a bit in it but that was it.

Newspaper cutting of the translators allocated to each team in their pink uniforms from a player scrapbook.

Afterwards

'The following year, in 1972, I got married, becoming Mrs Taylor, and had my daughter in 1973 and then my son in 1976. When my daughter started school I got involved, and suddenly there were all these eight- and nine-year-olds wanting a game of football. But there were no teams for them to play against. So they'd play against ten- or eleven-year-olds, and get beaten. It was fun and we enjoyed it, and I would then be playing on the rec on a Saturday afternoon.'

Conclusion

This chapter has included just some of the players from the 1971 Mexican tournament. There are many more stories to tell, as there also are of the women and girls who played in Italy and did not go to Mexico, for various reasons.

These oral histories are a redress to the lack of knowledge about a forgotten England team. As they show, the excitement of Mexico was lost upon their return for almost fifty years. So the interviews begin to address that gap in our knowledge. These kinds of player testimonies are still vital methodologies in addressing gaps in our knowledge of women's experiences of football.

In spite of the acclaim that followed the 1971 unofficial women's World Cup in Mexico itself, the players returned to a resounding lack of recognition for their efforts. As the player testimony indicates, the schools who had agreed that young women could go to Mexico for a month at the beginning of an academic year were seemingly embarrassed by the athletic distinction that the England players had bestowed upon their institutions. Given that this is within living memory, it perhaps reflects how influential the 1921 'ban' on women's football was, even in 1971.

Certainly, as the player testimony indicates, Harry Batt and the Chiltern Valley club were 'banned' by the WFA from its activities. The WFA was in a precarious position with regard to its diplomatic situation in mediating between the women's football community and the Football Association. Patricia Gregory, who was a stalwart of the WFA at the time, recalls the main funding as comprising:

In the accounts of 1971–1972 the £665 grant is listed as Department of the Environment grant. From 1972 to 1973 it is called the Sports Council grant. You could check when the CCPR became the Sports Council as I am not sure of the transition date. What I do remember is that we had to be careful not to jeopardise the grants which we got because we could only govern amateur players [...] The FA didn't initially give us any money – there is money listed in 1975–76 as Admin and Coaching grant from the FA. I imagine at that time they might have stipulated that we only govern amateur players.

So, although Harry Batt's England did not necessarily reflect the strength in depth of women's football at the time, particularly from Fodens or Manchester Corinthians, a partly self-funded and partly FIFF-funded England squad were very proud pioneers for their country.

The reunions of the England players now has an international element as the football associations of Argentina and France are now promoting these players as pioneers, including trips to the 2019 Women's World Cup in France. UEFA hosted the England players at the same tournament as their guests. Ildefonso Apelanz, a feminist academic working at Albany

The 1970 and 1971 Harry Batt teams at our reunion in 2019.

University in New York State, has met several women in Argentina who identify themselves as 'Las Pioneras (The Pioneers)' as they began playing football back in the fifties. Among them is Betty Garcia, and other players who participated in Mexico 1971. This large group of women are leading a movement to uncover and publicise the history of women's football in Argentina. Lucila Sandoval is leading these efforts to group, document, and reunite the players. In 2020 she contacted four players from 1971 and also reached out to a Mexican player, so there is a possibility of a larger reunion, possibly also incorporating France, Italy and Denmark. This is exciting, but bittersweet that it should have taken almost fifty years to honour these pioneers.

Chapter 5

The Women's Football Association and the Women's National Team

The Formation of the WFA

A carpenter from Kent, Arthur Hobbs, organised an experimental football tournament for women in Deal in 1967, in which eight teams participated. The following year it was repeated, this time increasing in size to thirty-two teams, including Manchester Corinthians, Chiltern Valley and Fodens. As the tournament grew so did the idea of a national governing body, amongst dedicated volunteers like Gladys Aiken of Corinthians, and Harry Batt of Chiltern Valley. In 1963 Flo Bilton formed Reckitts FC, from Reckitt and Colman where she worked, and led a ten-team Hull League, before becoming a stalwart on various committees to establish a governing body. June Jaycocks from the Brighton GPO was another dedicated volunteer, as was Patricia Gregory, who played for the White Ribbon team from London. In 1969 forty-seven teams took part in The Deal Tournament, which had become international. At the conclusion, the participants agreed to form The Ladies Football Association of Great Britain.

The first meeting, at Caxton Hall in London, took place in November 1969 with representation by thirty-eight of the fifty-one clubs affiliated to the Women's Football Association (WFA). Olive Newsom, of the Central Council for Physical Recreation (CCPR), suggested ladies play golf and women do athletics and play football, so the more archaic term was dropped in favour of the Women's Football Association. A steering committee drafted a constitution. Further working party meetings were held on 13 December 1969, 31 January 1970 and 4 April 1970.

At the first Annual General Meeting, on 6 June 1970, the following committee members were elected: chair, Patricia Dunn; vice chair, Pat Gwynne; honorary secretary, Arthur Hobbs; honorary assistant secretary, Patricia Gregory, treasurer, Charlie Cooke. Kevin Gaynor of the FA of Ireland represented the unaffiliated women's clubs in Ireland. Of the fifty-one then in membership, forty-four clubs, organised into seven leagues, were present on that day. The regional leagues were: Kent, Midlands, Northampton, Southampton, South East of England, Sussex, and West Mercia., although more clubs sides joined without a league affiliation.

The FA gave the WFA no funding initially, which meant that the only money available was from the Central Council of Physical Recreation (CCPR), which in turn only funded amateur sport. Although the ban on women playing was lifted, it took a campaign by the WFA to be able to use FA pitches, so there was still a very grudging acceptance of women's football. They were also financial problems: subscriptions of £2 totalled £150 in 1970.

The founding clubs were, in alphabetical order: Arland (Luton);Bantam Ladies FC (Coventry); Bedworth Rangers (Warwickshire); Boreham Wood (Hertfordshire); Bosom Buddies Utd (Essex); Brighton General Post Office (Sussex); Chiltern Valley (Luton); Cycle and General (London); Deal and Betteshanger Utd (Kent); Dundalk (Ireland);

Poster advertising the Deal International Football Tournament in 1968, for 32 teams.

Edgware (London); Farley Utd (Luton); Gillingham (Kent); Hamstreet (Kent); Harlesden Athletic (London); Hartwell (Northamptonshire); Hellingly Hospital (Sussex); Hull Ladies FC; Kays Ladies (Worcester); Keresley (Coventry); Lan-Bar Ladies FC (Warwickshire); Leicester City; Macclesfield (Cheshire); L'Oreal Golden Ladies (Bedfordshire); Manchester Corinthians (Lancashire); Manchester Nomads (Lancashire); Medway Ladies FC (Kent); Nuneaton Wanderers (Warwickshire); Patstone (Southampton); Rainbow Dazzlers (Burton-on-Trent); Ramsgate All-Stars (Kent); Rapide Ladies FC (Worcestershire); Real Ladies (Southampton); Reckitts (Hull); Romford (Essex); Rye (Sussex) Spurs Ladies FC (London); Spurs Supporters (London); Swindon Spitfires (Wiltshire); Talon Elite (Luton); Thanet Utd (Kent); White Ribbon (London); Wilton Dynamos (Hampshire) and Yardley Hastings (Kent).

As well as the clubs listed above, including Dundalk, Welsh and Scottish clubs joined the WFA in 1970, each paying £2. The first problem was whether the WFA could allow teams that were affiliated to it to play against non-affiliated teams. Hobbs did not want to upset the FA and so declined the chance to play against unaffiliated teams. In response the FA found it could not help with a planned coaching course because the WFA itself was 'unaffiliated.' As Sue Lopez explains in her book *Women on the Ball*, the WFA asked Fodens player, Joan Briggs, who was a PE teacher, to run the course, overseen by the FA's director of coaching, Walter Winterbottom.

Similarly, planned exhibition matches at the Empire Pool in Wembley were not covered by the BBC because the FA did not respond to their request to broadcast from the events. A series of five-a-side matches between Manchester Corinthians and Southampton were played just before a men's final in front of crowds of 8,000 people in April 1970, sponsored by the *Daily Express* and the *Evening Standard*.

A national cup competition was a good innovation, with eight regional groups competing, and later rounds at Watford, with the final at Crystal Palace National Sports Stadium.

There were also Europe-wide developments. On 3 March 1970 the global governing body, FIFA, sent Circular Letter No 142 to ask member national associations about the status of women's football in their particular country. Both for statistical reasons and for the promotion of women's football in *FIFA News*, this was the first global effort to understand the size and scale of women's football in each member association. Repeated letters of enquiry to FIFA in 1969 and 1970, primarily from referees asking to officiate at women's games, indicated that there was a gradual assimilation of women's football rather than widescale and rapid change. The questionnaire was short, and asked for the numbers of registered players, the number of cup competitions, and whether there was a national championship.

The following countries did not reply to circular No 142 (but though FIFA concluded this meant there was probably no women's football in that national association, unofficially there may well have been enthusiasm and activity): Central Africa, Chad, Ethiopia, Gambia, Guinea, Lesotho, Liberia, Mauritania, Mauritius, Niger, Senegal, Somalia, Tanzania and Togo (Africa); Aden, Afghanistan, Bahrain, Burma, Ceylon, Indonesia, Iran, Israel, Jordan, Korea DPR, Lebanon and Syria (Asia); Bahamas, Cuba, Dominican Republic, Haiti, Honduras, Nicaragua, Panama, Puerto Rico, El Salvador and Surinam (CONCACAF); Bulgaria, Czechoslovakia, Germany DR, Republic of Ireland, Northern Ireland, and Turkey (UEFA); Bolivia, Ecuador and Uruguay (South America).

Some countries responded to the circular saying that they did recognise women's football at all. These included: Algeria, South Africa and Upper Volta in Africa; China, Singapore and Thailand in Asia; Guatamala and Jamaica in CONCACAF; and in Europe, France, West Germany, Sweden and Wales. In England the FA responded that they had recently decided to allow women's football to be played on Football Association pitches, officiated by registered referees, but had decided by a small majority not to bring women's football under their direct control.

Intriguingly, the following number of women referees was noted: one in Kenya; two each in Japan and Austria, 2; 100 in the Netherlands; one each in Uganda and Bermuda; fifteen in Sweden; twenty in Switzerland; three in New Zealand. France and Jamaica reported that they had referees but did not give a number. Why there were so many women referees in the Netherlands remains to be known, but often female teachers were encouraged to take their refereeing licenses to officiate at schools contests, so that may explain the numbers.

Alongside these positive transnational developments, there were missed opportunities, and reactive moves on behalf of the WFA which prevented

First Game of the Tournament. She and I, on your behalf, and also on behalf of the charities to

		Jersey	Trunks
1	MINSTER (County Youth Club)	Claret and Blue	White
2	DEAL (County Youth Club)	Red and White	
3	HAFFENDEN (Sandwich)	Royal Blue and Amber	
4	RAMSGATE (County Youth Club)	Yellow and White	
5	AYLESHAM (Youth Club)		
6	HERNE BAY	Tangerine	White
7	PATSTONE UNITED (Southampton)	White	Royal Blue
8	BILDESTON (Suffolk)	Black with Red V Band	Red
9	THE SAINTS (St. Augustine's Hospital, Canterbury)	Amber and Black	
10	BOBBY'S (Margate)	Green	Navy Blue
11	MARKS & SPENCER (Ramsgate)	Navy	White
12	PFIZERS (Sandwich)		
13	ORIENT GOLDEN GIRLS (London)	Gold	Black
14	DOVER G.P.O.	Amber & Black Stripes	
15	HARTLEY WINTNEY (Hants.)	Blue and White	
16	IPSWICH	All Blue	
17	NORTH DEAL	Amber and Black	
18	BIRCHINGTON	Green and White	White
19	DEAL HOCKEY CLUB	Green and White Qtrs	
20	MARKS & SPENCER (Canterbury)	Red and White	Navy
21	WHITE RIBBON GIRLS (London)	Sky Blue	White
22	MANCHESTER NOMADS	All White	
23	BOBBY'S (Eastbourne)	Burgundy Gold	
24	SPURS SUPPORTERS LADIES (London)	White	Navy
25	SANDWICH (County Youth Club)		
26	RAMSGATE ALL STARS	All White	
27	SPURS BYRDS (London)	Navy	Navy
28	MARKS & SPENCER (Eastbourne)	White	White
29	BRIGHTON G.P.O.	Red	White
30	WOULPIT (Stowmarket)		
31	REED LADIES (Maidstone)	Black and White	
32	MANCHESTER CORINTHIAN	All White	Red White

Programme notes detailing the 32 teams who attended the Deal International Football Tournament in 1968.

further international growth. Firstly, the Butlin's Cup promoted by Hughie Green, compere of the popular talent show *Opportunity Knocks*, was developing a business dimension, with sponsorship from the holiday camp company. Today, this would be the equivalent of Ant and Dec promoting women's football on primetime television in conjunction with a major holiday chain, and in sponsorship terms an extremely valuable commodity. The WFA responded by launching its own national cup competition, sponsored by Mitre Sports, the WFA Mitre Cup, which was first contested in 1971 and won by Southampton. This struggled on until 1976, casting around for sponsors. The cup benefited from the support of several companies, including Showerings, manufacturers of Babycham and Pony alcohol drinks, CWE, Trimtape, Niagara Therapy, and Mycil. In some years there was no sponsorship and the biggest profit made by WFA was £180. Perhaps they should have stuck with Hughie Green and Butlins.

The first official England team trials were held in 1972, partly to negate Harry Batt's involvement with FIFF. England played a single match against Scotland that year. A reported profit of £250,000 from the tournament Batt attended in Mexico was considered by the WFA to have jeopardised the players' status as amateurs. This did not prevent him from taking an English team – many of whom were Chiltern Valley players who had been 'banned' by the WFA before returning to play in other teams – to a tournament in Italy in 1972. His involvement with such activities, and his links with a planned Women's World Cup in England in 1972–73, are likely to have prejudiced an already wary WFA against the enterprise.

Sue Lopez writes about her meeting with Geoff Hurst, Alf Ramsey and boxing promoter Jarvis Astaire, who assured her that the planned World Cup would be sponsored to the tune of £150,000, and that the England team would receive coaching to develop their skills ahead of the tournament. Arthur Hobbs, Gladys Aiken, Norman Holloway and Sue Lopez were in favour of the project. David Marlowe and Pat Gregory were not keen. In March 1972, at the Royal Lancaster Hotel, a meeting convened to discuss the project was voted against by WFA chair Pat Gwynne, who carried a second vote with a Scottish representative voting against the proposal, and endorsed by Gwynne's casting vote. Not only was this undemocratic, but it was pointedly unaware of the promotional value of the tournament, backed by journalist Ted Hart.

The commercial supporters of women's football were not always treated with due respect during the WFA years, though the Metropolitan Police, *the Daily Express* and Pontin's holiday parks fared a little better.

In the 1970s *The Daily Express* sponsored a five-a-side competition for professional men's clubs at the Empire Pool, Wembley, in which the WFA provided the interval entertainment in the form of an exhibition match. In 1980 The Met followed suit, organising a five-a-side competition that included women's and girls' teams, with a finals night at the Empire Pool, Wembley. The WFA launched five-a-side and nine-a-side competitions in 1977 at Brean Sands and Prestatyn, in collaboration with Pontin's holiday parks, and in direct competition with the Butlin's Cup.

Gradually, Scottish and Welsh associations formed in 1972 and 1976 respectively. Sadly, Arthur Hobbs had stood down from the WFA himself in June, 1972, due to ill health, and died in 1975, after seeing the rapid subsequent expansion of the organisation that he had helped to build. However, his role in seeking FA approval had effects on the careers of other WFA officials.

The coaching department of The FA recommended in 1972 that Eric Worthington, a senior lecturer at Loughborough College of Physical Recreation, FA Staff Coach and former professional footballer, should become the first England women's manager. After a series of inter-league matches, Worthington chose a squad of twenty-five players to a development weekend at Loughborough College, and fifteen players were selected to travel to Scotland for the inaugural official WFA international match. England won by three goals (Sylvia Gore, Lynda Hale, Jeannie Allott) to two (Mary Carr and Rose Reilly).

Though fixtures were few and far between, in August 1974 a number of England players successfully completed the first ever women's coaching course at Lilleshall, working with England manager Tommy Tranter. These included Carol McCune of Hull, Pauline Dickie of Southampton and Jayne Talbot of Spurs, who were all successful in achieving the FA Preliminary Coaching Award. Tranter invited Carol McCune for England trials, and she won her first cap on 7 November 1974 when she came on as a substitute, at Wimbledon, playing against France, aged nineteen. Then, to Carol's surprise, in May 1976 Tommy asked her to take on the captaincy from Sheila Parker just weeks before her twenty-first birthday. She would go on to become the first woman to win fifty caps for England, almost all as captain. This was no mean feat as there were just six England women's matches in 1976, five in 1977, and three in 1978.

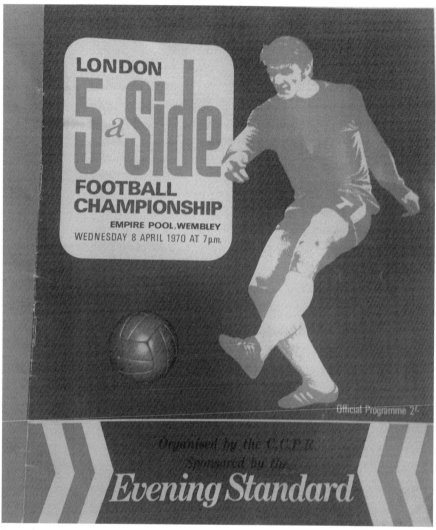

Programme for the 5-a-side match between Southampton and Manchester Corinthians, 8 April 1970.

Two key things affected the ability of the WFA to grow women's football in its twenty-three-year history. The first of these was lack of money, and therefore a voluntary workforce. The second was a policy of continuing to hand out bans, and to regulate women's football in a high-handed manner. This caused many volunteers to either be excluded by the WFA or to leave women's football altogether. Combined, the WFA legacy would be modest. The number of clubs throughout the 1970s and '80s fluctuated, with a rapid expansion to 269 in 1972, but increasing to only 373 by the time the WFA was preparing to hand over control to the FA at the end of 1992.

The European Confederation, UEFA, was by no means convinced that women's football was in a place to take forwards a competition of national women's teams, and, at its first conference to discuss the issue in 1973, reinforced this opinion. Importantly, not all of those who attended this meeting were people who had developed women's football, and some national representatives displayed a lack of enthusiasm. Notably, the Scottish FA, which was still voting not to accept women's football under its direct control in UEFA surveys as late as 1998.

A very important case for mixed football happened in 1978 when Theresa Bennett, an eleven-year-old girl who had played for North Muskham Primary School side in Nottinghamshire, and was invited to a trial for Muskham United's under-12 team. Nottinghamshire FA decided this was unlawful, and there was no women's team which was easily accessible. The Equal Opportunities Commission supported Theresa, as did her local newspaper. The case went to Newark Crown Court where she was initially awarded £250 in compensation, but the FA appealed to the High Court, and subsequently won. The process was not egalitarian. As Theresa later said:

> We weren't told when the court date was – it was kept quiet. We then suddenly had a phone call at 5.30am one morning to say the case was being heard that day at the High Court. Get yourself to London. My parents couldn't drive but we booked a taxi and caught the train. We arrived at the High Court and they just said: "All sorted. Decision made. The FA won their appeal and you lost." That was it. It was ridiculous. I was on the steps outside the High Court and had no chance to say anything. The FA was obviously more powerful.

This meant Theresa got nothing in compensation, and the maximum age for mixed football was set at the age of twelve for decades as a result, moving to eighteen years of age only in 2015. In supporting the FA, the WFA's view was simple: if Theresa was to be allowed to join what had been until that point an all-boys team, there would be nothing to prevent boys from joining girls' teams. There was, however, no evidence that this would be a problem. An alternative interpretation of the case can be found in a booklet by David Pannick, a leading QC, who released *Sex Discrimination in Sport* with the Equal Opportunities Commission in 1983. Pannick argues that, given the number of boys' football teams relative to girls' football teams in 1978, it was highly unlikely that boys would wish to join new teams, and if they did it would be a matter of personal choice.

That said, there were real points of innovation and transformational change which should be acknowledged. The first, in 1981, involved a trip to Japan to the Portopia tournament. The six-month-long Portopia Festival had been established to celebrate the completion of the construction of a new town on reclaimed land in Kobe, Japan. This was, at the time, the largest artificial island in the world. A journalist, Kagawa Hiroshi, a proud native of Kobe City in Hyōgo Prefecture, persuaded the chairman of the regional football association, Takasago Yoshiyuki, to travel to England and watch a 1–1 draw with Sweden in Leicester on 17 September 1980. Yoshiyuki, was impressed by the large number of spectators at the match, and by the use of standard FIFA rules. Takasago felt that the advances made by women in England and elsewhere in Europe could be replicated by the Japanese, and the Japanese Football Association agreed. On 22 January they announced that England, Italy and Denmark had accepted invitations to visit Japan. The three European teams were certainly among the best in the world at this time. Denmark had won the unofficial European Championship in 1979, beating hosts Italy in the final match. England finished fourth, losing on penalties to Sweden in a play-off for third place.

Each team would play two matches. Denmark, in front of 5,000 spectators, drew 1–1 with Italy. Then some 7,000 spectators saw England beat Japan 4–0 with two goals from Angela Gallimore, and one each from Debbie Bampton and substitute Vicky Johnson. For England, Terry Wiseman played in goal, behind Carol Thomas, Angela Gallimore, Sheila Parker, and Linda Coffin. The midfield was Linda Curl, Debbie Bampton, and Liz Deighan, and Tracy Doe, Eileen Foreman, and Janet Turner were the strikers.

A vastly experienced Italy then defeated Japan 9–0, and Denmark beat England 1–0, with both games drawing crowds of 3,000. The England party consisted of six officials: Pat Gregory (chef de mission), Flo Bilton (assistant), Annabel Hennessy (welfare officer), a team doctor, Tony

Brightwell (squad physiotherapist) and Martin Reagan (manager), along with sixteen players. The Japanese had spared no expense in staging the tournament. Each squad member was given a tracksuit and two full kits for the two games each team were to play. Also, every player was given a pair of Japanese brand trainers and high-quality boots, a tee shirt and a

PONTIN'S
INVITATION WOMEN'S
FIVE-A-SIDE FOOTBALL

NORTHERN AREA

MAY 20th to MAY 27th, 1978

PRESTATYN SANDS HOLIDAY VILLAGE, NORTH WALES

Under the auspices of the Women's Football Association

GREETINGS FROM SIR FRED PONTIN

It is with great pleasure that I welcome you to our Women's Football Weeks. I am very proud that my Company is associated with the Women's Football Association in staging a worthwhile competition for women footballers and, we hope, helping the W.F.A. to achieve some of its aims for women's football.

I am most grateful to everyone who has helped to make these weeks possible - the W.F.A. and their officials - especially to Miss Pat Gregory and Mr. David Hunt, and to the Clubs taking part for their participation.

I am sure we shall see some great football and with so many clubs taking part in these two weeks the standard may surprise many people. I trust the weeks will be happy and enjoyable for players and spectators alike.

My good wishes to you all.

SIR FRED PONTIN.

NORTHERN AREA CHAMPIONS 1977 - DROITWICH ST. ANDREWS

Your Northern Area Controller for the W.F.A. is Mr. RODGER E. BREN

Pontin's Management Details:
PRESTATYN HOLIDAY VILLAGE
Central Beach, Prestatyn, Clwyd, North Wales LL19 7LA
Tel. Prestatyn 2267/8/9/70
Village Manager: Mr. J. F. MALLINSON
Secretery: Mr. B. S. TOUHLADJIEV
Entertainments Manager: Mr. G. SMITH

Programme for the Pontin's Invitational 5-a-side tournament at Prestatyn in 1978, with a greeting from Sir Fred Pontin.

personal travel bag. Although the England team came third behind Italy and Denmark, with Japan in fourth, it was to prove useful international experience for the squad in 1984 and 1985, when they would win significant victories.

The England team's rivals continued to diversify, managed for much of the 1980s and the 1990s by Martin Reagan. Reagan was both popular with the England players I have interviewed, and strict in his discipline, due to having a military background. England's greatest success to date came as runner's up in the final of the 1984 UEFA European Competition for Representative Women's Teams (the forerunner of the official European Championship). This was followed by victories in the 1985 and 1988 Italian Mundialito competitions, and the first appearance at Wembley Stadium in 1989. There was no doubt that an underfunded, amateur England side were very good. There was also clear evidence that other nations were catching up and overtaking the self-funded England players. For instance, although England beat the USA 3–1 in their first match on 23 August 1985, and again 2–0 on 27 July 1988 on the way to the Mundialito victories, when the sides met for a third time, on 9 August 1990, USA won by three goals to nil.

Along with the inherent conservative ethos of the WFA, financial problems continued. In 1982 the WFA became a limited company, in direct relation to a number of problems with the previous accounting system. This improved rigour was rewarded with a seat at the FA on the same basis as one of the county FAs, and Tim Stearn served as representative. The factionalism continued, though, and the FA, the Football Trust and the Sports Council became increasingly certain that the WFA was too reliant on volunteers in its constitution. By early 1993 the WFA's financial position was again unstable, having accrued considerable debts. England were knocked out of the UEFA competition in the quarter-final stage, and John Bilton stood down as the manager. The FA would appoint the next England manager. So, who were some of these key personalities, and why were some more acceptable to the FA than others?

Pat Dunn: the First Chair of WFA, 1969–1970

While Arthur Hobbs has often been credited as the godfather of women's football by the WFA, particularly in relation to the Deal international tournament, the WFA organisation was complex and prone to infighting, with many factions and schisms. Hobbs may have held sway at the WFA, but the treatment of Pat Dunn, who was the WFA's first chair, is instructive. Having been democratically elected, she was asked to resign in October 1970. This was also short lived. In 1972 Gwynne reverted to the position of vice chairman, but was concerned that there was a potential conflict with his refereeing activities, and so he resigned in 1973. So why was Pat Dunn considered a controversial choice by the FA, and why did Hobbs request her resignation in person?

Patricia Alice Lewis, better known under her married name Pat Dunn, was born in 1933 as the youngest of four children to Henry and Rebecca. Her brother, Arthur, was the eldest, followed by her sisters, Doreen and Miriam, who was known as Joan. All were very close, as their Mum died when Pat was just two, so Joan in particular really bought Pat up. Joan reported that as a child Pat was sickly and determined to make something of her life. At the outbreak of the Second World War in 1939 Pat went to Weymouth, in Dorset, as an evacuee from Elephant and Castle in London.

Pat and Joan played football for fun while growing up on Weymouth Old Rec, but the younger sister was more enthusiastic than the elder. Women's teams from the Second World War disbanded, but it was not long before Pat joined Stroud Green FC, in Newbury, Berkshire, in the season 1958–59, at the age of fifteen. She was the only girl in the team and the other players did not hold back. On one occasion Pat returned home with seven stitches above her eye, along with several cuts and bruises.

Pat worked as an account clerk at the *Dorset Evening Echo*, but football ruled her life. Her niece, Deborah, who has helped so kindly with this profile, remembered as a child being slightly embarrassed by her pioneer aunt because people used to ask, 'Is that your Aunty, the one who plays football?' Pat seems to have played in an organised way for women's teams, firstly for the newspaper work's team versus a local team, in around 1966. Pat worked for the newspaper for thirty years, and its support was helpful in promoting her as a pioneer of women in football. She lived in Chickerell Road, Weymouth with husband Alf, who, unsurprisingly, had been a former footballer for Chickerell and other teams. 'I couldn't have married anyone who wasn't interested in football,' she is reported to have said.

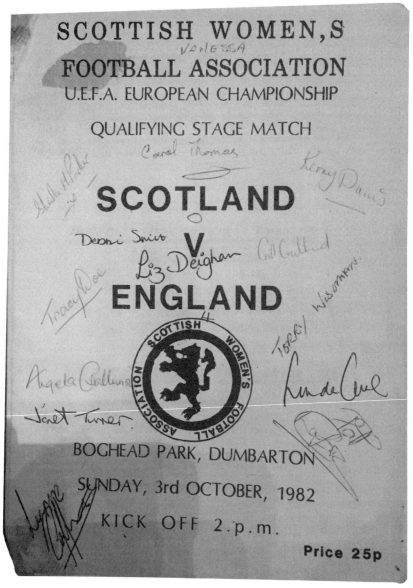

Autographed programme for a 1982 England versus Scotland game, to mark a decade since their first 'official' fixture.

However, it was Pat's wish to referee that upset the FA quite so much, since they did not have a rule banning women from refereeing: in their view, it was inconceivable that a woman should even try. Beginning by running the line, Pat soon wanted to officiate in the middle of the park, and began in youth football and friendlies, where a formal refereeing certificate was not needed. In 1967 Pat told the *Daily Mirror* newspaper that she had begun to referee 'as a joke' in 1965, at the age of thirty-four, when asked by her office team, and had accepted the half-hearted invitation.

In 1967 Pat refereed the auspicious-sounding Southern Newspapers Knockout Cup, between *The Dorset Evening Echo* and *The Bournemouth Times*. By 1967 she was refereeing local matches and was part of the football scene in Dorset. She had by then applied to take the FA examinations to become a qualified referee. There was no doubt in her mind about the attitudes of the FA, but she was determined to become a pioneer. In one local match she was officiating she saved a player's life when he broke his wrist and fainted with shock, then swallowed his tongue when unconscious. Pat gave mouth-to-mouth resuscitation until the ambulance arrived.

Perhaps the national news coverage of Pat's wish to become a referee embarrassed the FA, as a local spokesman said he had not previously been aware of a woman refereeing a men's game and did not think it would be allowed. Unsurprisingly, Pat considered this to be 'a load of bunkum', and told so to the *The Sun* newspaper Less than a month later, on 18 February 1967, the Dorset County Football Association (DCFA) sent a letter, signed by secretary Mr J. Hodges which opined that: 'the referees feel no useful purpose would be gained by you taking the examination to be a referee. It has always been the purpose of the county referees' board to hold examinations for the purpose of the registration of referees to serve on the county referees lists. In your case this would not, of course, be possible.'

An appeal to the FA was met with the ruling that, 'we do not recognize ladies football so it would be ridiculous to accept lady referees.' Pat continued to protest until she was allowed to take the exam in early September 1967. A letter to Southern Newspapers congratulated her on 'becoming a fully-fledged referee', but the congratulations would be premature. Upon passing, Pat was informed that 'no certificate would be issued because the examination board had found that a) women are not allowed to play football, and b) you wear glasses.' Combining sexism with disability discrimination in one fell swoop, this ruling neatly ignored the numbers of bespectacled male referees. Three months later, the FA passed a ban on women officiating in FA or league matches: 'The meeting decided to adopt recommendation that regulations for the guidance of referees, Country Associations, Leagues and Competitions be amended, <u>COUNTY ASSOCIATIONS SHALL NOT REGISTER FEMALES AS REFEREES'</u>. (Underlining and capitalisation as in the original document).

Pat wrote to the Minister of Sport, Denis Howell, and the queen to object, and had a photograph taken of the reply from the Palace, which made the national news. *The Daily Express* characterised her as 'The Ponytail Ref' and 'The Lipstick Ref'. Undeterred, Pat refereed many matches, including the prestigious Deal Women's International Tournament, featuring sides from Austria and Czechoslovakia. Again in 1970 she was rebuked by a letter from the FA: 'You are not permitted to referee women's football teams played on grounds under the jurisdiction of the Football Association as females are not permitted to be registered by County Associations!'

This degree of publicity that Pat had achieved clearly riled the FA, who in 1969 accepted control of women's football, at the instigation of FIFA. It was begrudging. When Pat was elected the chair of the newly formed Women's Football Association, her tenure was to be shortlived. She was asked to resign as chair shortly after, specifically referencing a phone call from Arthur Hobbs requesting her resignation. A male referee, Pat Gywnne, was more acceptable to the FA as chair, and particularly to the secretary of the WFA, Arthur Hobbs.

Pat Dunn confessed to being mystified, having pioneered important aspects of the women's game, as this summary has shown. For instance, the WFA did not take up the issue of women refereeing until 1973. From the 1973 season women referees were able to register with the WFA to officiate at women's matches only, and were awarded a halfway certificate by the WFA, which didn't accredit them to officiate at male matches.

It took the Sex Discrimination Act in 1975 before women referees could register with their County FA, once successful in passing their refereeing qualification. This delay did not deter Pat Dunn, who was finally allowed by the FA to officiate at an auspicious fixture between male teams, Rolworth Rangers and Free Wheelers, in the Dorset League on 5 September 1976.

Pat continued to referee for a decade before giving up on football altogether. Given how she had been treated, we might be surprised that she volunteered her time and enthusiasm to the sport for so long. The

Trailblazing ladies footballer recalls High Court battle

By Elizabeth Hambidge
e.hambidge@newarkadvertiser.co.uk

A WOMAN footballer who took on the Football Association 30 years ago for the right to play with a Muskham boys' team believes her battle helped pave the way for the current success of ladies football in England.

Theresa Bennett, 42, who hung up her competitive boots only two years ago, said a lot had changed in the game since her unsuccessful fight as an 11-year-old schoolgirl against the governing body.

She said: "It raised the issue and it did get a lot of press all over the world. I believe it helped to promote female football and the progression to where today's England ladies are playing in the World Cup."

The row also inspired Theresa, of Balderton, to go on to a successful sporting career in football, hockey and cricket.

She contacted the Advertiser after she was mentioned in an article about Newark's role in promoting women's football.

Her part in the history of women's football was researched by Collingham author Helena Pielichaty, who recently published a book called Here Come The Girls!

Theresa was 11 when she trialled for Muskham Colts under 12s, a team made up of boys. She was successful and was asked to play for the team, but FA rules would not allow her to compete.

Disappointed with the decision, Theresa took her fight to the High Court, which eventually ruled in the FA's favour.

Theresa said she had wanted to play with the boys' team until she hit puberty, when her team-mates would have become stronger than her.

She said: "I understood the reasons why (the FA wouldn't let her play) but my view was that I'd played football at my school with the boys and I was playing at a better ability than some of them.

"It would just have been for a couple of seasons."

Despite this early setback Theresa was not deterred and, after a seven-year break from the game, went on to play for a team in Nottingham.

After leaving school she worked at

> ❝ It was quite awe-inspiring going from living in a small village and then being thrust into the public domain . . . it was ground-breaking at the time. ❞
>
> **Theresa Bennett**

Newark Ambulance Station, before joining the Army as a personal trainer, where she was selected to play football.

Theresa holds the record for the quickest goal scored at the Army's ground in Aldershot, netting against a German team after 23 seconds.

She also played at Arsenal's former home, Highbury.

Football was not the only sport at which she excelled. Theresa played hockey for the Army all over the world, and cricket for both Nottinghamshire and Ireland.

Theresa said she believed her early setback with the FA inspired her to go on to achieve so much.

She said: "It was quite awe-inspiring, going from living in a small village and then being thrust into the public domain. I obviously got positive and negative comments from many people.

"There were a lot of girls out there who were in the same position as I was and who were not able to do anything about it. It was ground-breaking at that time.

"The experience gave me a never say never attitude, which has stood me in good stead through to this day.

"I'm pleased with my career and I've achieved an awful lot."

● THEN AND NOW: Theresa Bennett, above, pictured in her football kit when she was an 11-year-old trying to play for boys' team Muskham Colts under 12s. Right, Theresa, now aged 42, pictured still ready to play women's football, a sport which has advanced in recent years thanks partly to her famous High Court battle with the FA.

More children adopted	New bid to fight crime will get up	Last chance to speak up
THE number of children who have been matched with adop-		THERE are just four days left for residents to have their say

Newspaper clipping of the Theresa Bennett case, reported when Theresa was 42 years of age.

likes of Wendy Toms, Amy Fearn and Sian Massey-Ellis owe Pat Dunn a huge debt of gratitude and she should be in the National Football Hall of Fame. How many more women have been lost to the sport due to this kind of discrimination is likely to remain a large and ultimately unanswerable question.

It was not of course just women who were treated badly. Infighting led to increasingly acrimonious bans on individuals, such as Harry and June Batt, who attempted to develop women's football, as we have seen in a previous chapter. In 1971 Pat went to the unofficial women's World Cup in Mexico, as the team coach and trainer. On their return from Mexico, Harry, June and The Chiltern Valley club, which they led, were given a 'lifetime ban' by the WFA, which barred them from any involvement in women's football. Perhaps Pat felt any hint of a ban was already redundant considering how she had already been treated, but at least she got to experience the wonderful atmosphere in Mexico.

More WFA Personalities: Florence 'Flo' Bilton

Flo Bilton was born in 1921, in Hull. She worked for Reckitts and ran its women's football team from 1963, playing for a while in goal, plus founding the Hull League. She later helped local players Carol Thomas, Gail Borman and Gill Coulthard progress to the England national team, with Carol and Gill becoming England captains. Flo Bilton was included in the Lord Mayor's Centenary Awards in Hull to recognise her significant achievements in the city as a player, and in 2018 a commemorative plaque was unveiled in her honour.

An influential figure and founding member of the Women's Football Association, Bilton took on various thankless tasks for the WFA with enormous good humour and patience. She seemed to have possessed a Trojan work ethic on behalf of the WFA, with her many and varied duties including promotional activities such as producing the WFA newsletter, becoming membership and development secretary, as well as sewing by hand the international caps for the England team when the WFA could not afford to have them produced. This typified her determined, industrious and creative personality. Bilton reportedly borrowed a badge from her neighbour, Raich Carter, who had played for England men's national team, and copied it by hand. Many England women internationals I have interviewed spoke about their single badge, with some receiving one for their first representative game, and a wooden plaque to mark their last. Flo Bilton also kept the England women's team's records from 1972 onwards, and was made an Honorary Life Vice presidentof the WFA in 1990. She was a diplomat who did not always respond to the sniping of the WFA committees, but was nevertheless plain speaking. All the players remember her with enormous affection and admiration as their chaperone on overseas tours. She died in 2004.

Patricia Gregory

Patricia Gregory was in many ways the protégé of Arthur Hobbs. She was initially the volunteer assistant secretary of the WFA, until taking over as secretary from Arthur Hobbs in 1972. Gregory held this position until 1981, when it became evident that a full-time official was required. Inspired by England winning the World Cup, and Tottenham winning the FA Cup, Patricia wrote a letter about women's football to her local paper and received several replies about playing.

Having set up a team, White Ribbon, Gregory was not noted for her football skills, but her administrative legacy was considerable. She eventually managed to hire a pitch and ended up running both her club and a women's football league. Gregory also had a challenging full-time job as a secretary in the BBC's Sports Department, which she had joined in 1970. Running a club and a league, as well as duties for the WFA, proved too much for her, however. Once Linda Whitehead was appointed on a full-time basis, Gregory was invited to become a member of the UEFA Women's Football Committee in 1979, serving seven terms until 1993.

Gregory then joined ITV in 1978 as their first Network Sports Coordinator, before returning to BBC Sport in 1993 until her retirement in 2010. Prior to becoming an Honorary Life Vice presidentof the WFA in 1984, until the dissolution of the WFA in 1993, she served for a year in each role as liaison officer and chair, often working with the FA's Denis Follows. After the WFA was dissolved, she served on The Women's Football Alliance Committee of The FA.

June Jaycocks

June Jaycocks – born in 1936 – somehow found the time to work full time, run a league and a club, as well as volunteer for various WFA offices. The

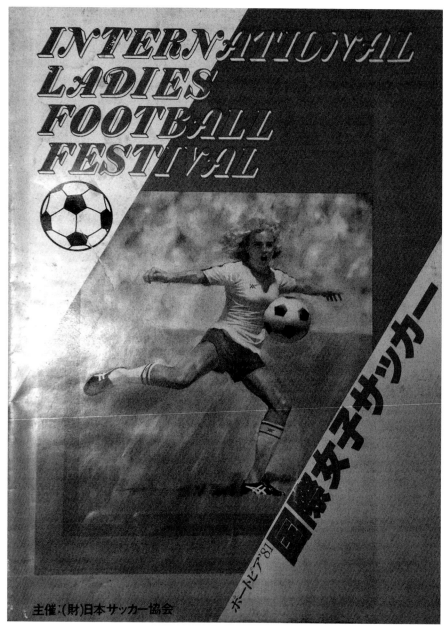

Programme Cover for the Portopia tournament played in 1981, in Japan.

support of her late husband, Jimmy, was key. At club level, Jaycocks began her involvement with the Brighton General Post Office team, formed in 1967, from workers at the telephone exchange. In 1969 she founded and chaired the Sussex Martlet League, to which Brighton General Post

Office affiliated. By 1975–76, the team name had changed to Brighton & Hove Albion. As Brighton and Hove, they reached the Women's FA Cup semi-final, but were beaten 8–1 by Southampton WFC. Another name change followed when the club signed a sponsorship deal with sports retailer Clapshaw and Cleave Sports, becoming C&C Sports during the 1979–80 season. They have now reverted to the name Brighton and Hove Women's Football Team, managed by Hope Powell, and have been led by a number of England internationals down the years, including Julie Hemsley, Angie Banks and Tracey Doe. But it is clear that in terms of club football and the regional league, Jaycocks was a tireless role model and pioneer.

In terms of the WFA administration, June served on the executive from 1971 until 1978 and was briefly assistant secretary in 1979–80 and vice chair from 1980 to 1983. Like Flo Bilton, June was remembered by players as having a warm, lively personality and a great sense of humour, which made her very popular. Hers was an easy-going, smiley diplomacy, much needed by the WFA, who could often appear somewhat frosty. But even this good humour could not hide the financial pressures of the WFA. Jaycocks administered the England team between 1982 and 1991, resigning following two very poorly attended but innovative matches against USSR at The Dell in Southampton and Brighton's Goldstone Ground. She then became an Honorary Life Vice-President.

David Marlowe

David Marlowe benefitted women's football through his expertise in PR for the vacuum company, Hoover (one of the prominent Scottish teams at that time was the Cambuslang Hooverettes). Marlowe brought a passion for rules and regulations, which led to the rather punitive approach of many of the decisions that the WFA made for its members. Marlowe was chair from 1972 to 1977, and rules co-ordinator from 1982. There is no doubt that, for all his voluntary work, Marlowe held back women's football personally, and as a figurehead at the WFA: his aspirations were to manage and control, rather than promote. England's first women internationals had to be amateur, and were prohibited from being professional in either their outlook or preparation. For this reason, many had to choose between playing for their country or playing abroad, as Sue Lopez has already

Pat Dunn snapshot in her refereeing uniform.

outlined. Marlowe reiterated a commitment to amateurism as the most desirable future for the women's game in 1975, and in subsequent meetings.

By 1982 the FA had granted the WFA £3,000 per annum, possibly rising to £4,000 by 1985, for its expenses. Nevertheless, the WFA meeting that recorded this historic breakthrough also noted that it was not uncommon to spend over an hour discussing the thorny question of expenses and subscriptions, with fines issued to players, individual teams and to leagues. An invitation to play in Norway in 1982 was declined due to lack of finances, and women who wanted to avail themselves of a coaching experience in New Zealand, including future England captain Debbie Bampton, were advised to self-fund.

By 1983 the WFA had become a limited liability company, and Marlowe became company secretary from the inauguration of the WFA as a limited company in 1982, but was unable to accept the accounts in 1984 and resigned. Ultimately this did not end the WFA's penury, and financial problems and irregularities were at least one of the reasons that the FA took control of women's football in 1993. Combined with a volunteer workforce, this financial instability would eventually limit who was, and who was not, involved as a WFA officer. Marlowe oversaw a WFA constitution, established standing orders, and standardised league and club rules. The disciplinary system was thorough and comprehensive, as is evidenced from Marlowe's papers, minutes and newsletters in The British Library. Marlowe was created an Honorary Life Member in 1977 and died in 1999.

Conclusion

It is important to remember that the formation of the WFA in 1969–1970 took place at a time of real social division about gender equality, enshrined in the problematic legislation of the 1970 Equal Pay Act. The Sex Discrimination Act followed in 1975, and the Equal Opportunities

Soccer-mad housewife accuses FA

Pat Dunn refereeing a local match at Weymouth.

THE WORLD of football-crazy housewife Pat Dunn crumbled yesterday.

Officially, 37 - year - old Mrs. Dunn, who has battled for the last five years for the cause of women's soccer, resigned from her post as chairman of the recently - formed Women's Football Association.

Resignation

But Britain's first-ever qualified woman referee made it plain that she had been forced out of the job.

And now she is wondering whether officials of the all - male football Association were behind the move to get rid of her.

For Mrs. Dunn, who has travelled more than 8,000 miles round Britain to referee women's soccer-matches, has often clashed with the F.A.

Pat, foster mother of two young boys, posted her resignation to Arthur Hobbs, secretary of the W.F.A. last week. It was officially accepted at a meeting of the association's executive committee in London yesterday.

But Mrs. Dunn claimed she had been asked to resign without any reason being given. She told me: "I was elected president when the W.F.A. was formed last year. Then, in June this year, I was made chairman.

Rebel

"But only two or three weeks later, Mr Hobbs phoned me and said he had been advised to ask for my resignation. He would not give a reason nor say who his advisers were.

"After all I've done for women's football, I was absolutely shattered."

Mrs. Dunn first clashed with the F.A. when she applied to take the official referees' examination. At first she was refused permission to sit the test but eventually won her way. But after passing the exam she was refused registration as a referee in Dorset where she lives.

Pat Dunn newspaper clipping: 'Soccer-mad housewife accuses FA'.

Commission was established in 1976, defining and promoting intersectional politics more obviously in every- day life. The 'second wave' Women's Liberation Movement, from 1970 onwards, focused less on campaigns for the vote, as the 'first wave' had done more than fifty years before, but on the more intimate politics of statutory campaigns around maternity and abortion rights, employment, and personal freedoms to make choices. As we have seen from the Theresa Bennett case, individual women and girls interviewed for this project would not necessarily identify as feminists, but tried to exercise their own personal choices as pioneers, whether or not society was ready for them to do so.

This chapter is not a comprehensive history of the WFA, as that would entail a book in itself. Perhaps we should celebrate how much was achieved by the tireless volunteers, rather than how little progress was made, if we judge by club numbers alone. Perhaps it was entirely to be expected in the early days of women's football's absorption by established governing bodies that some factions with different perspectives should emerge. This remains the case today, when confidence in the FA's handling of England women (as with the men's) remains contested in the mainstream and social media. Certainly the departure of male coach Mark Sampson, and the long and somewhat arbitrarily planned departure of Phil Neville in 2020, or what some commentators are calling 'Nexit', are grounds for thinking that the FA have more money, if not always more sense, than the WFA.

There are many more WFA personalities who came and went due to the voluntary nature of the organisation, and there has not been space to do them all justice here. For example, David Hunt was the second treasurer of the WFA from 1972 to 1977, as well as running a club, a league, and, along with his wife, Marianne, promoting the WFA Mitre Cup competition. He served as chair from 1977 until 1982, and became an Honorary Life Vice President. Richard Faulkner, originally associated with The Football Trust, was elected to the WFA chair in 1988 until 1990. Such voluntary work was recognised when he was created Baron Faulkner of Worcester in 1999.

The WFA were so cash strapped that it did not get a permanent funded secretary until 1980 when Linda Whitehead joined the team. When Linda moved into the Corn Exchange offices in Manchester in the 1988– 89 season from a tiny office in Hyde Park, London, a key purpose was to forge closer links with the Professional Footballer's Association's Football in the Community Programme. The move was moderately successful, with twenty-six new clubs joining the WFA, particularly in the North West of England, to bring the total to 249 affiliated clubs. In twenty years this was a modest and very incremental growth.

The WFA move north was short-lived, and had limited success, mainly because of a lack of funds, and their own financial problems which had led, by this time, to several splits and departures (as we have seen). In spite of her hard work, dedication and entrepreneurial spirit, Whitehead was made redundant when The Football Association took over the running of women's football from the WFA in 1993. She was replaced by recent graduates in sports development roles who had little connection to the existing structures of women's football, and led to the departure of many volunteers who had worked so tirelessly. This did not stop those newcomers from celebrating the voluntaristic structures of women's football as their own creation, and receiving distinctions such as MBEs.

Because the WFA knew that the FA viewed women's and girls' football in much the same way that it viewed boys' football, as a potential financial liability rather than an economic asset, Football in the Community seemed a good way to draw in funds so that professional football could subsidise women's teams. Hence the likes of Manchester City, in setting up its 'Ladies' team as a sign of community goodwill and outreach, effectively confined it to charitable patronage rather than it being aligned with the overall club brand.

As previous chapters have shown, one of the more successful clubs of the 1990s, Arsenal Ladies, imported an existing women's team that was led by the former first-team kit man, Vik Akers. The fact that Akers and others are now often called the 'revolutionaries' of women's football, founding the club in 1987 and so on, neglects all the voluntary work before he took over.

When we look in more detail as to how the teams were funded, with loaned old kit, and playing on grounds well away from the limelight, we should be careful to consider how successful this Football in the Community strategy has been over the last thirty years. There is no doubt that Akers and others helped women's football immeasurably. He received an OBE in recognition of this. However, many dedicated individuals have not been rewarded in this way.

Snapshot of Pat Dunn refereeing men's football teams in 1976.

Debbie Day has kindly shown the author a photograph of the hand-stitched WFA caps that were awarded to each player on her first appearance. Sheila Parker was the first England captain, between 1972 and 1976, winning thirty-three caps. Carol Thomas was awarded her fiftieth cap by Sir Tom Finney. Debbie Bampton, MBE, shared the England captaincy and was a roommate of Gill Coultard between 1985 and 1993, winning ninety-five caps in all, with the changeover due to injury, illness and controversy. Coultard became the first woman, the fifth ever England player (male or female) and the only amateur to reach 100 caps in October 1997. Before a 1999 World Cup qualifier against Holland at Upton Park she was presented with a silver cap and silver lion memento by Sir Geoff Hurst.

Bearing in mind that the WFA was so cash strapped that they played just eleven internationals in 1990, when Gill first took over as captain, eight in 1991, and six in 1992, before the FA took over in 1993, Gill Coultard's career represents an incredible resilience. As an amateur with a full-time job and limited access to top-flight football, this should be recognised as a momentous achievement. Fifteen years later, the FA presented her with a gold cap, as it had done for men who reached the century milestone. Perhaps they could have been more gracious.

In 1992, just as the WFA folded, ten-year-old Tracey Wright appeared in *Born Kicking*, a BBC One Screen One production by Barry Hines, featuring protagonist Roxy Reddy, the first woman to play professional football for fictitious league side EPR. Forms of professionalism had already been pioneered before the programme was aired, but the pitch of the script as a 'futuristic drama' shows how important amateurism was to the WFA during its twenty-three-year reign over women's football in England between 1969 and 1992. Importantly, women's football was perceived as ideally amateur in nature in Britain. No home nations qualified for the first Women's World Cup in 1991, and it would take until the second Women's World Cup in Sweden for a more organised approach to be adopted. Amateurism had an important part to play in the acceptance of women's football from 1949 to 1969, and this changed only gradually up to 1992. The more recent takeover of women's football by the FA in 1993 has seen a very steady rise in numbers of participants, while football remains a sport practiced by girls mainly outside of school, rather than in PE lessons.

Chapter 6

The First England Women Captains 1972–2000

This chapter focuses on the careers of the first four women England captains. Sheila Parker became the first England women's football national team captain in 1972. Her successor, Carol Thomas, would become the first woman to earn fifty international caps in an era when there were very few games.

These were fast changing years for women's football in England and Carol led the team to the Portopia tournament in Japan 1981 and to finish narrowly second to Sweden in the first women's Euros in 1982–4. After Carol's retirement from international football, Debbie Bampton took over for the remainder of the 1980s. Gill Coultard then swapped the captaincy with Bampton, first receiving the armband in 1991.

The controversy over the television programme, *I Lost My Heart to the Belles*, meant that Coultard gained, then lost, then regained the captaincy as the first England appearance at a Women's World Cup approached in 1995. In 1996 Atlanta hosted the first Olympic women's football tournament, and though this expanded the number of international opportunities at the highest level, it would take until 2012 for the Great Britain women's team to be constituted. Coultard went on to become the first woman to reach 100 caps for England, the first amateur to win so many caps, with a final total of 119, and only the fifth English person to do so behind Billy Wright, Bobby Moore, Bobby Charlton and Peter Shilton. To cover this period of time in some depth, each woman was interviewed about how she began to play football, some of the key events in which she was involved, the feelings associated with captaining her country, and how she approached that honour.

Sheila Parker, 1972

The first England game, against Scotland at Ravenscraig Stadium in Greenock on 18 November 1972, resulted in a 3–2 victory. The referee, J. Clelland of Glasgow, officiated a tight and exciting game. The welcome was warm for 'the auld enemy', but conditions were icy and bitterly cold. Sylvia Gore, who had previously played for Manchester Corinthians, and then joined Fodens, opened the scoring for England. Scotland equalised through Mary Carr, and then went ahead with an impressive Rose Reilly goal direct from a corner kick. Two late England goals from Pat Davies eventually won the match. It was to be the only England international in 1972. This was an impressive debut as the Scotland team, managed by Robert Stewart, was strong: It included Janie Houghton in goal, defenders Jean and June Hunter, Linda Kidd and Marian Mount. Captained by Margaret McAulay, the midfield also showcased the outstanding talents of Sandra Walker, Rose Reilly and Edna Neillis, with strikers Mary Anderson and Mary Carr. The substitutes for Scotland were Angela Creamer, Mary Davenport, Linda Cooper, Diane McClaren and Irene Morrison.

Reilly, just seventeen, and a player for Westhorn United of Ayrshire, would go on to a professional career in Italy, and an unofficial World Cup title as captain of the Italian national side. She remembered: 'I was just a kid, basically. It was baltic, it was freezing.' Captain McAulay, also a Westhorn player, would go on to win twenty-three caps for Scotland, but she pulled a ligament so was substituted in the second half. She later became a referee, was the first woman to be

Programme from first England v Scotland game, Ravenscraig, Greenock, 18 November 1972.

officially awarded an SFA certificate in Lanarkshire, and amongst the first in Scotland. Elsie Cook, the first secretary of the Scottish Women's Football Association, sewed the badges – which she paid for with an instalment loan – on to the shirts.

The England team had little better financial preparation, and resources were just as sparse. Managed by Eric Worthington, players included Southampton's Sue Buckett in goal, and a strong defence in Morag Kirkland, Sandra Graham and Janet Bagguley. The midfield included Captain Sheila Parker, Paddy Mc'Groarty, Lynda Hale, Sylvia Gore and Pat Davies. The strikers were Jeannie Allot and another Manchester Corinthian Jean Wilson. The bench indicated strength in depth and included Wendy Owen, Julia Manning, Eileen Foreman and Susan Whyatt.

Sheila Parker remembered:

I signed for Dick, Kerr's in 1960, aged thirteen, and later made my debut on 10 June 1961 against Oldham, who we beat 6–2 at Cleveleys. I so enjoyed playing the game and played wherever I was asked, except in goal. I just loved it so much, playing at the local 'rec' at Chorley and picking up bits from the men, like how to slide tackle. In 1963 I signed for Foden's of Sandbach, Cheshire, and played alongside some greats including Sylvia Gore. Most often, I played in midfield or defence, but I didn't mind where, I just preferred to be playing. By 1969 the Women's Football Association (WFA) had formed in England and Foden Ladies won the English Knock Out Competition final against Westhorn United of Scotland, a sort of Scotland v England before full internationals. As captain of Fodens, I was part of the team that beat the up-and-coming Southampton side, which had several players who would later become full England internationals, 5–1.

Another career highlight was in 1970 when the North West Women's League was formed comprising eight teams. In 1972 I captained the first ever WFA England side in a 3–2 win over Scotland, with Sylvia Gore scoring the first goal. I was made captain by manger Eric Worthington the night before the match. I was already married and returning to football after the birth of my son. I went on to play under four England managers: Eric Worthington, John Adams, Tommy Tranter, and Martin Reagan. All through

1973 England remained unbeaten in five matches that I was captain. As England team players we travelled to several overseas countries, which in those days was a marvellous honour, as we were all so down to earth and loved playing the sport. In 1974 I also won a WFA cup medal with Fodens in the 2–1 win over Southampton; a hard fought game.

There seems to be some confusion as to whether Hale or Allot or Davies scored the remaining two goals in 1972, and there are notes on programmes to that effect. In fact, there was just one England international in 1972, four in 1973, three in 1974 and three in 1975. So opportunities to represent at the highest international level were sparse. Little wonder, then, that Sheila's obvious pride in captaining her country also led her to rely on club football and domestic honours for most of her distinctive achievements. Even so, it took ten games for England to be defeated: Sweden were the team to inflict a 2–0 home victory in Gothenburg on 15 June 1975.

The interview with Sheila continues:

I signed for Preston North End Ladies FC in 1975 scoring fifty-one goals in fourteen games and helping them to the Division One Championship. 1976 was another career highlight as England won the first ever home international championships, and Preston North End retained the League Championship, in which I scored forty-two goals. In 1977 I won a third Division One Championship medal with PNE and we did the double in the first ever League Cup final. A great year since I also scored the only goal against Italy at Wimbledon to win that international. A header, if I remember rightly. I was so happy and proud!

In May 1976 the manager Tommy Tranter had asked Carol Thomas to take on the captaincy, which she held thereafter. However, Sheila's England career was far from over. By the end of 1977 England women had played Scotland, France, Northern Ireland, the Netherlands, Wales, Switzerland, Sweden, and Italy, with their first game against Ireland in May 1978. The Ireland fixture marked England's twenty-third official international match, and was on this occasion sponsored by Pony Wine, with the match ball donated by Mitre.

Snapshot of Sheila Parker in her trademark cap with badges from her travels with England.

Sheila was to go on to score important goals for England, including coming off the bench to score against Switzerland in Sorrento during an international tournament organised by the Italians. The 1979 tour seems to have been the most sustained and well organised by the WFA up to that point. It also seems to have been an extremely social affair. The touring team was managed by Cleveland Spartans manager John Simms, as Peter Warburton could not travel due to commitments with Altrincham. Dorothy Carr acted as interpreter and the team stayed at the Britannique Hotel, after refusing to lodge at a hostel. They used the San Germano Hotel swimming pool; both Pat Chapman and Linda Curl had birthdays and there were parties around the pool. John and Jenny Bruton came out to support the team. Flo Bilton helped with arrangements, as did Jane Talbot. England beat Finland 3–1 in their first match on 19 July 1979, then beat Switzerland 2–0 on 23 July. They lost four days later 3–1 to Italy in Naples, with Curl scoring a birthday consolation goal, and drew 0–0 with Sweden two days later in Scafati.

Sheila Parker remembered her continuing England and club career:

My club and England career continued, winning in 1978 a League Cup winner's medal and part of the newly formed North West Regional Squad. Again in 1979, Preston won the League Cup and the League Championship, a double double for the club. In 1980 PNE won the Championship, and League Cup, narrowly missing out on the treble of the WFA Cup by finishing runners up to St Helens. I was voted Player of the Match though. We played a really attacking style of football: five forwards, full-backs who could get forward, a playmaker centre half, and attacking midfielders.

The next year was one of mixed emotions. After thirty-three games for England I retired from the squad on 22 May 1983 when we had a 2–0 win over Scotland in the UEFA Cup qualifier at Elland Road. I was voted Division Two Player of the season after signing as a player for my home team, Chorley Ladies FC, and then becoming manager in 1984. In 1988 I received a loyalty award from the North West Women's League. But I couldn't leave it there. In 1989 I signed for Second Division Wigan Ladies FC, winning a Championship medal and intermediate cup finalist medal in 1990. I captained Wigan in the restructured North West Women's League to a second championship and promotion to Division One. Thirty-four years on, aged forty-six, I decided to retire from football, playing my final years for Clitheroe Ladies FC.

In concluding this case study on Sheila Parker, this personal testimony illustrates a common pattern that would follow through the other interviews, and three key themes emerge. Firstly, football was a lifelong passion that players pursued when it cost them financially, emotionally, socially and in terms of family life. Secondly, we can see that, although not overtly political in their views, there was a strong practical feminism in Sheila's actions. The extremely makeshift nature of women's football at the time meant playing on the worst pitches possible at the least convenient times, and with the most basic and uncomfortable facilities and limited resources, be these changing rooms, transport, hygiene or playing kit. The discomfort of the activity was integral to its culture for women players. Thirdly, the idea that there was any concession to 'feminine' styles of play, or stereotypically female conventions of comfort and decoration, or a preference for the social aspects of the game over the competitive requires serious reconsideration. Conversely, something about the extreme nature

The first official England women's national team, captained by Sheila Parker in 1972. Front row L to R: Jeannie Allott, Janet Bagguley, Sue Buckett, Pat Davies, Eileen Foreman, Sylvia Gore, Sandra Graham. Back row L to R: Linda Hale, Morag Kirkland, Julia Manning, Paddy McGroarty, Wendy Owen, Jean Wilson, Susan Whyatt and Sheila Parker standing next to manager Eric Worthington.

of the privations of women's football, at a personal and collective level, engendered a real solidarity and camaraderie, which meant players often felt obliged to ensure that future generations did not have to suffer the same privations. This was as much the case for the next England captain, Carol Thomas, as for Sheila Parker, and remains an important theme even today.

As Sheila herself says of her post-competitive career in football:

Refereeing helped to fill the gap that football left in my life and I became a Class 2 referee in the Saturday Alliance League, and Sunday League in Chorley. Football was the centre of my life still. I kept fit by jogging and training on the rec. By the time of my National Football Hall of Fame notification in 2013, I had finished playing for quite a few years. I was inducted alongside great male and female players, from Lily Parr onwards to Matthew Le Tissier, Cliff Jones, Jack Taylor, Eddie Gray, David Clarke, and Mike Somerbee. This was the best honour, and one that will last forever.

Carol Thomas

Born in 1955, Carol McCune (née Thomas) was part of a sport-loving family, along with her two brothers, and her dad, Percy, in particular, playing football in Hull. The inimitable and indomitable Flo Bilton ran a women's team nearby, called Reckitts and Coleman, one of several women's works football teams in the region, including British Oil and Cocoa Mills (BOCM). At eleven, inspired by England's World Cup win, Carol took her football more seriously and joined the women's team, BOCM, just as pioneering leaders Flo Bilton and Pat Gregory were forming the Women's Football Association (WFA). Flo had played as a goalkeeper for Reckitts since the 1940s, and developed women's football around Hull.

A move to Hull Brewery Ladies followed, and saw her regional selection for Hull and District Representative team, and a call up to the North of England squad. As well as Tottenham Hotspur women, Carol also played for Preston Rangers in Lancashire, CP Doncaster Rangers, and Rowntrees (York), an indication of how far players had to travel to maintain fitness at the highest level. Carol played until 1985, when she retired to have her children. Before then she had the good fortune of Hull City allowing her to train with the male Under 19s on Tuesdays and Thursdays to keep her skills and fitness sharp. As a valued Northern Dairies employee, her employer was also supportive.

Carol went to her first England trials, and in August 1974 successfully completed the first ever women's coaching course at Lilleshall, working with England manager Tommy Tranter. Tranter invited Carol for England trials and she won her first cap on 7 November 1974, when she came on as a substitute, at Wimbledon, playing against France, aged nineteen. Carol summarises her feelings: 'It was absolutely amazing just to get the letter telling me I had been selected. Then to go to England training at Crystal Palace, to pull on the shirt and sit in the dugout made me so proud, so when I actually got onto the pitch, it was my footballing dream.'

In 1974 Moët and Chandon supplied the winners – England, by two goals to nil – a magnum of champagne by way of celebration and the squad who shared the celebration that day against France was: 1. Sue Buckett; 2. Maggie Miks; 3. Maggie Kirkland; 4. Wendy Owen; 5. Sheila Parker (C); 6. Janet Bagguely; 7. Sandra Choat (debut cap); 8. Pat Firth;

ENGLAND

Colours: White, Navy Shorts, White Stockings

BUCKETT

KIRKLAND   GRAHAM

                                              M'GROARTY
BAGGULEY   PARKER
                  (Capt.)

HALE   GORE   DAVIES   ALLOTT   WILSON

Substitutes: Owen, Manning, Foreman, Whyatt

Even before the formation of the Women's Football Association in 1969 the aim of the organisers was to promote women's football at International level. We now see the realisation of this aim with today's game. The England squad were selected from regional competitions and final trials, and at a training weekend the present squad were selected.   ERIC WORTHINGTON, England Manager.

ENGLISH TEAM

SHEILA PARKER (24), Centre Half and Captain from Fodens L.F.C. Housewife with young son.

JEANNIE ALLOTT (16). This blond striker also stars with Fodens and is a brilliant opportunist.

JANET BAGGULEY (17). From Buxton and plays for Macclesfield L.F.C.

SUE BUCKETT (28). Southampton keeper for five years. Toured America two years ago. One of the most experienced keepers in the game in England.

PAT (Thunder) DAVIES (17). Also from the crack Southampton team and earned her nickname for her shooting power.

EILEEN FOREMAN (18). A prolific goal scorer from Warminster in the West Country.

SYLVIA GORE (28). The most experienced player in the side, with 14 years of football behind her; a crafty inside forward from Fodens L.F.C.

SANDRA GRAHAM (28). A hard-tackling left back who lives and plays in Blackpool.

LYNDA HALE (18). Also with Southampton L.F.C., a strong and determined Outside Right.

MORAG KIRKLAND (15), youngest of the side and the fourth member from Southampton L.F.C.

JULIA MANNING (21), lives and plays in Lowestoft. Also plays representative Hockey.

PADDY M'GROARTY (25). Cousin of Pat Crerand, English born, but lived for many years in Scotland. Reckoned to be the George Best of Ladies' Football.

WENDY OWEN (18). "The Joker" in the pack, but takes her football seriously, presently a student.

SUSAN WHYATT (16), from Macclesfield and is reserve keeper.

JEAN WILSON (23), from Manchester Corinthians, and a bank clerk.

ERIC WORTHINGTON, Manager. F.A. coach, Senior Lecturer at Loughborough College. Is former professional player and is responsible for team selection.

Programme notes on the players in the first official England women's national team, captained by Sheila Parker in 1972.

9. Pat Davies; 10. Sue Lopez; 11. Jeannie Allott; substitutes 12. Elizabeth Deighan (debut); 13. Carol McCune (debut); 14. Lorraine Dobb and 15. Annette Matthews (debut). Davies and Lopez were the goalscorers in the second game against France: the first had been on 22 April 1973, a 3–0 victory to England with two goals from Pat Davies and one from substitute Eileen Foreman.

How did it feel to be awarded the England captaincy just weeks before her twenty-first birthday? Carol replied: 'I could read a game and see what people were going to do, even before they did it, or perhaps knew they were going to do it. But also I was a good trainer. I worked hard, and I listened to what the coaches were saying, trying always to improve my game. I was a calming influence and I tried to lead by example.'

On 31 October 1978 Thomas became the first captain to lead out an official England women's side to play on a Football League First Division ground at The Dell, home of Southampton FC. Sponsored by Martini & Rosso, who had long supported women's football, and in front of a crowd of 5,471, England beat Belgium 3–0, with Thomas providing the cross for Elaine Badrock to open the scoring for the home nation, followed shortly after by her second. A Belgium own goal completed a satisfactory occasion for the England squad, which was: goalkeeper Sue Buckett, who had twenty-two previous caps according to programme notes; defenders Carol McCune, seventeen caps, Maggie Pearce, nineteen caps, Lorraine Dobs thirteen caps and Linda Coffin twelve caps; midfielders Linda Curl, five caps, Elaine Badrock, twelve caps, Sheila Parker, eighteen caps and Eileen Foreman nine caps; the strikers were Sue Lopez, sixteen caps and Pat Chapman, eight caps. The substitutes showed strength in depth with Liz Deighan having eleven previous caps, Alison Leatherbarrow, fourteen caps, a young Debbie Bampton one cap, while Theresa Wiseman and Julie Brown were yet to debut under manager Tommy Tranter. Carol maintained her captaincy when Martin Reagan took over as England manager from 1979 to 1990 and stayed in charge for ninety-six matches.

Fifty England caps followed at a time when there were very few England women's matches (six in 1976, five in 1977, and three in 1978). It was an amazing achievement by an amateur player, before her international retirement in 1985. Carol married her husband in 1979, and flew out later that weekend to Italy for a fortnight with the England team to play in a tournament, which was her version of a honeymoon. In the penultimate match, against Italy in Naples which England lost 3–1, the players threw the fully clothed referee into the hotel pool afterwards in protest at his poor decision making.

Thomas was even more pioneering as the captain of an England women's team to visit Japan in 1981, well before England men had made the same trip. She recalls the trip in vivid detail from the build up to the event itself:

For some years discussions had been held about a World Cup for Women. Whilst I didn't know what was being discussed, it had already assumed an unofficial name Mundialito or 'Little World Cup' without a ball being kicked. Of course, every international woman player of every nation wished for it and it was not until early 1981 that rumours started to circulate that we (England) were to be invited to a Football Festival that would include teams from around the world. What's more, the Japanese had made a suggestion ahead of Italy, as part of the 1981 Kobe Portopia Festival.

By June 1981 I had become an England regular, with twenty-eight consecutive caps to my name (twenty-three as captain) and having led England into two previous tournaments (the Home Internationals in 1975 and the 1979 Unofficial European Cup). Whilst many would assume my position was secure, as every international player will tell you, we never take anything for granted. The lead up to each and every international match had its dread, but given the era and location, this was dread on steroids! Had I done enough over recent internationals to warrant selection? Had I performed consistently over the league programme to warrant selection? Had I done enough in the regional trials competition? Would I be picked for the squad? Would I play in the tournament? Add to this the new England manager, Martin Reagan, who had been appointed in late 1979, had only five internationals in charge. In effect all the established players were still trying to prove themselves to him and justify their inclusion in his squads, whilst he was openly lauding the skills and potential of the youngsters starting to emerge around the country. Indeed this tournament would see Martin experiment with his selections, players and formations, as well as introducing new and unique styles of play.

A couple of days after my birthday I received my selection letter. Phew! I had been selected and Martin confirmed to me that I would be captain for the tour, but he did say that he had every intention of using every player on the trip during the tournament. That meant every player could expect to be substituted or be a substitute over the ten days away, without exception! (Ouch – he wasn't a Tank Commander during WW2 for nothing!) But this was a reasonable approach given the unique experience this trip would give to the girls. To most of us it would be a once in a lifetime opportunity.

This trip has to be put in context. In the modern era it is easy to dismiss a trip to Japan as just another holiday destination. Back in 1981 the world was not only a different place but a much bigger place. Japan was a place that only existed in films. In 1981 a girl from a northern backwater could only dream of visiting there. To me it was not just another country or another world, it was another planet! The six-month-long Portopia Festival had been established to celebrate the completion of the construction of a new town on reclaimed land in Kobe, Japan.

For the first time as a squad, we agreed an official uniform for the trip should be worn; a skirt, blouse, and blazer. Of course, this was an expense that would have to be met by the players, but it helped establish a feeling of professional pride. Also, as a squad, we had agreed to attend two training weekends in the lead up to the festival. As all the squad members will tell you, Martin was an absolute stickler for fitness. Fail to meet the expected standards and he became ruthless; your England days were numbered despite our amateur status!

Carol Thomas, the first woman to 50 caps, captaining her country against Sweden in the second leg of the finals for the inaugural Women's European Championship in 1984 at Luton Town.

The first training session would be held in Richmond upon Thames on the weekend of 1–2 August, where we had coaching sessions each morning/early afternoon and then played a match against a South of England Representative side each afternoon. The second was held in Leicester on 22–23 August, again with a similar format, coaching followed by matches against a Midlands Representative side two days running. Then back to work the following day on the Monday morning. However, the sting in the tail was that due to the lack of available finances at the WFA, a lack of sponsorship, and disinterest from the FA, we had the pressure of self-funding these two training weekends as well. Given the financial situation of many of the girls, this was turning out to be a considerable cash liability and was a real ask of individuals. Couple that with the fact that, in footballing terms, this meant no real 'close season'. Players were asked to keep training as best they could after the season, throughout June, July and August, to maintain our fitness to play the tournament. We would then return home and go straight into the domestic season!

In addition, many of the girls had to forego family holidays, and, given it was a ten-day trip to the other side of the world, possibly beg their employers for extra time off work. It became a significant sacrifice for each and every one of us. Back home the news in the press started to relay the significance of the trip to the women's game, although these tended to be restricted to the more local and regional papers and not the large nationals. Of course, TV displayed its usual distinct lack of interest.

Before going on to examine more of Carol's experiences as captain, we must first examine why the Japanese came to host the Portopia tournament in 1981. This would be the first England women's national team tour outside of Europe, and so the link with Japan was not immediately obvious, although the Asian Ladies Football Association (ALFA), or Confederation (ALFC), was a leading international force in campaigning for more FIFA approved international matches and tournaments.

In a 2019 interview, Veronica Chan who became president of the ALFC, and whom Sepp Blatter later called the 'Mother of Women's Football', gave the reasons for her enthusiasm as rooted in a childhood love of the game: 'My five brothers and their friends played and I wanted to be part of their group. So I would be the goalkeeper. I loved being keeper and I played this position growing up. My football heroes were Pele, Maradona and George Best.'

So why were England, along with Denmark and Italy, invited as the leading European teams at the time? David Hanley, who has written a history of women's football in Japan, gave a brief overview in our interview:

The organisation of women's football in Japan developed significantly in the 1960s and 1970s. Leagues were run on a local or regional basis, and an unofficial annual national championship was first held in early 1976. In 1979 the Japan Football Association (JFA) began registering women's teams and their players, and it also established its own official championship.

While the JFA provided funding for women's activities, they left the day-to-day organisation of women's football to the newly founded Japan Women's Football Federation (JWFF), whose members had already been running the sport for some years. As a result, the JWFF was largely free to organise competitions as they saw fit, and until the 1981 season (which began in April), teams competing in the All Japan Championship and most regional leagues fielded only eight players. The ball used was smaller than the regular size, and the pitches were also smaller. The main reason for this situation was that most senior players were in their early teens, and playing for ninety minutes on full-sized pitches would have been too much to ask of them.

Aside from domestic football, the JWFF also endeavoured to organise a national team. Although women had played football in east and southeast Asia since the early twentieth century, the sustained organisation of competitions (especially international matches) did not develop until the 1960s. In 1961, Tunku Abdul Rahman, the prime minister of Malaya (and after the forming of Malaysia in 1963, its first prime minister) decided to arrange women's matches to raise funds for charity. The matches were a great success, and Tunku encouraged the founding of teams across the country. His wife, Tun Sharifah Rodziah, thereafter took responsibility for developing

The England Women's Team arrive in Japan in 1981.

women's football, and in 1965 she led a representative team to Hong Kong, where they would play the first international matches in Asia.

To prepare a side for the event, the Hong Kong FA approached Veronica Chan, a businesswoman involved in men's football with her husband, to organise a women's team. The better-prepared Malaysian side won all three matches, but the more important outcome was that Veronica Chan became wholly devoted to the promotion of women's football: over the coming decades she would spend enormous sums of her own money to ensure the sport's growth.

In 1968 the Asian Ladies Football Confederation was founded, with Sharifah Rodziah as president and Veronica Chan acting as one of three vice-presidents. Little progress was made until 1974, when Chan became president (Sharifah Rodziah became honorary president) and a number of new members joined, bringing the total to eight: Hong Kong, Malaysia, Singapore, Taiwan, Australia (actually just New South Wales), Indonesia, Thailand, and New Zealand. Six of the eight members met in Hong Kong for the first Asian Cup Women's Football Championship (Indonesia and Taiwan did not) in August 1975. The winners, who never again took part, were New Zealand.

The ALFC thereafter held their Asian Cup tournament at roughly two-year intervals, though not without difficulties. Neither FIFA nor the Asian Football Confederation would incorporate the organisation, and both sought to disrupt its activities. An additional problem, which would take some years to resolve, was that many countries, including Japan, did not maintain formal relations with Taiwan.

Prior to the founding of the JWFF in 1979, the JFA had not endeavoured to form a national side, though they did give Tokyo's FC Jinnan, the first club team founded in Japan (in 1972) permission to take part in the Asian Cup in 1977. The players, who wore the national flag on their sleeves rather than on their chests, were beaten by both Taiwan and Indonesia, but they were most appreciative of the chance to travel overseas, to meet fellow players from elsewhere in Asia, and to gain an appreciation of the wider world.

No Japanese team travelled to the third Asian Cup, but by the time of the fourth tournament, held in June 1981, the JWFF was ready to send an official team for the first time. The trip was not without its issues – the JFA refused to provide any financial backing, and only through a combination of funding from overseas foundations, sponsors, and the players themselves, was participation possible at all. Japan's entry onto the international stage prompted a change in domestic football, as eleven-a-side matches on full-sized pitches became the norm. Not everything changed – the players still used a smaller-than-standard ball, and matches were far from ninety minutes in length – but these deviations from standard football would also disappear over the coming years.

The Japanese were disappointed with their performances at 1981's Asian Cup, with just one win over Indonesia providing some cheer. They lost to the two eventual finalists, Taiwan and Thailand. What most concerned the players and coaches was that the Japanese players were not only technically inferior to the neighbours, but also physically inferior, and players from farther afield were hardly likely to be any smaller or weaker.

Having entered international competition, the JWFF's next mission was the successful hosting of an international tournament in Japan, and the first chance to do so would come in September of that same year. However, the suggestion that the country should host such as tournament had first been made in January 1980, when three influential journalists had discussed the possibility of inviting overseas teams in a leading football magazine. One of the journalists involved was Kagawa Hiroshi, a proud native of Kobe City in Hyōgo Prefecture, and he insisted that 1981's Portopia Exposition, an event to celebrate the construction of the world's largest artificial island, would provide an ideal backdrop for such an occasion.

The chairman of Hyōgo Prefecture's football association, Takasago Yoshiyuki, travelled to England and watched the home side play out a 1–1 draw with Sweden in Leicester on 17 September 1980. He was impressed by the large number of spectators and by the use of standard FIFA rules. Takasago felt that it would be most desirable if the advances made by women in England and elsewhere in Europe could be emulated by the Japanese, and the JFA agreed. On 22 January they announced that England, Italy, and Denmark had accepted invitations to visit Japan.

The three European teams were certainly among the best in the world at this time. Denmark had won the unofficial European Championship in 1979, beating hosts Italy in the final match. England finished fourth, losing on penalties to Sweden in a play-off match for third place. Each team would play two games, and there was never any suggestion that it would be a round-robin tournament. The first matches would be held on 6 September in Kobe. Italy would play Denmark, and Japan would take on England. In Tokyo, on 9 September, Japan would play Italy, and Denmark would play England. The matches would be eighty minutes long, and they would use standard-sized balls and eleven players per side.

The Leicester match in 1980 inspired the organisation in Kobe, and the longstanding rivalry between Sweden and England provided a close, hard fought competition. Since a later chapter deals with the major tournaments of the 1970s, 1980s and 1990s, suffice to say here that England did not distinguish themselves on the pitch in Japan. Debbie Bampton, who had made her England debut in 1978 as a sixteen-year-old, went to Japan as a development player, and remembered: 'When we used to go abroad, to Japan and so on in the eighties, Flo Bilton and Pat Gregory used to come, and so did June Jaycocks and Linda Whitehead. Almost like chaperones,

England versus Sweden in 1984 with Deborah Bampton centre, front row.

but we had a good time all of us anyway. After all, we were amateurs and giving up our time for our country and the WFA never had any money.'

There is a range of voices and experiences to examine as part of being 'on tour' with England, and later chapters will describe these. But how did Carol Thomas remember England's results?

> The games themselves were played late in the evening to avoid the worst of the humidity in front of massive crowds. Our game on 6 September against Japan was played in front of 30,000 and was televised live across Japan. We won 4–0 with two goals from Angela Gallimore and one each from Vicky Johnson and Deborah Bampton. We then lost to Denmark through a second-half goal from Inger Pedersen. Our performances were not the best it has to be said. However, I always maintain that given the new introductions to the squad, a relatively new manager, the change in playing style, squad rotation and the humidity, I believe we did well. We finished third behind the eventual winners, Italy, and runners-up, Denmark. Sadly, it wasn't a true round robin tournament so we never got a chance to redeem ourselves against the mighty Italians after the Denmark loss.

In drawing this case study to a conclusion, perhaps Carol Thomas' finest international achievement, beyond her fifty caps, was almost winning the inaugural UEFA European Championships in 1984 as captain. This remains, at the time of writing, the highest the England women's national team has reached in a major tournament since FIFA, and then UEFA, officially recognised international women's football as coming under their remit. The first UEFA European competition for women's football, launched in 1982, culminated in a dramatic penalty shoot-out success, which ended 4–3 to Sweden, held at Luton Town FC. The pitch was atrocious, the match closely fought as each team tried to make history by winning, well before an official FIFA World Cup was organised in 1991.

The resonance of the Luton game was felt throughout Europe, with the creation of the first UEFA women's championship in the 1982 season, which led to the first official German Federal Republic versus Switzerland match, in Koblenz, which the home side won 5–1. However, there had previously been regional developments which heralded a strong showing from the Nordic countries and the outcome perhaps reflected their longer history. Sweden were traditionally well drilled as a team, and with a 2–0 victory in Gothenburg, had inflicted England's first ever defeat as a national side on 15 June 1975. It was England's tenth international match.

In the sixteen-team qualifying round in 1982, England were joined by Belgium, Denmark, Finland, France, Germany, Iceland, Italy, the Netherlands, Northern Ireland, Norway, Portugal, the Republic of Ireland, Scotland, Sweden, and Switzerland. Each of the four groups had four teams. Sweden led group 1 to meet the victors of group 3, Italy, in the semi-finals, while England, the winners of group 2, met Denmark, winners of group 4, in the second semi-final. Played over two games, one home and one away, Sweden defeated Italy 5–3 on aggregate to get to the final, with Carolina Morace's brace of goals for Italy seeing her second in the race to win the golden boot, behind Pia Sundhage for Sweden with four goals. Stars of unofficial women's World Cups, such as Italy's Elisabetta 'Betty' Vignotto, also joined the leading scorers board.

In their semi-final, England first defeated Denmark 2–1 in Crewe, followed by a 1–0 victory in Hjorring, to take the fixture 3–1 on aggregate. Unusually too, the final was played over two legs, first in Gothenberg, where the home side were victorious by a single goal scored by Pia Sundhage, and then, on the return in Luton England, where the home side returned the favour with a strike from policewoman Linda Curl.

Introducing The Dons

GRAHAM NEWNHAN
Second Team Manager

GARY RUMBOL
Coach

MALCOLM MAPES
Coach

DEBBIE BAMPTON
Dons Skipper

Bampton had an impressive career as a coach, and captained her club, as well as playing at the highest level internationally.

And so to the penalty shootout. Sweden goalkeeper Elisabeth 'Lappen' Leidinge kept the fourth England attempt out, and it was left to Pia Sundhage, whose international career had started in 1975 and would last until 1996, to seize her moment in history. Also victorious in winning the golden boot as well, Sundhage remembered: 'I took the last shot. We won the final. It was a marvellous success.'

Debbie Bampton, by then an integral member of the squad, recalls now that this second place is often overlooked in comparison with England's recent form in the twenty-first century: 'A great occasion that we are not always credited with, from that era was the European Cup Final in 1985 at Luton. Well, first it was a big achievement to beat Denmark over two legs to get into the final, then we held Sweden to a 1–0 lead in Gothenburg, then we equalized in the second leg at Luton, losing 4–3 on penalties. Pia Sundhage was some player!'

This is how Carol now sums up her career:

The year 1985 was significant for me. Just a year before I had played in a UEFA Final for National Representative Women's Teams (this was its formal title, it could not be simply called the European Nations Cup!) and now, one year on, I was winning my fiftieth cap. We played at Deepdale, the home of Preston North End, against Scotland. It was cold, the pitch was frozen, hard as a skating rink, with snow brushed off to behind the goals. In the current era the game would have been called due to safety issues. After a slow start we ran out 4–0 winners.

After the game, I was privileged to have Sir Tom Finney award me my cap. Wow! A living legend of the English men's game, and here he was presenting me with my fiftieth England cap. I had to pinch myself. It was only when I got home that I had time to start reflecting on what I'd achieved so far. England player at nineteen, England captain by twenty-one, and a leading player for an unbroken eleven years, first English woman to reach fifty caps, a European finalist and the prospect of leading England into another Mundialito (Little World Cup). Not bad for a girl from a footballing backwater! I also realised that my fiftieth cap as England captain was also within my reach. How that sounded, and what a driving force: the first English woman to captain England fifty times. My media appearances started to increase and I realised I had to promote our game. Short appearances in all the media, national and regional, were frequent. I like to think I gave our game its rightful exposure, albeit small written articles and timeslots, and given the attitude towards our game. The birth of my first son saw me make the decision to retire with fifty-six England caps to my name.

But it wasn't long before I returned to help create a local side. I carried on, with no thought of an international return, but just to enjoy myself and hopefully pass on some knowledge and experience. Eventually I was asked to captain the first East Riding County FA Women's squad when I was well into my forties. I eventually retired in 2009, aged fifty-four. The legs were 'going', actually; the bruising was taking longer to disappear. I had too many mountains to climb and two grandsons to help to nurture.

My involvement with our game has never really stopped. I have made several guest appearances at discussion groups, award ceremonies, and so on since my 'retirement', and my most recent involvement, in November 2019, has seen me being appointed as the first Club Ambassador and Lifetime Honorary Member to Hull City Ladies AFC, with the aim to 'spread the good word' about our game (and our club, of course). I hope I moved the women's game forward, if only by a fraction. Given the era, a fraction would equate to giant leaps compared to today's exposure.

Deborah Bampton

Deborah Bampton, who had travelled to Japan in 1981 as a relative international novice for England clearly benefitted from Martin Reagan's policy of introducing new players, even if, in her case, it was a 1–0 loss to the more experienced Danish team. Following a second successful *Mundialito* campaign in 1985 in Italy, which England won, Carol Thomas retired and Bampton was awarded the England captaincy. How did she begin to play football and what were her major influences?

Born in 1978, Bampton recalls:

I was the middle child of three daughters and my dad was football mad. My sisters played a little bit, and we all watched but my dad played for a men's team. From the age of five up to ten I played in the primary school playground. At secondary school I was not allowed to play, but I did all the sports available to me anyway. One head teacher had me in the office to tell me not to play football, and I wonder what she would have thought of my England career later? I

204   The History of Women's Football

used to have my football socks and my shorts under my other clothes and would play at break time, so although I was discouraged, it did not really make any difference.

I was the mascot for my dad's club for a while and then, when I was eleven (this would be the early Seventies), we discovered that there was a women's team nearby, and we hadn't heard of women or girls playing football before in a club, so I joined. I was a midfielder, and my team was in Maidstone in Kent, where I played for five years, becoming, you know, my own person. I was called up for England aged just sixteen, and made my debut against Holland away, which was quite daunting to be playing against full grown women when you are in your teens. But I loved the challenge. I kept playing at Maidstone, where my dad had become the manager. But you know how people can be and some people were saying: "Oh, you do alright because your dad is the manager," so I joined Lowestoft at about the age of twenty for a while. There was a semi-final for the WFA cup, Lowestoft versus Maidstone, but I missed my two clubs meeting because of a knee injury that was to plague my career later.

The WFA had a scheme where you could be sponsored for overseas opportunities, and I was offered to go to New Zealand when I was about twenty-one and I took the chance. But I had done my knee for the first time just before, so I went on crutches, and, well they butchered me really, operating on my knee and it wasn't right from then on. I was out for five months and, aged twenty-two, I missed about a year playing for England. I was made captain on my return by Martin Reagan.

In fact the England debut against the Netherlands, when Bampton came on as a substitute, showed again how international standards were improving in the late 1970s, because the home team won 3–1, with the England scorer, Pat Chapman, by then a very experienced player. Bampton has been to Japan, as we have seen, and was also integral to the 1984 European squad that lost so narrowly in Luton, scoring one of England's three successful penalties, along with Angela Gallimore and Kerry Davis. After winning a third place play-off against Belgium by 2–1 in the second *Mundialito* in Italy in August 1984, thanks to Linda Curl and Marieanne Spacey, England were again reminded that international standards were becoming increasingly competitive. West Germany were left to compete with Italy in the final. However, in the third *Mundialito*, also in Italy, in August 1985, a defeat 1–0 to Denmark was followed by a 1–1 draw with Italy and a 3–1 win over the USA, with goals from Linda Curl, Angela Gallimore and Marieanne Spacey. An exciting final against Italy saw England victorious thanks to a brace of goals from Spacey, and a third from midfielder Brenda Sempare, with Ida Golin scoring two for Italy. England also won the fifth and final *Mundialito* in 1988, again beating USA on the way and Italy 2–1 in the final, but could not always be so consistent in subsequent UEFA European competitions.

A civil servant and then a driver by profession, Debbie played her club football for Millwall Lionesses, and already had over thirty caps to her credit. Debbie was one of two players in the England squad from Millwall, along with Hope Powell, then a teenager. Her hobbies were weight-lifting, squash and badminton. This typified the amateurs of the England team at the time, as most held jobs that allowed them to train for football (although there were exceptions like animator Theresa Wiseman who would later move to Hollywood to pursue her profession). A typical England squad of the late 1980s would comprise: Theresa Wiseman in goal; in defence Sue Law (sport development officer), Loraine Hunt (bank clerk), Deb Bampton, and Jackie Sherrard (customer service representative); in midfield, Gill Coultard (ancillary worker), Brenda Sempare (postal worker), Joanne Broadhurst (leisure centre attendant) and Marieanne Spacey (recreation assistant). The prolific goalscorer Linda Curl was a police officer, while forward Kerry Davis was the only professional footballer, and, perhaps unsurprisingly, England's top scorer. As we have seen, however, professional status could be for extended periods or quite short-lived.

Debbie maintained her own fitness, as she reported:

I had another knee operation, aged twenty-seven, and then I played for England until the age of thirty-seven, mainly by keeping myself really fit. I used to train twice a day.

Another milestone was when we qualified in 1995 for the Women's World Cup in Sweden, and the likes of myself and Brenda Sempare could not have envisaged that we would be doing that when we started playing as little girls. It was really special to represent your country. I had a season at Trani with Kerry Davis and Rose Reilly, who had a sports shop, so she did really well. In all I played for my country for twenty-one years. I finished under the FA, and manager Ted

Copeland, and whereas we used to get a plaque of all our games under the WFA, I didn't get a memento. No "Thank you for your services" letter, nothing. Bearing in mind we were strictly amateurs, and had to keep ourselves in shape mostly, doing that until the age of thirty-seven was difficult but I loved football and I would have carried on.

I had strong opinions about out fitness and training more and I expressed these to Ted Copeland after we had lost to the US. When the US started playing we used to beat them, and we could beat them by a few goals. But they improved so much so fast and took it very seriously, training every day. I didn't play again after that for England, as it wasn't always welcome to have an opinion.

Then I moved on after my last game for England to Croydon as player-manager, then in the Bromley league managing Park. I had knee replacement surgery eight years ago. I was also fortunate to become the first woman player to be awarded an MBE, which I like to think of as a thank you to my mum and dad, for driving me all over all those years and supporting my interests. Even now, my dad is eighty-seven and still refereeing. If there is a game on I know we will be thinking the same thing over the tactics and so on.

In concluding this case study, it would seem that England's results vindicated Bampton's concerns. By 1990 the USA, who England had beaten previously several times, were now becoming a powerhouse of women's football, mainly thanks to Title IX, an educational equality act which stipulated parity of resources within US schools, colleges, and universities, including in sporting provision. Not only did England lose to rising European nations like Norway and West Germany in 1990, but also suffered a resounding 3–0 loss to the USA, and relative newcomers like USSR held England to a 1–1 draw the same year. Poor performances meant that England did not qualify for the first Women's World Cup in 1991, and Ted Copeland adopted increasingly dictatorial attitudes to his players during his spell as full-time manager.

It was in this precarious time of change, as the FA began to prepare to take over full control of women's football from the WFA in 1993, that Gill Coultard became England captain. That she would negotiate increasingly choppy waters into the 1990s to eventually win 119 England caps is testament not only to her professionalism and quality as a player, but her determination to play football at the highest level, whatever the political challenges. And the ordeals would be many.

Gill Coultard

Gill, born in 1963, started playing with her siblings – four brothers and four sisters – mainly on the green spaces outside her house. She would go on to become the first woman, and the first amateur, to win 100 caps in an era when the WFA, and then the FA, funded about four internationals annually. Most of her twenty-year England career took place before the first World Cup, in 1991, and the first Olympic women's football tournament, in 1996, after which internationals became more routine. Her achievement of 119 caps would stand until 2012 when Rachel Yankey, playing in the era of increased professionalism and more numerous internationals, won 120 caps.

In a road about a mile long, the green outside Gill's house would be the 'home' pitch, while those further down the street were designated as 'away.' Tournaments up and down the road included football, cricket, and a range of other sports. Gill's first proper club was the junior school team, and she had signed with the famous Doncaster Belles by the age of thirteen. At that time she also began to trial for England, attending 'North versus South', 'Possibles versus Probables' and several other training camps.

Her first England cap came in May 1981, when she came on as a sub in a 3–1 win over the Republic of Ireland, along with Angela Gallimore.

Gill Coultard, the first woman to 100 caps for England, and team captain.

This was not the only first. The flight to Ireland was the first time Gill had been on a plane, and the first time away from her family. The camaraderie of the England team more than made up for these life changes. Like Carol Thomas, Gill's first England cap was homemade at the hands of Flo Bilton and issued by the WFA (the FA did not yet want to take full control of women's football).

Gill's captaincy began in 1991 when Debbie Bampton, with whom she roomed as an England international, was injured. She describes the experience as 'surreal [...] to play football for your country, to play at Wembley, and to captain your country, you ask yourself, wow, is it really happening?'

But huge sacrifices were required on a personal level. Like many women at the time, Gill had to travel increasing distances to play at the highest level in order to keep her England place, including a five-year spell at Rowntree Ladies in York, and travelling to Castleford for club football. The usual format was twice a week club training, and personal fitness, on top of working five days a week on the production line at a Pioneer factory in Castleford, and sometimes weekends. Gill was one of the fortunate ones, as her employer allowed her to use paid leave for time off for internationals, valuing the fact that she was representing her country.

'We had eleven captains for England, every time we played,' Gill tells me, 'everyone was a captain.' Gill's style of play could be described as '110% committed': a box-to-box midfielder, robust in the tackle, a winner who disliked losing, and one who felt the responsibility to help others on the team as part of her leadership legacy. Gill couldn't remember her fiftieth cap, as no special celebration took place. Her hundredth cap came against Scotland, and in October 1997, before a 1999 World Cup qualifier against Holland at Upton Park, she was presented with a silver cap, and silver lion memento by Sir Geoff Hurst. Fifteen years later, the FA presented her with a gold cap, as it had done for men who reached the century milestone. The first woman, and first amateur to reach the distinction, Gill was also only the fifth person to reach the milestone of 100 caps for England after Bobby Moore, Billy Wright, Bobby Charlton and Peter Shilton. Considering how few games were played during her era, and that England did not qualify for a Women's World Cup until 1995, this is an incredible achievement, and one which deserves greater honour in public life.

Chapter 7

Professional Pioneers 1972–2022

Introduction

In many ways the history of the UK's women players is a globally pioneering one, and this has long been the case, although the college amateurs of the US and Canadian systems perhaps challenge this today. So who were those pioneers, and what forms of professionalism developed, and at what times? Football as a sport has often stood for modernity since its codification from 1863 onwards and the acceptance of professionalism in 1885. The Football League was established in 1888. In terms of professionalisation, the women's game began as a commercial enterprise in 1881 and there were amateur leagues, so the format was different to men's football. It is also often helpful to look outside the logic of sport, at the wider context of female patterns of employment. How have football's gendered labour-markets shaped opportunities for individual women, whatever their personal motivations for pursuing a career?

The chapter begins in the late 1960s and early 1970s when, as women's football was no longer banned, players could seek professional futures in the new leagues in Italy, in college soccer in the US and Canada, and the Scandinavian countries. We examine the careers of England's Sue Lopez and Dot Cassell of Southampton, as well as that of Scotland's Rose Reilly and England's Kerry Davis. Davis was one of the first mixed heritage players to put on an England shirt: her father is Jamaican and her mother white British. Both Reilly and Davis played professionally in Italy just as different forms of commercialism saw the leagues established, in the case of Reilly, and develop, in the case of Davis. Reilly would play abroad professionally from 1973 to 1995, and become an Italian citizen. Although consistently recorded in the England programmes of the time as a professional footballer, Kerry Davis played for four years in Italy from 1985 to 1989, in between spells with Crewe Alexandria.

The chapter then moves into the twenty-first century, looking at the period between 1999 and 2022, where more professionalism has been evident. The players we study here are England internationals Kelly Smith and Eniola Aluko, who both played in the US. Smith played initially as a student-athlete, before joining the new US professional leagues, and Aluko joined a professional US club after graduating in the UK. We examine their different England and club careers, looking not only at the role of gender but also race and ethnicity in shaping their experiences. The life chances of players like Eni Aluko reflect the wider lack of diversity in the England women's team in the twenty-first century, compared with the men's team, which is based on the professional academy system. The chapter therefore explores individual agency in shaping a professional career, compared with the structural forces at play.

The number of women who earn a full-time living wage entirely from their football playing career is in the hundreds, rather than the thousands. But professionalism can take many forms, and there are new opportunities. The ancillary occupations around the sport (coaching, sport development, public relations, media, administration, physiotherapy and sports psychology for instance) enable women to increasingly support themselves from related earnings.

As we have seen during 2020, football can be a precarious industry. Away from Europe's top five leagues, football is as varied, transient and short-lived an occupation for the many men and boys who work in it as it can be for women. It is important to note that sport, and particularly the economics of football, has changed considerably during the timeframe focussed on by this chapter. Labour migration in sport has gathered pace and spanned more widespread geographical areas for an increasing number of people. The clubs and leagues into which the women have migrated have also changed. The following explains some of those changes and some of the continuities.

Sue Lopez and Dot Cassell

Sue Lopez first began playing in the South Hants Ladies' Football Association League created in 1966 by women inspired by the 1966 World Cup victory. Each club affiliated for the equivalent today of 50p,

Rose Reilly.

players registration cost 35p and an WFA player affiliation fee was just 15p. Transfers of players between clubs cost 12p in administration. Family influence was important, as Sue tells me: 'I'd been a big football fan of English men's football since about the age of nine or ten when my grandfather would take me to some Saints matches. My Mum would buy me a football magazine to feed my love of the game, and she was a big fan, too.'

It is clear that Sue and her teammates had their eyes on European football as the Royex team, for whom she first played (an office team based on the Royal Exchange Assurance office in the town), had changed their name to Real FC in 1967–8. Following the Deal international tournament in 1967, a larger thirty-two team event the next year and fifty-two entries in 1969, Lopez became aware of more European sides: these included Start Praha and Slavia Kaplice from Czechoslovakia, and a side from Vienna. Cambuslang Hooverettes, the Scottish champions from Glasgow, also participated. In the 1970 Deal tournament Cambuslang lost to Southampton on penalties in the final to give Saints their first title. Combined with the Butlin's Cup, jointly organised by the holiday camp chain, ITV and the *Daily Mirror*, the Deal tournament provided some international rivalry at club level. As we have seen in previous chapters, there was no official WFA England team until 1972, but Sue first travelled to the FIEFF tournament in Italy in 1969.

Why was Italy so important? After the Second World War, the country would become an important centre for the revival of women's football, especially the professional leagues, with business and commercial sponsors. By 17 May 1968 nine Italian women's football teams had announced the formation of the *Federazione Italiana Calcio Femminile* (FICF) in Viareggio: it comprised Ambrosiana, Cagliari, Fiorentina, Genova, Lazio, Napoli, Milano, Piacenza and Roma, with Real Torino joining a year later. The *Federazione Femminile Italiana Gioco Calcio* (FFIGC) was established in Rome in 1970 with fourteen teams. Through the stories of Reilly and Davis, spanning the 1970s to the 1990s, we can see how players had to be entrepreneurs, as the professional structures were fragile, and negotiating them challenging. There were other players in Italy, such as Jan Lyons and Dot Cassell, who were not full professionals but had semi-professional and amateur careers, so comparisons enable us to see the different living and working conditions.

Sue Lopez told me:

In 1968 there were several active women's football teams in large cities such as Rome (Roma, Lazio), Florence, Turin, Milan, Naples, Genoa, Piacenza as well as Cagliari in Sardina. Next year there was a championship with ten teams, and a national game against the Czechs. So by the time of the Turin tournament in November 1969, women's football was being taken seriously in Italy, hence their national team was well provided for. By appearance and conduct on and off the pitch, the French and Danish also looked serious about the game, too.

The English team for the 1969 tournament had the bare basics. Harry Batt, manager of Chiltern Valley and a member of the WFA, who had received the invite to this tournament from FIEFF, brought a second-hand kit of red shirts, red socks and white shorts (most of us brought our own shorts!) We all wore our own tracksuits: some sewed on little Union Jack flags to give a sense of national pride! The Italians and French had quality looking national team replica kits and the Danish wore a 'professional' looking all-white strip. Most of them were from the Danish Femina club, who wore white, so maybe it was their kit. Harry and his wife had a first aid kit, but I can't vouch for their medical knowledge.

Food, accommodation and travel in Italy were very good. All was free of charge, including travel to Italy (by train). Training facilities were better than most of us experienced at home. Our match versus Denmark was played at Valle d' Aosta, near the accommodation we shared with the Danes. The Italy versus France match was at Novara, (in the vicinity of Turin). The final and third place play-off was at the outstanding Stadio Comunale in Turin attended by 10,000 spectators. In the final Italy beat Denmark 3–1, and we beat France 2–0 to take third place. I scored one of the goals, and captained the team again. This was by far the most professional atmosphere I'd played in. Even the Aosta local pitch was very good, but the Turino Stadio Comunale was at least similar to a good Championship or Division One ground in England.

Despite being a group of players from two or three clubs who hadn't played together before, England certainly performed in a competent manner, but by comparison we looked very much the 'poor relations'! Reflecting back on the *Corriere delo Sport* cuttings of the tournament, they illustrate how important women's football was to the Italians, way back then. There was serious, comprehensive coverage, with super photos.

We were accommodated with the Danes and as several spoke good English we found that they also had the basis of some organisation in their country. Their better players were looking to play professionally, and after the tournament two of the Danish team, including Maria Sevikova (who was in fact a Czech) stayed on with me in Turin to trial for Real Torino.

I was fêted by the organisers as one of the top players in the tournament, and was very happy to be guests of Real Torino for a few days, while our teams went straight home after the final games. I returned in March 1970 with Dot Cassel to play in a trial friendly game against Verdon (a Lausanne team) at the Stadio Communale again, and we won 10–0. I scored five goals. By this time the English and Italian national press was regularly reporting about my possible move to Italy.

This led Lopez to sign for Roma, and she suggested in our interview that Italy was the most important European country for the development of professional women's soccer at the beginning of the period.

Businessmen started a league in 1970 with nine, then ten teams, and in 1971 it grew to fourteen. In December 1972 it seems that this league merged with another to form a Serie A and Serie B League system. After I returned home to consider the move, Roma started phoning me and inviting me there, which of course I subsequently accepted. Torino had not been very specific about the deal, whereas Roma were very persuasive regarding accommodation, travel, and they were at the time quite a successful club.

My impression at the time was that Italy offered the opportunity to play competitive full-time football to a good standard in an organised national league at no cost to us. I felt respected by my manager, trainer and colleagues, and fans. I was absolutely amazed that the national sports paper *Corriere dello Sport* reported all our matches in a full, serious and respectful way. They had a dedicated sports reporter in Gianni Bezz. He was a charming man who treated us with great respect whenever we met him at matches: he attended most of them. And, of course, Italy was an attractive country in which to live. I never knew what kind of money was offered to players at Roma or elsewhere. I was very happy to be a full-time player.

For Roma, Medri and skipper and centre-back Lucia Gridelli were international players. The team played a passing game of football, and some had outstanding ball control. Probably another reason I liked it in Italy, though some of the Southampton teams I played in were very skilled, which is why there were always five or so of them in the national team! Our opponents in Italy also had some good international players, especially our main rivals, Piacenza, who won the league when I was there, and we came second. I scored in a crucial game against them but we lost 2–1. I think it was them that wanted to sign me, or Bergamo. It would have been interesting to have discovered how Italian players became so good.

I had accommodation within walking distance of Mira and Franco Bellei's apartment at Ostia Lido, a short train journey from the centre of Rome. I took my main meal of the day with the Bellei's and they arranged breakfast at a local café. I lodged in a one-room apartment. Monika Karner, an Austrian striker, lodged at the Bellei's, where she occasionally assisted them with certain off the field club duties.

At the end of the season, we had an all-expenses paid trip to Bangkok. Roma had been there before, too. We played at the Palasuka National Stadium after a men's match between two arch rivals, including the local champions. Our first match was against a local Under 18 Bangkok select boys' team. We lost 8–1 as the boys were fitter, and stronger than us! We played another game two days later against a less good boys' team but I can't remember the score! The price of tickets ranged from 15–30 baht (about £1–2). On arrival at Bangkok airport we were received by our local hosts, and each garlanded with flowers beside the plane, and inside the airport. Photos were taken by the local press and our visit and two matches were reported in the Bangkok Post. We stayed in a first class hotel, and were escorted on a tour of the city, temples and the floating market, and an official visit to a local children's hospital.

After returning to Rome I went home early in the New Year. At the time I was being lured away to one or two of the northern Italian teams for the new season (spring time), but I was also being told by

Back row left to right: Josie Clifford (Assistant Manager), Anita Dines, Sammi Wilson, Donna Smith, Louise Cooper, Alex Cottier, Tina Mapes, Caroline McGloin. **Front row left to right:** Columbine Saunders, Tara Proctor, Brenda Sempare, Hope Powell, Kerry Davis, Carole Osborne, Debbie Bampton (Player Manager)

Kerry Davis with her club side Croydon.

the WFA that players playing abroad wouldn't be considered for the impending first ever official England team, so I didn't return.

I realised playing in Italy that I was one of the best players, and, as a successful striker, valued and respected by everyone I encountered – unlike in England sometimes. There were absolutely no hassles and I loved the Italian way of life. It was a very difficult decision as I was patriotic and very keen to see the game develop here in England, and I believed it would develop more quickly than it did! Also, my colleagues at Southampton were keen for me to return as there was a upcoming national cup.

As we know, Lopez was a proud member of the first England team and went on to win several caps. But did she have any regrets in leaving Italy?

Women's football was still not being taken seriously in England and I can only say that my whole football experience in Italy was enjoyable and positive. By contrast, it was a constant battle in England to have the game recognised as a serious female sport, not dependent on players paying their own way for most things. Belatedly, I realised that the pleasure of playing in Italy was not to have all the distractions that players had to put up with here.

Despite an England team starting, there weren't any official tournaments like now. And the unofficial ones were soon banned. Also, the local and national political battles impacted on players. I guess if I'd known how slow it would be to develop in this country, and without the threat of a ban if I played abroad, I would have returned to Italy to maybe a bigger club in the north, learnt the language, and made a career there. But I wouldn't have played for England, presumably, nor had the thrill of winning eight FA Women's Cup Finals.'

In conclusion, we can see that Lopez was careful to play in Italy as an amateur, in the sense of not receiving a salary. Some players in the Italian leagues reportedly earned upwards of £40 a week at the time (about £450 in today's money). Lopez emphasised that she was paid only living and travelling expenses.

She played a leading role in the England team, along with goalkeeper Sue Buckett, Morag Kirkland, Sandra Graham, Janet Bagguely, Syliva

Gore, Sheila Parker, Paddy McGroarty, Wendy Own, Lynda Hale, Pat Davies and Jeannie Allott, Jean Wilson, Julia Manning, Eileen Foreman and Susan Whyatt. However, she retired in frustration from international football fairly soon after in 1979.

In spite of being only one of seven women to hold the highest A Licence coaching certificate, Lopez was overlooked for the England national team coach appointment in favour of a woman with no qualification at that level when Hope Powell was appointed in 1998. Instead, Lopez earned a living from her coaching, and continued as an academic and teacher of physical education, but has had to negotiate a career path that has seemingly always involved multiple roles in order to support herself. She told me:

> Since writing my book, *Women on the Ball*, I left my role as coaching and development officer for Hants FA, where I organised and delivered the FA licence course for the county, and, in 1998, ran the newly evolved post of Director of Saints Girls Centre of Excellence. In 2000 I joined Southampton FC full time as Head of Women's Football, running the Premier League women's team, reserve team, the academy, and the centre of excellence, before the whole women's programme was cut when the men's first team were relegated in 2005. During my time in that role twenty-seven girls were in the England Talent Identification group, several went on to represent England at various youth levels, and one became a full England player.
>
> I then became a part-time tutor of FA courses for Hants FA and local higher education establishments. I have received several honours since: the 1999 *Sunday Times* Sports Sportswoman of the Year; Coach of the Year; an MBE in 2000 for service to women's football; the third female inductee into the National Football Museum Hall of Fame in 2004; and, in 2006, an Honorary Doctorate from Southampton University for services to women's football.

Currently living with dementia, which she has said stems from repeatedly heading the ball in training sessions and games, Lopez has provided many other women and girls with opportunities as a leader and role model.

As we have seen, Sue was one of many British short-term migrants to the Italian leagues, but this does not mean that the move was any less important in their lives for being temporary. As Sue Lopez's teammate, Dot Cassell, told me in our interviews:

Born in 1953, I am from a family of three brothers and three sisters. Football was my life early on, but it was always with boys. I didn't play women's football until I was fourteen or fifteen. I was in the school team, as I was good enough and school could not *not* let me play, if you see what I mean.

I was one of five Southampton players picked to go over to Italy in 1969 with Harry Batt, including Barbara Birkett, Sue Buckett, Jill Long and Sue Lopez. We played the likes of Germany, the Netherlands, France and the Danish. The Italian teams were watching us, and Sue Lopez and I were invited to a charity match at Turin, at the Stadio Olympico Grande Torino, also home to professional club Juventus, alongside Maria Scevikcova, of Czechoslovakia and Birgit Nilsen of Denmark. We won 11–0 against a side from Switzerland, and I was called *Il Topolino*, little mouse, or Mickey Mouse, by the newspaper journalist Gianni Rivera.

I went to play in Italy after the unofficial European tournament in 1970. Harry Batt, who was running Featherstone ladies, took an unofficial England team that was made up with his players and some from Southampton, of which I was one. We played in the mini-tournament against Italy, France and Denmark. We came third after losing a close game 4–3 against Denmark. Surprisingly, Harry never sought players from Fodens or Corinthians to go and I am sure that if he had we would have fared much better.

In May 1971, after Southampton had won the inaugural WFA Cup competition, Sue Lopez left for Italy, having signed for Roma. In June, I signed for a second division league club called Trastevere, from the oldest part of Rome. The club was very professionally run and was supported by Lubium, a men's tailoring company, and run by Mr Troii who ran an insurance company. The sponsorship and marketing was key.

I moved to Trastevere on my eighteenth birthday. I was approaching my eighteenth birthday and had started a new job. My sister's twenty-first birthday was approaching and it was also to be her engagement party. My parents had bought me a bracelet, and we exchanged this for a suitcase. It was quite a move for me to make. I played for them from June 1971 to 1972.

I arrived not speaking Italian and was greeted by my new manager at the airport who did not speak English. Thankfully we were able to converse in French and we arrived at his house where I was greeted by his wife and two children. When we went inside I was presented with a birthday cake with eighteen candles and I knew at that point I was going to be okay in Italy.

From 1972 to '73, I played for a team called Lubium, also based in Rome. Several of our matches were played on gravel pitches. Sue Lopez was also in Rome at this time and playing for a team called Roma. I also enjoyed every moment of my time playing in Italy and became semi-fluent in Italian. I'm still able to speak it today almost forty-nine years later. I lived in a flat owned by the club. The Lubium goalkeeper, Theresa Catallari Ribenzo, was always over with her family. I do remember playing against Piacenza and having Luciana Meles, Tizziana Meles and Rosa Rocca in Lubium. They were all ex-Piacenza players. It became a second nationality really. I went back thirty years after leaving, and met Theresa's son.

I had two wonderful years there and returned to England after I had an accident on a moped. I served a year-long ban from the WFA for supposedly being a professional and then decided to join a club in Southampton and to get a job. I don't think Sue picked up the language. Jill Clements also came over for about six months, but went back and didn't return. She has since died of a brain tumour. Later Rose Reilly signed for Milan in 1973 and stayed.

Rose Reilly and Kerry Davis

Rose Reilly was born in 1955, in Stewarton, Ayrshire, into a large working-class Catholic family, and knew from an early age that she was physically gifted. However, things were slightly different in Scotland, Wales and Ireland than in England because each FA took a slightly different view of women's football. Although there had not been a full Scottish FA ban in 1921 to mirror the England case, the SFA did issue a ban in 1947, and only grudgingly lifted it in 1974, having been the lone vote against accepting women's football into the national associations in a

1971 UEFA motion to promote and integrate women's football. So this is the wider context to Rose Reilly's career, and, in large part explains why she had to play abroad, as much as wanting to play in Italy.

Having been given a doll at four, she swapped this for a football, and slept with it for a year. By cutting her hair short and calling herself Ross,

Women's Football is now better represented in museums and public spaces, such as this bronze statue in the National Football Museum, Zibo China.

Reilly was able to pass herself off in Stewarton boys' football teams before puberty. When a scout from Celtic expressed an interest in signing her, it was only being a girl that prevented the move. School did not want her to play. Rose said: 'They finally got exasperated with me and I got the belt, right across the back of my hands. The headmaster said to me, "You are never going to learn, are you?" I said, "Naw, it's youse that are never going to learn. I just want to play football, I'm doing nothing wrong." Back then sometimes I felt like I would be burnt at the stake for playing football.'

Continuing to play at secondary school level, Rose was eventually expelled and had to find work in a carpet factory, a job which she said she hated, but there were compensations. She daydreamed of playing professionally on the walk to work, and joined the men's team in nearby Howard's Park.

Rose was coached by both Kenny Philips and William Murphy. She was a natural athlete, a great all-rounder. Kenny always entered Rose for the boys' races, which she often won. At sixteen she was shortlisted to represent Scotland at the Commonwealth Games in the pentathlon. Her athletics career may have also been the source of her great speed, which in turn helped her football career, but having been told to give up football in favour of athletics, Rose chose football, much to her parent's confusion.

In women's football, Rose made her debut for Stewarton Thistle from the age of nine, having waited to join the team for two years. Stewarton reached the first WFA Mitre cup final in 1971, losing 4–1 to Southampton, but defeated them on the return fixture the following year to win the cup. Having been selected for Harry Batt's British Independent's team to go to Mexico in 1971, along with teammates Sofia MacDonald and Elsie Cook, the players were given an ultimatum that if they played in Mexico, Stewarton would fold as it was affiliated to the WFA. As we know, the WFA were fond of 'banning' players and clubs, and so Elsie, Sofia and Rose did not go, although they soon left to play their club football in Glasgow for Westhorn United, so perhaps they should have gone anyway!

By now Reilly had decided to move on from the athletics track and concentrate on her skills on the football field. She played with Stewarton Thistle Ladies and was part of the team that won the inaugural Scottish Cup in 1971. However, although part of the 1972 Scotland team that played England, this was regarded as a friendly by the SFA and her caps, ten in all, were awarded retrospectively years later. The last training session for the Scottish team before the fixture with England involved Elsie Cook flagging down a furniture van when the team coach broke down. Seated in armchairs and comfy sofas, the players laughed their way to training. This reflects how little support there was at the time. Reilly scored the second of Scotland's goals, direct from the corner, in a 3–2 defeat to England. However, Reilly's international fame would come not with Scotland but as captain of Italy.

Sponsored by *The Daily Record* newspaper and motivated by the signing by French club Reims of Irish midfielder Anne O'Brien, with whom she went on to win three French titles before moving to Italy, Rose Reilly and Edna Nellis went for trials to Reims, hoping to further their careers aged just seventeen. They were so good they were signed at half time. Reilly's subsequent list of achievements is incredible considering the obstacles faced by female footballers in the early 1970s.

In 1972 Reilly and Nellis won a French women's league title for Pierre Geoffroy's team, before moving to AC Milan in 1973. However, Nellis suffered from homesickness and returned to Glasgow. Determined to learn the language and stay, Reilly adapted. She played in front of crowds of up to 80,000 and would score the winning goal when Milan won the league in her first season with the team.

Although there was little communication with her family, there were reasons why a permanent return to Scotland would have been disappointing. Firstly, because the Italian national federation was not involved, the leagues were run by businessmen who raised large sponsorships and spent considerable sums on marketing and PR. Women's football was an unregulated market and so could take whatever form it chose. RAI TV and journalists made specific efforts to become knowledgeable. Moreover, Rose was enjoying a cosmopolitan lifestyle of nice restaurants, beauty treatments and professional football in the San Siro. Other players such as Nicole Mangas and Maura Fabbri had also made the move to Italy from France, and there was an international aspect to women's football culture.

Secondly, Reilly's personality suited the vivacious Italian street culture, and her teammates taught her Italian swear words as her first language lessons. Thirdly, this was the biggest league in women's football at the time, and the blonde Reilly was able to make a name for herself on and off the pitch. When one of the directors of Milan, Italo Ambrogio Qunitin, arranged an all-expenses trip home for Rose, concerned that she might be homesick, her mother got something of a surprise at how much her daughter had changed. Her twin sister Mary said, 'To me she was an Italian, she came back Italian.' To Italo Ambrogio Qunitin this trip was good value for money, as he considered her the number one foreign player in the country at the time, and she was soon made captain. This was the first distinction of many.

It should be remembered that Scotland had its first official women's national team in 1972, so representing her country provided very limited opportunities. After taking the Scottish team out to Italy to play against AC Milan at the San Siro, the manager Elsie Cook, and players Edna Nellis and Rose Reilly were all banned for life from the Scottish national side. There was never any explanation why. There was clearly an element of jealousy at their cosmopolitan lifestyle; a wish to prevent the players getting 'above' themselves.

It is also noticeable that Anne O'Brien, born in 1956, and just 5ft 4in tall, was a major pioneer for Irish women's football, but was never brought home to play for the national team, though did play once while home on leave in Dublin in 1990. She said, 'I was never looked for. The only time I went home was in 1990. When I was at home I played for the national team because I got onto the national team when I was young. I was fifteen. I played about four matches with the Irish team. Then when I went away, I never got the chance to play for Ireland anymore.' In spite of being a professional player in the world's highest profile league, her achievements in Italy were not matched by her international career, although this reflects more on the national association than the player.

In a career spanning eighteen years, O'Brien played initially for Rome side Lazio, then other clubs including Napoli and Reggiana, winning a large number of league and cup titles, until her retirement in 1994. As a number ten, O'Brien played behind the strikers as a *trequartista*, or three-quarters, an attacking midfielder in Italian. This was especially the case at Trani where she formed an impressive front three with Carolina Morace and Rose Reilly. Returning to Lazio, she also played alongside Pia Sundhage. Along with Spain's Conchi Sánchez and Suzanna Augustesen, O'Brien was considered one of the best foreigners to play women's football in Italy. She later managed Lazio and Civitavecchia clubs, and worked as a coach in the Italian Football Federation, settling in Rome, before her untimely death, aged just sixty, in 2016.

Rose Reilly delayed signing on for Lecce in the south of Italy, getting the getting the president to first agree to grow a grass pitch instead of the red ash that the club previously played on. The team at Lecce was built around her, and she was given considerable leeway. This included permission to play Reims in France the same weekend she won the title with Lecce in the Italian league, and promptly helped Reims win the French title as well. Her emigration had clearly been Scotland's loss, not Rose's.

After five years, moves were made for Rose to obtain Italian citizenship, including initial suggestions that she should marry. But she did not need to do so as Giovanni Trabucco gave her his backing as the President of *Federazione Calcio Femminile* (FCF), as the Italian League was now called. Legendary Italian players like Carolina Morace supported the move to bring Rose into the Italian national team, one of the strongest in women's football at the time.

However, despite the fame and comfortable living this gave her, there were also challenges, such as the inevitable injuries. Rose nearly died in 1980 after eating raw shellfish at a post-match meal, and was also affected by hepatitis. Winning the 1984 *Mundialito Femminile* with Italy cemented Reilly's reputation. She was captain in the final against West Germany, with an assist for the first goal, and scoring the second in a 3–1 win. At twenty-nine years of age, and after eleven years playing professional football in Italy, Reilly was also now a World Cup winner.

In October 1984 she was voted best player in the Italian team that beat the USA in China in the final of the Asian Ladies Football Association Xi'an tournament, scoring ten goals in five games. She captained Italy and scored one of the goals as the Azzurri defeated the USA in front of a 90,000 crowd at China's national stadium. She was said at the time to be the best, and most famous, women's footballer in the world. At the 1985 edition of the *Mundialito*, Reilly featured in Italy's 1–0 win over the United States, and so was well established before the future stars of the US women's national team.

As well as two French titles, Reilly won eight Serie A titles, four Italian cups and was twice Serie A Golden Boot winner – with forty-three and a record forty-five goals respectively – during her time in Italy. Rose was capped twenty-two times for Italy, thirteen of those as captain, well before official FIFA World Cups began in 1991.

Her full list of clubs was: Stewarton Boys and Stewarton Thistle women in Scotland, Reims in France, AC Milan, Catania, Lecce, Trani, Napoli, Florence and Bari, finally finishing with AFC Agliana in the 1994–95 season, aged forty. Having moved to Italy in her late teens, she learned the language and was integrated into the local culture, owning a sports shop, Reilly Sport, for a time in Trani, and regularly appearing on television. Rose stayed in Italy until the age of forty-five and married Norberto Peralta, the Argentine doctor who had initially treated her for an injury. A little over a year later she had her daughter, Meghan Valentina. The family were content to remain in Italy, where Rose lived in a penthouse flat, until returning to Scotland to nurse her frail, elderly mother following a stroke. Nine years later she remained a carer for her mother, as well as a mother with a young daughter. Rose was inducted into the Scottish Football Hall of Fame and the Sporting Hall of Fame, where she was piped in by bagpipes in Edinburgh in 2007. She became the first female recipient of a special PFA Scotland Merit Award in 2011. The only Scottish footballer to win a World Cup, Rose was awarded an MBE in the Queen's New Year's Honours list in 2020.

Kerry Davis was born in 1962 in the Sneyd Green area of Stoke-on-Trent, the youngest of three children, with an older brother and sister. When she was ten the family moved to the village of Harriseahead, north of Stoke, where her brother delivered milk to the family of Tina Birchall, who played for a women's team called Sandbach Ladies in Cheshire. As Kerry was just eleven years old, Tina considered her to be too young to join the women's team, but took her to training anyway. Kerry stayed until she was sixteen, when she joined Crewe, a better team, where she remained until she was twenty-three.

Debuting for England on 19 September 1982 against Northern Ireland, Davis scored two goals, and was soon an integral part of the squad. She was a large part of England's success in the inaugural UEFA Women's Euros, held over two years between 1982 and '84, scoring twelve goals in ten games. In the finals England lost narrowly to Sweden on penalties over a two-legged final, with the second game played at Luton Town in 1984. Davis was one of the three England players to score her penalty in the penalty shootout. Pia Sundhage scored Sweden's fourth penalty, thus securing victory.

Although she missed the 1984 *Mundialito* in Italy, where England finished third, Davis was a leading forward in the 1985 competition, also held in Italy, with an important goal against the hosts in the group stages, and playing in the final, which England won 3–2 against the same opponents. Winning the *Mundialito* was widely reported back in England and also in Italy. Again prompted by the signing of Irish midfielder Anne O'Brien, Davis signed for ROI Lazio for one season, along with fellow England striker Marieanne Spacey, who did not enjoy the experience and soon returned home. Davis moved to Trani for two seasons from 1986 to 1988, forming part of the strike force behind Carolina Morace and Rose Reilly, with Anne O'Brien having transferred to Lazio by then.

While the league could perhaps better be understood as semi-professional, with several of the Italian players travelling across the country on night trains to play on a Saturday after working, the foreign players, like Davis, did not work and played football full time. Accommodation was also provided, with four players sharing an apartment, and there was full backroom team to provide support for the players. At Lazio this included a coach, a manager, a goalkeeping coach, a doctor and a physiotherapist. The teams were all sponsored by businesses, either national or international names, like Despar, the Italian brand of the Spar convenience store chain, or local businesses, often fashion or clothing brands.

Davis was already well established in England before she went to Italy, but had to pay for her own flights to join her national team members. She also remembered in our interview that she was expected to make matches for which she was selected, otherwise there was a real chance that she would not be selected in future. Kerry remembered her final year in Italy with Napoli as hard work, and decided to return to the UK. She got a job in a factory, which she 'detested', and played her club football for Crewe, Knowsley, and Liverpool, ending her sixteen years with England in 1998, scoring forty-four goals in eighty-two appearances. It was not until Kelly Smith overtook her in 2012 that this record was beaten.

It is remarkable that Davis is not more celebrated. She played in the first Women's World Cup that England qualified for, hosted in 1995 by Sweden, and was an important player at a time when generally there were fewer international matches than there are now. Along with Hope Powell and Brenda Sempare, she was an important pioneer for Black and Minority Ethnic England internationals (Powell was the first BAME vice-captain, then head coach, of the England women's team, in 1998).

Kelly Smith and Eniola Aluko

In order to understand why an alternative to the professional Italian leagues developed in the late 1980s and early 1990s, we first have to understand why an educational law called Title IX and its legacy would impact on the rise of soccer in the US as a mainly middle-class female sport. We explore these issues thought the stories of Kelly Smith, and Eniola Aluko.

Kelly Smith, born in 1978 in Watford, went to the US in 1997 to enrol at Seton Hall, where she broke records, having previously played for Garston Boys Club, Pinner and Wembley, before joining Arsenal to win the Premier League title in the 1996–97 season. Smith won a student-athlete scholarship to Seton Hall, and played for Seton Hall Pirates from 1997 to 1999. After university, and playing professional club football for New Jersey Lady Stallions in the W-League, it looked as though Smith might stay in the US, as she then played three seasons in the Women's United Soccer Association (WUSA) League for the Philadelphia Charge. After returning to Arsenal for a four year period, which included a 2007 UEFA Women's Cup win, Smith returned to American professional soccer with the Boston Breakers in the Women's Professional Soccer (WPS) League. From 2012 to 2017 she returned to Arsenal for her third and final stint at the club.

Eniola Aluko, born in 1987 in Lagos, Nigeria, moved with her family to Birmingham at the age of six months. She grew up playing football with her brother, Sone Aluko, who would also go on to become a professional player. Aluko started her career at Leafield Athletic Ladies and signed for Birmingham City Ladies aged fourteen. She played for the senior team from 2001 to 2004, Charlton Athletic from 2004 to 2007, and Chelsea in 2007–2009. Although she is educated to Master's level, Aluko went to the US not as a student athlete – she had already obtained a law degree at Brunel University – but as a professional player for St. Louis Athletica in the WPS in late 2008. She was their top scorer in 2009, but the team ran into financial difficulties in 2010 and Aluko signed for Atlanta Beat. She was then traded to Sky Blue FC, and, at the end of the 2011 season, returned to Birmingham City, before moving to Chelsea in 2012. In 2018 she joined Juventus, where she ended her career as their top scorer, and retired early in 2020. To understand the new professional opportunities in the US for players born in the late 1970s and 1980s, we need to analyse the effects of Title IX.

On 23 June 1972 Title IX was signed into law as an educational gender equity programme, which mandated that equal resource should be a principle of the provision of educational resources. Perhaps unintentionally, this provided new impetus for physical education programmes, especially for girls and women, but also for some young men, by banning sex discrimination in all federally funded school programmes, including sports. High School and College sports programmes had been dominated until that point by large and expensive, although overtly amateur, male American football squads.

This obliged educational institutions to introduce sporting provision for young women that was perceived as less violent than American football, but which also had larger squads than the traditionally strong women's basketball and track and field programmes. Association football, or soccer, began to provide college scholarships for able female players, and was backed by high-profile athletes. In the media, tennis star Billy Jean King won her 'Battle of the Sexes' match against Bobby Riggs, two decades her senior, in 1973. This galvanized increased discussion of equality, combined with the first USA women's basketball Olympic gold medal in 1984, and the first women's Olympic marathon, won by Joan Benoit the same year. This inspired a whole generation of intelligent, college-educated female football players, who would go on to win the inaugural women's World Cup in 1991, led by Michelle Akers. (The was repeated in 1999 under the leadership of Mia Hamm).

April Heinrichs, captain of the US national team that won the first FIFA World Cup, and later coach of the US women's national team from 2000 to 2004, remembered the effect of Title IX Legislation on her career:

I was an early benefactor of Title IX Legislation. My high school had very good soccer and basketball teams, and I played both sports for four years. I was then offered a scholarship to play basketball at Colorado Mesa University in 1982–1983. I played one year while still hoping to be recruited for soccer at a top university. In 1983, I was offered a scholarship and played four seasons at the University of North Carolina. In short time, it was clear to me that I was training and competing against the best players in the country. When I heard there was national team try-out, I was full of confidence and made the US Women's National Team in 1985. In 1986, we played in the *Mundualito* in Jesolo, Italy. I was voted team captain for my first cap. Upon graduation, I returned to Italy and played professionally in the Italian First Division for Juventus in 1987 and FC Prato in 1988. After a few more years, it was clear I needed a full-time job. I was hired at the University of Maryland as head coach. We competed in the Atlantic Coast Conference in Division I NCAA college soccer and offered scholarships to our players in the early 1990s. As you can see, I benefitted from Title IX in literally every step in my career, for which I am eternally grateful and pinch myself even to this day.

Similarly, Megan Rapinoe, current co-captain of US Women's Soccer National Team, World Cup winner in 2015 and 2019, and Olympic gold medalist in 2012, also realised its effect.

Title IX gave me, and countless other women, the opportunity to chase our dreams and fully realize our potential. It's unfortunate that a law had to be passed to push for equality, but what our women's sports pioneers did with these opportunities, which have certainly been built on by the work and passion of several generations of wonderful female athletes, has been truly inspirational. There's still a lot more work to do in the USA, and especially around the world, but we're able to continue to push for more, in large part because of what Title IX started in 1972.

Another key feature to emphasise is how important collegiate soccer programmes can be in promoting the wider reputation of certain institutions in the US. By way of example, the University of North Carolina (UNC) at Chapel Hill began as a club team of students. The women players then asked to be recognised at varsity level for college honours and to play formally against other institutions. The team transitioned to varsity level, meaning that it was supported by the university, with coach Anson Dorrance, in the 1978–79 season.

The Association for Intercollegiate Athletics for Women (AIAW) followed this with a national women's soccer programme in 1981. Anson Dorrance began recruiting very strong individual personalities and very committed athletes, leading to a championship win in 1981 with twenty-six wins and no draws or losses. Having taken the initiative, Dorrance's motto became 'Let no one catch us'. Although this would be the last AIAW competition before The National Collegiate Athletic Association (NCAA) took over, the record of North Carolina remains intimidating. Dorrance would become a multiple winner of the NCAA national coach of the year, beginning in 1982. As well as April Heirnrichs, Mia Hamm, Cindy Parlow, Kristine Lilly, Crystal Dunn, Shannon Higgins, Tisha Venturini, Heather O'Reilly, Yael Averbuch, Carla Overbeck, and Lori Fair, there are sixty others from UNC who have become all-American first team players for the US Women's National Team. Little wonder then that by 2008 the UNC had invested $2.1 million in a new soccer centre.

To be in a position to move to the US, Kelly Smith had already had experience of club football at Arsenal, but her move was the result of chance rather than planning. Her autobiography *Kelly Smith: Footballer* details how she was spotted playing in the Watford Football Festival against an American side. The scouts wanted her to go to their college for a soccer scholarship.

At the time, playing for Arsenal, she was only training two evenings a week, and America represented the dream to become a professional player. But Smith found US College soccer a running game rather than a game of skill. She won both Newcomer of the Year and Player of the Year within twelve months, but social anxiety led to her drinking to excess. The relentless insistence on running resulted in anterior cruciate ligament damage, a meniscus damage and a broken leg. At the same time as this last, and most serious, injury, the Women's United Soccer Association, in which Smith had first played in 2000, had ceased to exist. Following the collapse of the league, Smith had chosen to play for the New Jersey Wildcats when the injury was sustained. On her return to England, she attended the Sporting Chance Clinic, and was able to resurrect her club and England career.

Smith was often injured. The number of stress fractures, including those to her feet, Achilles, and other health problems, reflected the lack of infrastructure around the England women's team, and in English women's club football. In comparison, the US college and professional programmes were well resourced. Had she been injured less often, Smith would undoubtedly have won more personal honours. Nevertheless, she finished third in the FIFA World Woman Player of the Year awards in 2009, fourth in 2007, and fifth in both 2006 and 2008, voted for by international coaches.

England were a very ordinary international team at that time, as shown by their results in the Euros and World Cups. Nevertheless, Kelly managed to score an impressive forty-six goals in 117 appearances for her country, and also appeared for Great Britain at the 2012 Olympic Games. Had she been born ten years later, when the FA put more money into women's football, particularly in preparing the national women's team, and the Women's Super League had become more professional, she would undoubtedly have been a superstar like Megan Rapinoe. She made a successful move into the media, in the US as well as the UK, and maintains an assured reputation as an insightful analyst of both men's World Cup and women's international soccer with ESPN and Fox.

Eniola Aluko's club and international career indicate how complex gender and ethnicity can be in determining access to sporting life chances. Born in Lagos, Nigeria, in 1987, Aluko moved with her parents, Sileola and Daniel, to Birmingham as an infant. Aluko's British-African identity is a key theme of her memoir. While Daniel returned to Nigeria to pursue a career in politics, Sileola worked as a nurse and then for a pharmaceutical company. Though originally an upper-middle class family in Nigeria, they were housed on an inner city estate in England, and Aluko has been vocal about the importance of her family values, and of her faith, in overcoming the challenges that she has faced.

Aluko started her career at Leafield Athletic Ladies (many women's football teams still call themselves ladies' rather than women's teams), and subsequently played for Birmingham City Ladies, along with future England teammate, Karen Carney. A strong forward player,

Aluko scored on her Birmingham team debut, aged fourteen. By 2003 she was named Young Player of the Year at the FA Women's Football Awards, before moving to Charlton in 2004 for three years, and, when that team folded, moving to Chelsea in 2007. In the meantime, she graduated from Brunel University in London, with a first class degree in law and continued her training as a lawyer. She has since continued with a master's degree in sporting management and has expanded her portfolio of skills considerably.

Aluko joined women's football in England at a time when new forms of semi-professional, and professional careers were now possible, with the establishment of the Women's FA Premier League as the top flight from 1991 to 2011, before the FA Women's Super League was launched. Over in the United States, several British players had obtained athletic scholarships. This could lead to lucrative and prestigious coaching and professional contracts once professional women's leagues were set up following the success of the 1999 Women's World Cup in Los Angeles.

The Women's Professional Soccer (WPS), established in 2009, was one of these iterations of professional leagues, and Eniola Aluko was signed first to St Louis Athletica, then Atlanta Beat and Sky Blue FC, illustrating how precarious the team finances and league structures could be. Aluko returned to Birmingham briefly, before her second spell at Chelsea until 2018, where her prolific scoring rate was matched by her assists.

Her final club football destination was Juventus in the 2018–19 season, after which she retired to work in the media, including being the first woman to appear as a pundit on Match of the Day, and in the US covering men's and women's World Cups, and as a sporting director of Aston Villa Women's FC. Other roles include acting as a mentor to elite athletes transitioning to a post-competitive working life, and as a motivational speaker, as well as writing for *The Guardian*.

Having chosen to play for England, and working her way through the talent identification system, and youth squads, Eniola's senior debut came in 2004. Aluko would go on to win 102 caps during her England career, mainly under long-time coach Hope Powell, herself a former international with over fifty caps, and one of the first black-British women to play for England women, along with Kerry Davis and Brenda Sempare. That women like Powell were changing the traditional look of British football is clear from her autobiography, *Hope*, in which she covers her Jamaican heritage, her working-class childhood in Seventies London, and how, in 1998, 'In one fell swoop, England got its first black manager, its first woman manager, and its first gay manager.'

This was time of major change in world football's attitude to women. The first Women's World Cup had taken place in China in 1991, followed by England women's first qualification for the second Women's World Cup, in 1995 in Sweden. Thereafter, women's football became part of the Olympic Games, in Atlanta in 1996, but, as a Great Britain squad, there has always been the problem of whether or not the home nations should supply a joint squad for the tournament. Fearing that this could change qualification rights for men's World Cups, this has been resisted. In the eighteen-strong squad for the 2012 Olympics women's football tournament, only two Scots, Kim Little and Ifeoma Dieke, were selected, with Wales and Northern Ireland not represented at all by coach Hope Powell.

So although the Women's World Cup and the Olympic tournament have a complimentary qualification system between the two events, it took a historic decision to promote British women's football through the London 2012 Olympics for Aluko and her teammates to appear. Women's football was an important curtain raiser for the entire Games, and therefore appeared to showcase the more diverse range of Olympic sports on offer.

However, after the Olympic Games, and the disastrous 2013 Women's Euros campaign, Powell's fifteen-year term as manager came to an end. When she left her position, Powell, who has Jamaican heritage, had become the first full-time England women's coach, the first Black-British England head coach, and the first openly gay England manager. She had previously become the first vice captain of the England women's team of Caribbean heritage.

But when Aluko became the first British-African woman to win a hundredth cap for England, it was under new manager Mark Sampson, an inexperienced coach with no international playing expertise or top management qualifications, who was employed by the FA in 2014. Sampson was thirty years of age; Aluko twenty-eight and now a senior England player. Although she achieved her hundredth cap, it was under muted circumstances. Aluko came on as a substitute in the second half and hastily handed the armband to mark a brief captaincy. Two matches later she was dropped from the England squad for 'Un-Lioness Behaviour'. What had changed for a player to win 102 caps for her country and then to be perceived as having an attitude problem?

In fact it was Sampson who had the problem. In 2016 Aluko filed a complaint to the FA which detailed bullying and examples of unfair treatment, as well as a broader culture of harassment and bullying in Sampson's approach to coaching the England team. The complaint also included details, which Aluko outlines in her 2019 autobiography, *You Can't Teach This*, about a racially offensive comment that Sampson had made in 2014 to Aluko before an England v Germany game. For a long time Sampson denied making the comment, and he was clearly defended by the FA. Mark Sampson was later sacked in 2017, not for these allegations, but for safeguarding issues related to his time at Bristol women's team, where he was known to have relationships with players while manager.

This has no doubt profoundly affected the way that the England women's football team, branded by the FA PR machine as Lionesses, is perceived. When Aluko was dropped and the allegations about her were being made in the media, Nikita Parris, a young Black-British England player, ran to support Sampson when she scored a goal in a 6–0 defeat of Russia in September 2017. The rest of the England squad followed. Subsequently, in the middle of the Black Lives Matter debate in July 2020, Parris would apologise to Aluko. Sampson also apologised in January 2019, the same month that he received payment for unfair dismissal from the FA.

Between 2016 and 2017, two internal FA inquiries had found no wrongdoing. However, the second led to an FA payout of £80,000 to Aluko for loss of earnings as a centrally contracted England player. This later led to a hearing of the Department for Culture Media and Sport (DCMS), which showed the levels of casual racism under Sampson's management, ending the career of both Lianne Sanderson, who had fifty caps until that point, Drew Spence, and Aluko. It had taken three investigations to prove that two incidents of abuse took place, and the Football Association held shambolic internal reviews. FA Chair Greg Clarke later apologised to MPs for having described issues such as institutional racism as 'fluff', and he fumbled and deflected his way through the DCMS hearing.

In her written statement to the inquiry, Aluko suggested that during the initial media frenzy the Football Association provided information to journalists to influence how the story was covered. The FA initially controlled the media narratives, a reminder of how powerful institutions can influence how less powerful people are perceived. However, the DCMS hearing showed the FA's ineptitude and their grudging attitude towards the player when it was revealed that £40,000 of the £80,000 in lost earnings had been withheld until the hearing on 17 October 2017. It was little consolation for Aluko when Greg Clarke admitted that not enough due diligence had been done on Sampson and he should probably not have been appointed in the first place.

The calm, clear and professional manner in which Aluko conducted herself was in marked contrast to the officers of the FA, who appeared confused over what exactly had happened and at what point. Aluko has written about forgiveness as a positive decision in her autobiography and remains gracious, if forensic, in her account of the situation. There is, though, the wider problem of the lack of diversity in the FA as an institution, and in British football generally, with racist and homophobic attitudes constantly needing to be challenged.

The wider issue from this particular case, beyond how the athlete themselves can choose to change their life chances as determinedly and wisely as Aluko, is that she was ultimately dependent upon the FA, and its choice of Team GB manager, for her selection, based not just on her club performances, but her fit with the wider England squad. That a Black-British, gay, woman coach who had also been an international player of the highest calibre would give Aluko her Team GB opportunity, and that an inexperienced, white, male coach, who lacked the sophistication to understand her heritage, would end her England career, tells us much about the continuities of British sport at the organisational and governance level. In January 2019, coinciding with a considerable pay-off for unfair dismissal, Sampson apologised to Aluko publicly.

In our interview I asked Aluko to tell me the individual to whom she most looked to define her career and her answer was surprising: Oprah Winfrey. So, with her move now to sports executive and media personality, there is every chance she will transcend the incident that ended her England career. Certainly she was able to do this on the pitch by going to Italy to play for Juventus, and continuing to score goals at the highest level.

The Future of Women's Football

There are many historical examples of intriguing stories, such as those told here and elsewhere. Mary Phillip is a pioneer on many levels in football. Born into a tight-knit family of two older brothers, a sister and one younger sister, Mary would play out on the Willowbrook Estate or at Burgess Park in Peckham. She played football, cricket, or whatever other game was going on, with friends and family. Mary's dad is part of the Windrush generation who came to England from St Lucia in 1962, and her mother hailed from Kerry in Southern Ireland. Although Hope Powell had previously become England vice captain, Mary Phillip would become the first Black-British England women's captain in 2003.

Always athletic, Mary remembered an occasion in primary school where the girls were being prevented from playing football in the playground and a lunchtime supervisor came over and took the ball from the boys, giving it to the girls so they could play. The boys never again excluded the girls from that day forward. Mary also recalled being asked by a teacher in an English lesson in secondary school if she was black or white. She did not dignify that with an answer, her complexion speaking for itself. Mary told me, 'I grew up in a family were we accepted each other and our difference, not to judge by color, creed or gender.'

In terms of organised sport, it was a choice between following her love of football or to pursue karate seriously at Wandsworth Youth Club. Competitions for football and karate took place on a Sunday, so she couldn't do both. At Patmore Youth Club, a youth worker named Audrey had formed a women's football team with a local called Ozzie as manager. Little did they know they had sparked the interest of a future England captain sufficiently that Mary gave up karate.

Wanting to improve her game, Mary moved to Millwall Lionesses, after winning the Anniversary Cup with Lambeth Women's FC (based at Patmore Youth club) against Arsenal women's third team. At Millwall, Mary learned an awful lot about top-flight football. This included how to be a gracious winner, and, more importantly, being a dignified loser. She also learned how to bounce back, how to build team cohesion, and a desire to learn and grow. Having joined Millwall in the beginning as a centre-forward, or midfielder, it wasn't until she was somewhat randomly played at centre-back that she found her true position. Unusually for women's football at the time, she had the combination of pace, vision and understanding of the game to read opponents, and to marshal the defence.

Her first England call up came at the same time as Millwall teammate, Tina Lindsey, and her next call up was into the 1995 World Cup squad in Sweden. This could not have been more exciting, as England had qualified for the Women's World Cup for the first time in 1995. As part of the squad led by Ted Copeland, Mary learned a lot from the experienced England players around her. After the birth of her first child in 1995, Mary was dedicated about regaining her fitness, and was rewarded with her England debut in 1996.

Several more internationals followed before a group of players at Millwall seemed to fall out of favour in the England set up. Along with Pru Buckley, Louise Waller, and Julie Fletcher, Mary was dropped, despite being in good form for her club. In 2000 she joined Fulham (on a professional contract), and this soon revived her England career. After Hope Powell took over as England coach in 1998, Mary was recalled, on 24 February 2002, after her two sons were born, in a game against Portugal. She also played in the Algarve Cup for England that year. She became a regular and quickly reached fifty appearances.

In 2003 she was also asked to captain her country, on 13 November against Scotland at Deepdale. After this there were regular occasions when Mary would take the armband, including on her fiftieth appearance against France, where England secured passage to the 2007 Women's World Cup in China, making Mary the first England women's player to reach two World Cups. Mary decided to retire from football internationally in the 2007–08 season. (I am still researching exactly how many times Mary captained England between 2003 and 2007, but we think it is into double figures.)

Having been the first woman onto the YTS programme at Millwall in 1993, Mary obtained her UEFA B Licence coaching qualification. She then decided to dedicate more of her time to coaching, initially in a voluntary capacity. On retiring from playing in 2008, Mary looked into doing her A Licence. She was coaching voluntarily at Peckham Town FC at step seven grassroots level, which was suitable for A Licence work, but the financial cost was too high.

In 2016 the PFA held a women-only course for international players, led by Jim Hicks. With the likes of Lou Newsted and Casey Stoney, Mary took this opportunity. Having coached at Peckham Town FC for several years, and helping grow its youth segment, she started to help coach the senior players in 2014, and took over the senior team in 2015.

In 2016 she was finally able to start her A Licence and began to help coach the first team, becoming the manager in 2019–20. They went on to win the senior London Cup for the first time in the club's history in her first season in charge. However, in February 2017 Mary fell ill a week after being hospitalised. Shortly after her fortieth birthday she was diagnosed with MS. She told me: 'That blew me for six! It took me a couple of months to recover from my relapse. I started to refocus and evaluate life, and, although this slowed me down slightly in completing the A Licence, I now have the qualification.' Mary is proud of her London Cup victory with Peckham, giving back to the local community that she values so much. Her players have said what an honour it is to be coached by an England captain with over fifty caps to her name. But while undoubtedly a pioneer in the game, the difficulty of obtaining paid employment in football is evident from Mary's story.

International representation can also still be fluid. For instance, Wales' Sian Williams, a stalwart captain of Arsenal FC women's side, had one game for Wales, aged seventeen, in 1985, before going on to win twenty caps for England. How did this come about? As John Carrier details in his research about women's football in Wales, Sian was offered a full-time contract in Italy for Serie A side Juve Siderno FC. The then Wales manager Sylvia Gore warned that she would not pick Sian if she went to Italy, in spite of the Italian side offering to fly her back for international games. In the event Wales had no international games for the two years Sian was in Italy, but Sylvia would not pick her on her return to Arsenal. So, with the help of Arsenal, the FA and the then England manager John Bilton, she made the switch to play for England. Sian was then approached to become the manager of Wales women's national team while still playing for England, an irony that John Carrier's research revealed. Williams was also coaching the England University Women's team, and working full-time at Arsenal's academy. She has continued to coach in the US and Israel since leaving the FA of Wales, after criticising them for not funding the women's team to play in the qualifiers of the women's Euros held in England in 2005.

There is a gradual but widening public recognition of women who pioneered professional and semi-professional roles in football, in part due to the increasingly European-wide practice of electing key individuals to respective halls of fame. At the National Football Museum in Preston, female inductees are Debbie Bampton, Pauline Cope, Gillian Coultard, Sue Lopez, Lily Parr, Hope Powell, Brenda Sempare, Marieanne Spacey, Karen Walker and Joan Whalley. At the Scottish Football Museum Rose Reilly was inducted in 2007. Others, like Welsh international Karen Jones, have been awarded honours, in this case the Member of the Order of the British Empire (MBE) for services to football as an administrator and volunteer. With more time, and space, it would surely be possible to compile a more comprehensive list of the growing number of women across generations who have been recognised for their contributions to the sport and to society more widely.

Jess Fishlock, MBE, the first Welsh international player, male or female, to reach 100 caps is one of football's more cosmopolitan travellers, having played for Reading, where she is currently on loan from OL Reign. She has previously played for Bristol Academy in England's FA Women's Super League, AZ Alkmaar in the Dutch Eredivisie, Glasgow City in the Scottish Women's Premier League, Melbourne Victory and Melbourne City in Australia's W-League, in addition to FFC Frankfurt in the Frauen Bundesliga in Germany. In addition, Fishlock has coached Cardiff City WFC, and won a title as player-coach with Melbourne City in the W-League, an amazing achievement. She also campaigns for gay rights, and has a number of endorsement deals, so is an important example of an athlete using her platform for social change. Perhaps if there is a Team GB women's team at the 2021 Olympic Games, she has made herself impossible not to pick?

The road to build the Women's Super League (WSL), in which Fishlock currently plays, has been long, winding and difficult to sustain. She has been critical of the WSL England, and would have stayed in the US had not the Covid-19 situation made the UK more attractive that the US. Several high-profile US Women's National Team players, such as Alex Morgan, Tobin Heath, Rose Lavell and Sam Mewis, have signed to

WSL clubs, in the case of Morgan outselling male players in shirt sales. So what has the WSL story been?

Kelly Simmons, speaking at the 2003 FIFA Symposium in Los Angeles, reported that in the previous five years the FA had invested £1.2 million in women's football, the National Lottery had granted £8 million and the Football Foundation £2.25 million: a total spend on girls' and women's football of £11.5 million. In addition, £60 million had been put into grassroots football. The additional grants and funding had been leveraged through health, crime, drugs, education, community cohesion and social deprivation projects. Having spoken with Mary Guest, Tessa Hayward, Rachel Pavlou, Kelly Simmons and Zoe Wishman of the FA, it is clear that licensing by the national association was the model for the newly launched Women's Super League (WSL) of eight teams.

At around £3 million spent on the project by 2011, the national association was also the major stakeholder. This was the culmination of fourteen years of work since the FA approved the first Women's Football Talent Development Plan in 1997. This levered new funding to establish a network of fifty FA Girls' Centres of Excellence across England licensed by the national association. Having used a series of five-year development plans to lobby for more funding from the governing body, women's football has helped the Corporate Social Responsibility programme of the association, in addition to its equity and diversity agenda, by targeting areas of government concern to draw in external income streams.

English women national team players were also offered central contracts for the first time in the 2008–09 season. Twenty England women's contracts of £16,000 per annum were available, issued by the FA and annually negotiated from 1 December to 30 November each year, and paid in monthly instalments. The contract covered training requirements, national team image, national fixtures and some promotional rights. A player could only work up to twenty-four hours a week in another job, and hence, rather than being a full-time professional agreement, it was seen as providing the 'freedom to train'. The fitness of so many England players was in need of improvement because of their need to hold down employment while training in what free time was left. Freedom to train was not, however, an entitlement to play or a right to selection. The application process for this was handled by the Professional Footballers' Association as so few women have agents, though the union considers the players semi-professionals. This has gradually changed in the last ten years, with more players having agents and more negotiating sponsorship deals.

None of the American-based England national team players for 2009–10 had central contracts (these included Kelly Smith and Alex Scott at the Boston Breakers, Eniola Aluko at Saint Louis Athletica, Anita Asante and Karen Bardsley at Sky Blue FC, and Karen Carney, Ifeoma Dieke and Katie Chapman at the Chicago Red Stars). However, the Chicago Red Stars had to suspend operations for the 2011 Women's Professional Soccer season, and while some players negotiated contracts in the United States as 'free agents', others, like Karen Carney, returned to England.

Slow and conservative growth was the key message of the Women's Super League in 2010. Then, each club could pay four players each year in excess of £20,000 (central England contracts were excluded). If any player earns more than basic expenses, they must have a written contract. Three sources of income were therefore available under the Women's Super League payment scheme: one a central England contract; two, the club contract, and three, additional duties, such as administration, ambassadorial work or coaching. Three ambassadorial posts per team were part-funded by the FA; these are subject to the salary cap and the non-playing obligations were part of the contract.

A draft system was thought to be good for competitive clubs, but unpalatable for players, and limiting overseas players would have been gender-specific, so also problematic legally. Though a player would need a work permit in order to play as a non-EU citizen, to get that work permit a player would have to have played a percentage of national team games in a period stipulated by the Home Office, and that national team would have to be ranked in the top 100-or so in the world. This has slowly changed over the last ten years. At the moment the key change is that the FA want to pass responsibility for running the WSL to the Premiership, thinking that top-flight men's football is the best way to develop the commercial strategies of the women's game. At the time of writing, it feels a little like 'pass the parcel.' However, there are real chances for change with more brands aware that women's football brings with it different messages than for men's football.

Finally then, as we look forward to England hosting the women's Euros again in 2022, there is a chance that when we talk about football coming home, it means women's football as much as men's as it has been pioneered across the UK and Ireland over the last one hundred and fifty years. Let's hope we see that change. After all, rather than 'thirty years of hurt' as the song goes, women's football, as a historically neglected and derided sport, has always been about the victory of the underdog. Perhaps in the future it can be part of a more inclusive and celebratory football industry.

Bibliography

Patrick Brennan, *The Munitionettes* (Donmouth 2007, ISBN 9780955506307).

Eduard Hoffmann & Jürgen Nendza, *Verlacht, verboten und gefeiert* (Landpresse 2006, ISBN 9783935221528).

Sue Lopez, *Women on the Ball* (Scarlet Press 1997, ISBN 3034313152).

Gail Newsham, *In a League of their Own* (Scarlet Press 1997 (first published 1994), ISBN 1857270290).

Laurence Prudhomme-Poncet, *Histoire du football féminin au XXe siècle* (L'Harmattan 2003, ISBN 2747547302).

Jean Williams, *A Game for Rough Girls?* (Routledge 2003, ISBN 0415263387).

Jean Williams, *A Beautiful Game* (Berg 2007, ISBN 9781845206758).

Jean Williams, *Globalising Women's Football: Europe, Migration and Professionalization* (Peter Lang 2013, ISBN 3034313152).

David J. Williamson, *Belles of the Ball* (R&D Associates 1991, ISBN 0951751204).